BURN BUDGIE BYRNE

—FOOTBALL INFERNO—

BURN BUDGIE BYRNE

—*FOOTBALL INFERNO*—

Brian Belton

'the archetypal soccer hero of the 1960s, looking as good as he was effective; a compact ball of flame, capable of doing the unexpected and making the conventional look revolutionary.'

breedon **books**
PUBLISHING

First published in Great Britain in 2004 by
The Breedon Books Publishing Company Limited
Breedon House, 3 The Parker Centre,
Derby, DE21 4SZ.

ISBN 1 85983 392 6

Printed and bound by CROMWELL PRESS,
TROWBRIDGE, WILTSHIRE

Contents

Dedication

This book is dedicated to the memory of the
most gifted player ever to have the Hammers
over his heart and an instinctive freedom fighter
Johnny 'Budgie' Byrne
and to his wife Margaret and their children
Kevin, David, Mark and Karen.

Acknowledgements

I have roamed around the world talking to so many
people connected to West Ham over years that have
changed my life. I have spoken to those who played
for the club from the 1930s to the present day and
to those who have done no more than watched,
cheered and wondered. This is the fifth book that
has grown out of this process, but in many ways it is
the culmination of this pilgrimage, as the man it
focuses on represents West Ham United so well; he
was the Hammers personified. I have spoken to
those who knew him from his earliest days over now
nearly three decades. I thank them all, but most of
all I thank Johnny Byrne.

Foreword
by Leslie Grantham

I would like to thank Brian Belton for asking me to write something about the late Johnny Byrne.

Ron Greenwood said it so eloquently and far better than I ever could when he called Johnny the English Di Stefano. For me, Budgie, along with Ronnie Boyce, was one of the finest players ever to wear a West Ham shirt. He was on a par with Bobby Moore, Geoff Hurst, Martin Peters and Johnny Sissons in those heady days of the 1960s. Yet, maybe in part because of England's World Cup victory, Johnny never got the praise or the credit he so richly deserved.

It was during Budgie's time at West Ham that the club built their reputation for quality football. Yet we flattered to deceive after Johnny left the Boleyn Ground, something no one has ever addressed to this day. Oh how we need a Johnny Byrne at Upton Park now! He was a class act, as every defender in the country during his days with the Hammers would have testified. He ran them ragged. John made goals, scored goals and never shirked from a tackle when the goal was in sight... he loved the opposition's goal area.

Budgie worked his magic on grounds that were like quagmires. He would have revelled in today's pitch conditions and the strike partnerships of the imagination are mouth-watering: Byrne and Di Canio, Byrne and Defoe, Byrne and anyone! Still, enough of 'All our Yesterdays', Johnny 'Budgie' Byrne was loved by the West Ham fans and hated by the opposition. He was a player who never gave any less than his best. As player and man he graced the greatest arena in football during the Hammers' golden era and entertained us claret and blue fans with his football skills and his banter. Johnny is gone but will never be forgotten by the supporters of West Ham, Crystal Palace, Fulham and England and in South Africa, among those who cheered on Durban City, Hellenic FC and that country's national side, he is a legend.

He worked his magic, and magic never dies. Rest in peace Johnny.

Foreword
by Ken Brown

When West Ham manager Ron Greenwood introduced me to 'The Budge', he asked me if I'd room with him on away trips and tours. I was delighted, partly because Ron thought that I was the right person to take on the responsibility of looking after a new young talented player, but also because it seemed like a strong indication that I was going to be in the side.

Budgie and I hit it off straight away. He always wanted to be doing something, he really just couldn't keep still. He always seemed to be thinking 'what can I do next?' Maggie, Budgie's wife, kept his feet on the ground; she was a big influence on him and hated anyone calling him Budgie. For her it was always John. She would tell the likes of me off if we called him anything else. (She was great for him.) That's not saying he never relaxed, he just loved life and was a lively, busy bloke. For example, on the morning before our FA Cup semi-final game at Sheffield in 1964 against Manchester United, he woke me up and told me that it had been raining all night. I said 'haven't you been asleep?' He said 'no, I couldn't'. He was so full of energy and nerves.

It's true that Budgie, like a lot of us, liked a drink, but he was very dedicated to training. However, like other great players I've known, for instance Trevor Brooking and Martin O'Neil, Budgie could do things in the competitive game that he just couldn't do in training. It might be something to do with needing the adrenaline that can't really be replicated on the training pitch. He had a sixth sense that enabled him to play with his back to goal, a rare quality in the game. He was never frightened and had a great touch. He really had a feel for the game and loved playing. For example, take our record win against Leeds United, he couldn't be touched. Jack Charlton was the Leeds centre-half that day. Jack was playing at the heart of the England defence at the time and was one of the most respected and feared defenders in the world. It was a great Leeds side, perhaps their best ever, but Budgie did what he liked during that match and ran rings around big Jack.

Budgie was always happy, except when we got beat. Sometimes he was very annoying, but never anything other than a great player and friend. Football lost a lot when 'The Budge' passed on. I still miss him a lot, as does everyone who knew him.

Ken Brown – West Ham United and England

Byrne in letters

THIS book is about the life and times of Johnny 'Budgie' Byrne. I have chosen to tell John's story though football, the game he loved and lived for. The tale begins with his footballing childhood and his first days at Crystal Palace and moves on to encompass John's contribution to some of the finest games West Ham United has ever played and all his goals for the Hammers, his return to Selhurst Park, his short stay at Fulham and his life in South African soccer. I have resisted the pressure to portray Johnny Byrne as a sort of lovable rascal, a type of scallywag or ne'er-do-well. This is the kind of treatment that has been meted out to the likes of Alex Higgins in snooker, and of course repeatedly to George Best. In truth, in John's case, it would be a relatively simple task to emphasise, magnify and manufacture scandal by insinuation, allegation, rumour and hint. The world, its wife, husband and second cousin twice removed has a story about Budgie. Many of these fables are made up of elements of truth, but some, if not most, are urban myths or forms of wish fulfilment. However, a book that made the most of Byrne's reputation would have lived up to the all too prevalent prejudices about self-destructive poor (Irish) boys not being able to handle success and that would have demeaned what John did and who he was. It would be like seeking to sum up the work of the glorious renaissance artist Caravaggio by focusing on his private misdemeanours. Such an exercise would tell us nothing at all about the magnitude of his art or its gargantuan impact and it is not too much to claim that Johnny Byrne was the Caravaggio of the high craft of football.

As such, the pages that follow do include some tales about John, the people he worked with and many of his exploits beyond the field of play, but on the whole I have tried to highlight the context in which he glowed and what he achieved in order to demonstrate the brilliance of his contribution to football and more importantly, the struggle of South African society to cast off the curse of apartheid, discrimination and segregation. He hardly knew it, but John contributed to human freedom – something that the way he played depicted and as such was natural to him. There is so much about Budgie that is not known and that is unappreciated, and it is the hope of this book that it will, by your reading, illuminate the burning spirit of Johnny Byrne.

Introduction

KWASUKA[1] I used to go to reserve games at West Ham's Upton Park ground. They don't do that anymore; the pitch is saved, in the main, for first-team games. I started attending reserve games when I was about five or six. My four or five mates and I would play for the Hammers against Spurs, Arsenal or, for some reason I can't recall, Estudeantes de la Plata in the FA Cup final in Castle Street, E13, waiting for the gates to the North Bank to be opened at half-time allowing us to flood into the near-deserted edifice. The North Bank stood where the Centenary Stand now overlooks the Irons' sacred turf and from its forsaken, yawning entrails we'd watch snatches of the game between mimicking first-team match days, crushing up together behind a single barrier, shouting warnings like, 'stop bumming me' and loudly questioning, 'who's pissed in my pocket?' while imploring the claret and blue second string to 'Coom-on-uuu-Iiiiionnnnzzz!!!'.

Other distractions from viewing West Ham's twilight regiment of future and past being pulverised included games of 'he' and standing directly in front of lone pensioners. We would look at these old boys in counterfeit shock as they pelted us with a comfortably predictable deluge of verbal filth. We would also mime 'crowd riots' (a challenge for such a small group with a collective age of 35) or line up one behind the other and 'do pushers', sending each other tumbling down the stand like over-coated dominoes. Another favourite pastime was doing the conga up and down the concrete terrace chanting, to the tune of the Seven Dwarfs classic, '*Hi-Ho!*'; *Mile End, Mile End, Mile End, Mile End, Mile End…* (such performances could go on for near to 20 minutes and occasionally more than an hour). This was the mantra of the 'Mile End Mob', a collection of youth gangs that would meet at Mile End underground station to become West Ham's travelling buccaneer army of the 1960s. The 'Mob' was made up of the young tribes of weekday rivals from Stepney, Canning Town, Whitechapel, Dagenham, Hornchurch and all the 'villages' north of the river, east of the Tower, an area still then pock-marked by the ravages of the Blitz and

[1] Zulu equivalent for 'once upon a time'.

continuing poverty. Come the next first-team game, this conglomerated crew would crush together onto the North Bank to renew their collective allegiance to the mighty Hammers. One day we would join their ranks and carouse around the urban wastelands of England celebrating being 'us'. But on that winter's evening, as the floodlights of the Boleyn Ground broke through the icy mist that shrouded London's Docklands, maybe 500 dawns into the swinging decade of the last century, we were far too young to be part of that. Our ambitions were set on becoming 'Snipers', the under-13 (more or less) cadet core of the 'Mile End'. It was just after singing and swaying to the Sniper hymn, *Snniiiipuzzz! Snniiipuzzz!* that I got knocked unconscious.

In time with our homage my little choir pointed towards what was then the enclosure where visiting supporters would be directed, the despised South Bank (that would eventually metamorphose into the Bobby Moore Stand). The South Bank would be transformed into the 'home end' in a rather lame effort to break the cult of the 'Mile End' and control match day trouble. The tactic was to mark the end of the MEM, but it gave rise to its more vicious, malicious successor, the 'Intercity Firm', for whom violence was an end in itself; sadistic sickness replaced aggressive solidarity as the hard boys moved on to be replaced by the hit-and-run yob culture, reflecting the Thatcherite sect-of-the-self.

Our 'Sniperian' sonnet had been going some moments when the ball was killed by the chest of West Ham's Johnny Byrne. The stained sphere fell, seemingly as slow as a leaf, to receive a mighty belt from the Byrne right boot. The shot screamed towards the goal, but with the lightest kiss atop the away side's bar, the oscillating orb cannoned on… straight towards me. I don't know how, when or why I decided that I would head the ball back at Byrne, but spreading both arms wide, I pushed my colleagues aside and flung myself towards the oncoming missile. I saw it spinning in the air and I knew I would make contact; I would meet this challenge and connect with my team. I would be totally Hammered! The last thing I remember before leather met cranium was marvelling that so much turn could be applied at such great force; then the lights went out, at least in my diminutive, infantile nut anyway. In the expanse of my childish unconscious I had a little dream wherein Percy Dalton (the peanut man) was arguing with the West Ham manager Ron Greenwood about the state of the buses, Ron was calling in Yogi Bear to arbitrate, him being smarter than the average bear, when illumination was restored. I awoke looking into the face of Johnny Byrne. England international, most expensive footballer ever, Johnny Byrne! 'You okay sonny?' he asked, looking concerned. My modest firm were standing round in awe, and little Colin Jones, the amazing two-foot Trinidadian, smallest giant in the East End, was mutely holding out a crumpled piece of paper and a blue, betting office pencil. Byrne had jumped out of the fantasy realm of the pitch into the stark reality of the North Bank; he had crossed the divide of dreams and run up the terraces to where I lay. 'Yeah' I said, trying to pretend that my flight down 20 feet of terraced hardness had been deliberate. I was planning saying something like, 'I do that all the time John' when he remarked, 'Good header' and gave a little chuckle as he helped me to my feet. 'Thanks' I replied with all the nonchalance I could muster. He signed Tony's scrap of putrid papyrus and trotted back down to where the other players were, quite rightly, looking up at him from the other side of reality. That autograph would be with Colin 40 years on. He carried it into eternity in the top pocket of the suit he wore as he was cremated in little Catholic chapel in New York after a long battle with an evil illness.

My first conversation with Johnny Byrne would not be the last, but our next chat would be separated by the tumult of my teenage years and John's combustive reign in world football. But we never really parted. As I followed him and his West Ham, we were all Hammers. Incited by Bobby Moore, our coming was felt like the distant thunder of a Zulu army jogging, inexorably, across the veldt. At the best of times, just when the opposition thought it had heard the last of the Irons, the portentous presence of Moore would appear in the middle of the park and the buzz of swiftness around the ball would start: Byrne, Hurst, Boyce, Sissons and Brabrook would dazzle, dizzy and confuse to weave the Hammers back into contention. Sophisticated in assault out of defence, passing along the ground with intoxicating accuracy, rarely did the ball take flight; darting runs carried it to rock the enemy like lightning bolts from the claret and blue. A collusion of deft passing and on-the-ball skill was their only authority. That West Ham side had the ability to create an idyll of football.

Unfulfilled potential

John should have been one of England's greatest internationals and he would certainly have bettered his total of 11 caps if he had been picked for the 1962 World Cup in Chile. Indeed, during the 1961–62 season most pundits thought he had his place in the England squad booked. He had just made his record-breaking move to Upton Park from Crystal Palace, where he had been, justifiably, seen first as a prodigy and then lauded as a genius. However, after a game at the Hawthorns, where West Ham had won 1–0, defending for most of the game, having had Chuck Drury rattle their bar and all in all frustrating the Baggies, John got involved in a scuffle with the turbulent former England defender Don Howe. The shadowy powers that then ruled the Football Association and still inhabited the archaic 'international selection committee' during the early 1960s did not view Johnny's involvement with one of their favourites kindly, and they effectively blackballed Byrne. It is painfully ironic that the steely, pragmatic and destructive Howe would one day coach the English team, a role never to be graced by the soccer mind of Johnny Byrne.

England took quality but technically less talented centre-forwards to Chile in 1962: the likes of Gerry Hitchens and Alan Peacock. England, and in particular the young Bobby Moore, were to feel the lack. When he heard about the situation before the World Cup third-place match in Santiago, Milovan Ciric, the legendary manager of the Yugoslavian side, who contested that game against the tournament hosts, said, 'This is a game for men, not for saints and women.' Ciric had seen Byrne play and said of him: 'Byrne is the future of centre-forwards. He is a wizard; he makes something from nothing and he will only become more powerful. He is England's prospect, its hope.'

Ciric was certainly accurate in his assessment of Byrne. Johnny was a very modern attacker. He had exceptional balance and played with a rare finesse. John was adept at dropping off his marker, finding space and either launching a colleague with an inspired pass or using his own pace, skill and powerful right foot to score goals himself. He favoured the deep-lying centre-forward role, but was quite happy playing at inside-left, as he did for the English side that beat Wales 2–1 in 1964 at Wembley and during his last England appearance, the 2–2 draw against Scotland in 1965.

John was one of the final 28 players selected for the 1966 World Cup, but the injury he sustained against Scotland in 1965 had taken its toll and he was not in the group of 22 that would be available for selection during the tournament. Awfully, immorally, incomprehensibly, one of the most talented footballers England had ever produced, one who was made for the modern game, was never to play in a World Cup. For all this, what follows will concentrate on what John did more than what he was prevented from doing, by himself and others, as that is the most remarkable chronicle.

Viva Johnny Byrne

Johnny Byrne lived life to the full. He was the archetypal soccer hero of the 1960s. A creative artist on the field, looking as good as he was effective, he was a compact ball of flame, capable of doing the unexpected and making the conventional look revolutionary.

Read this well: Johnny was stronger and more intelligent than George Best; he was at least the Irishman's equal in skill. At his peak Byrne would have learnt little from Pelé and could have taught the Brazilian a trick or eight. Johnny was like fire – unpredictable and able to have an impact in a split second. He really did need to be seen, live, to be believed. His feet and brain seemed to act in unison; he thought and moved with electric alacrity. The soccer temple, the mystic Academy of Upton Park, has produced the likes of Bobby Moore and Geoff Hurst, extraordinarily disciplined professionals, and in the case of Moore, a mind attuned to football. But these were self-made players, who became great as much by the force of will as anything else. The Boleyn Ground has also been blessed with many intrinsically gifted footballers: Martin Peters and Trevor Brooking, and latterly Joe Cole and Paulo DiCanio for instance, but wonderful though these performers were or might be – and Peters was nothing less than majestic – none could match the drama, personality, athleticism, natural equilibrium and sheer buoyancy of Byrne. He looked and performed like a football dream. Peters was a man of magic, a Merlin; Brooking was a maestro, able to orchestrate victory with the slightest movement of his body; DiCanio was a poetical predator – but Byrne remains a mythical god of a player, in every sense of the word: he was mercurial. You could see what he was doing but you could not easily explain how it was done.

Byrne ran circles round defenders, tied backs in knots, he made fools of those who sought to temper his heat and created boiling fear in the heart of every opponent he faced. Johnny burnt and was born to burn; go near him and he would blister you with his radiance. He was a huge talent; there was no one like him. He was the best attacking player West Ham United has ever had or will have, and was one of the most glorious talents the British Isles has produced. Sadly this has never really been recognised, probably because the beacon of his startling proficiency shone so briefly.

Johnny scorched off the field as brightly as he did on it. A gambler, a drinker and a rabble-rouser, he was never shy of letting people know the type of man he was. He did have regrets, but he made not a single excuse nor a solitary apology. He seemed to be on this earth to blaze hot and wild and that is just what he did in England, Europe and Africa. You took this footballing conflagration for what he was, and most people loved him despite his flaws. This is his story.

CHAPTER 1

Sacred Fire

J OHN Joseph Byrne was born in West Horsley in Surrey on 13 May 1939. Both John's parents were Irish and had migrated to Surrey from Dublin three years earlier in search of employment.

In the early part of the 21st century West Horsley is a picturesque commuter village just south of the town of Leatherhead, south-west of London. It is made up of desirable properties and a few shops servicing the same. In the late 1930s the same place was dominated by rural industry and the local aristocratic landowners. My own family, on my father's side, migrated to this part of the world in the early part of the 19th century as brickfield labourers, mixing with other families from Scotland, Ireland and all over England, supplying London with building materials for its great expansion that was to last until the second half of the 1900s. Other families and individuals came to the borders of the centre of the British Empire to serve the rich or bring their skills to facilitate the expansion of industry or the development of agriculture, which itself needed to become industrialised to feed the growing population of the south-east of England. As such, John was a product of this process. His first years were lived in the shadow of the most devastating war humankind had known and by the time he had grown to be a boy the world was being reshaped. Most of John's spare time in his youth was spent kicking balls about. He remembered: 'The kids used to traipse miles to a place called Sheeplease and we played long after dark. We used to plant torches in the ground.'

Thus the Surrey/Irish lad cultivated the intuitive skills that made him one of the finest touch players to represent England in the post-war years.

A shadow over Africa
In Britain the continuance of rationing and the recovery from conflict meant

that issues affecting the people of countries like South Africa did not come to everyone's attention. As such it is unlikely that the nine-year-old John Joseph Byrne would have noted the South African government starting to give official sanction to the limitation of black people's rights when it launched the apartheid system. No one then could have known how this madness would isolate South Africa, how cut off from the reality of the world it would become as it sank deeper into this self-destructive insanity. But already the seeds of the eventual struggle against repression had been sown. Two years after the imposition of the doctrine of white supremacy, Nelson Mandela and Oliver Tambo opened the first black legal firm in South Africa.

As the seeds of young Byrne's football talent were just beginning to germinate, the place where he would spend the second half of his life was also starting a new phase in its soccer development. South African soccer, like South African society, has a history structured by the racism that was in place long before the start of apartheid. The South African Football Association (later the Football Association of South Africa, FASA) was founded in 1892, but the association was a totally white entity. The participation of non-white people in organised football did not start until 1903 when the South African Indian Football Association (SAIFA) was inaugurated.

Almost from the beginnings of football in South Africa there had been large-scale resistance to race discrimination in the sport, but the game was soon implicated in the wider fight against segregation. Mahatma Gandhi, who was a lawyer in Johannesburg before he became a political leader in India, organised 'inter-racial' teams and matches that by their very existence challenged the racism of the time. One of the best remembered is the historic game played in 1910 at the Mayfair Ground of the Johannesburg Rangers, when a team of 'Passive Resistors' (Gandhi's speciality) from Pretoria met their Johannesburg comrades. The game was anything but an exercise in passive resistance, however: it was more a case, in the words of Malcolm X, of 'by any means necessary'.

In 1933, the South African Bantu Football Association (SABFA) was organised and the South African Coloured Football Association (SACFA) came into being at around the same time. The game was unified in terms of having one administrative body with the coming of South African Association Football Association (SAAFA) in 1935 and the 1940s saw the development of the Inter Race Soccer Boards, which organised matches between racial associations (whites didn't participate though there was no law against mixed sport).

The apartheid era officially began in 1948 and was to last for 46 years. In 1951 SAAFA, SAIFA and SACFA formed the 'multi-racial' (but not yet 'non-racial') South African Soccer Federation (SASF); the SABFA remained outside the Federation. Five years later the Minister of the Interior, Dr Donges, oversaw the process of bringing sport in to line with the apartheid policy of the South African government, directly politicizing sporting competition.

Palace Prodigy

Johnny Byrne emerged as a teenager in the grey days of the mid-fifties; a no man's land in time, when Britain and London were still reeling from the shock of global conflict.

If John had been an ordinary lad moving from boyhood to adulthood he would have become part of West London's post-war generation, caught up in the national economic modification that was transforming Britain from being the epicentre of world commerce and the dominant military power to an offshore European client state, a situation that was to endure until the mid-1970s. However, the young Byrne had a rare skill and a passion to develop the same. He had set his heart on a career in professional football and as a talented 12-year-old he was already turning heads when he had the chance to show what he could do. Ex-school teacher Jim Blore was one of the first to see John's potential when he turned out for Howard Effingham School. Known also as Victor and Vincent, Blore had played for Crystal Palace and had turned out nine times for West Ham United during the 1935–36 season, so it was with an experienced eye that he watched John's development as he moved to Epsom Town to be chosen for Guildford City Juniors and make a significant breakthrough when he was invited to represent his county at youth level. Byrne was never to forget Blore as it was the one-time professional who introduced John to the Crystal Palace manager, the former Tottenham goalkeeper Cyril Spiers, whose fatherly persona was much valued by the young Byrne as well as other younger players at Selhurst Park.

Johnny had cried when he left school at the age of 15. He reflected: 'I don't know why because if I'd had a good education I wouldn't have been a footballer.' But his education was just beginning

It's tough down south

As the youthful Byrne was becoming a noted young player in South London, in South Africa, the Congress of the People were producing a document demanding basic rights for black people. The finished article was presented to the People's Congress on 26 June 1955 in Kliptown, South Africa, and came to be known as the Freedom Charter. Many people were arrested and thrown into jail in connection with the Charter. On the eve of the Congress roadblocks were set up and hundreds of delegates were prevented from completing their journey. However, the delegates that did make it to the Congress managed to adopt the Charter. But the apartheid government saw the Charter as a communist tract (communism had been banned in South Africa during 1950) and ordered the arrest of African National Congress (ANC) leaders. This led to the famous Treason Trial, wherein the apartheid regime attempted to portray the ANC and its allies as being committed to a policy of violence and accused them of planning to overthrow the state, although in reality the Charter was a straightforward list of requests that embodied a vision of freedom for the future.

After he left school Johnny Byrne was also put under examination, a less threatening experience certainly than what was happening in the South African context, but nevertheless a life-changing process for the young man from West Horsley. Indeed, John was to see the moment that Cyril Spiers offered him a trial with Crystal Palace, a professional club, as one of biggest events of his life. But when Byrne left school at 15 he had to wait six months before he heard from the club. He started work as an apprentice toolmaker, but he never took his mind off of wanting to 'make football'. In all he had to take part in four trials before finally being taken on to the ground staff at Selhurst Park.

John's early days as a 16-year-old at Selhurst Park were hard work. There were three lads on the ground staff (this was in the days before apprenticeships) and together they had to wash out the dressing rooms, clean players' boots, re-stud them and endure complaints from the players if the state of their footwear did not meet the highest standards. John went home on one occasion with a thick ear when his boot-cleaning efforts were not up to scratch.

The lads also swept the stands and terraces, washed down walls and scrubbed floors. John eventually became the senior ground-staff member. The other two lads, like so many before and after them, were not chosen to join the ranks of the professionals. While on the ground staff John was not allowed to address senior players by their first names, and always referred to them as 'Mr'. At that time Palace were still in the old Third Division South. Post-World War Two the club were a struggling side. Selhurst Park saw a succession of managers as they sought re-election to the League three times.

From an early age John loved to see characters in the game. He recalled:

> When I first came into the game there were players like Len Shackleton, a truly magnificent player. His antics and clowning on the field were unbelievable, but his skill was unreal. Many a time he would play a ball off the corner flag and beat an opponent, or kick it against an opponent's shins and collect the rebound, or lob it over a defender's head and, as his opponent turned to give chase, the ball would spin back against Shackleton, who went away in a flash.

> Eddie Brown, a forward from Birmingham, was another who clowned his way through a game. I remember him once about to take a corner-kick. Near the flag stood a London bobby. Brown removed the policeman's helmet, placed it on his head, and then proceeded to take the corner-kick. It drew a roar of approval from the crowd.

The higher they build the barriers...

Making his way along the path trod so many times by professional players before and after him, John had no idea that as he was shaping his own destiny another part of his future was being dictated in far away South Africa. Early in 1956 a group of four soccer commissioners was appointed by FIFA to probe South African football's colour bar. The commissioners got their first taste of apartheid law when they landed at Jan Smuts Airport, Johannesburg. They were met on the tarmac by a large group of white people, representatives of the press and football officials. As they made their way through customs the commissioners did not see one black person. It was only later that they found out that only whites had been allowed any kind of access to them. However, as they came out of customs more than 200 non-whites, including soccer officials and reporters, gave them a heroes' welcome before they were whisked away by white officials for refreshments at a whites-only restaurant.

A few days after their arrival the commissioners met the representatives of the SASF at the Carleton Hotel in Johannesburg. They met the SABFA the following day at Kholvad House. The meetings were held in secret as the commission was in South Africa to generate a report to be delivered to the full congress of FIFA (to be held in Portugal the following June) who would decide whether or not to exclude the SASF from its membership. The SABFA had made its stand on the issue quite clear. As a body it was open to all races, irrespective of colour, whereas the SASF was for whites only.

FIFA's constitution stated that only one body could represent a country and it was clear that the SASF did not represent the majority of South Africans. Naturally, the SASF was on the defensive, taking the view that the question was a domestic one, and FIFA should not interfere.' But FIFA reserved the right to question the SASF on any issue that affected its membership. At around the same time Nelson Mandela was arrested on a charge of high treason, but following a lengthy detention he was found not guilty.

In common with Mandela's propensity to look to the masses for his motivation, early on in his career Johnny found those who followed football to be his inspiration and was soon to gain a reputation as an entertaining player, who looked to give the crowd what they wanted. By the conclusion of the 1956–57 season he had made 14 appearances for Crystal Palace, moving from inside-right to centre-forward, scoring just one goal (he netted in his eighth game for the club). Byrne signed professional forms in 1957 when Palace were struggling in the lower reaches of the old Third Division South. By then he had made the England Youth team on five occasions, having gained his first cap while playing for Surrey. Manager Spiers signed Byrne on the weekly wage of £7 with an extra £3 bonus if his side won and £1 for a draw. John's professional debut for Palace took place while he was still on National Service, at Selhurst Park. It was an October League game against Swindon Town; a disappointing 0–0 draw that gave little indication of the drama to follow during John's rollercoaster career. To complete an eventful period John married a local girl, Margaret, when he was half way through his 18th year.

In his first professional season Byrne scored seven times in 28 outings, gaining a regular place in the Glaziers' first team, but it was clear, when comparing his club experience with those of the young men he met during his international duties, that he wasn't being used well. Palace finished 14th, just below the dividing line that would have made them a member of the new Division Three to be formed the following term. In the closing weeks of the season, with five games to play, four of them at home, Palace had every chance of scraping into the top 12, which also included Southampton and Norwich, but three defeats meant that the Selhurst team had to be content with becoming founder-members of the Fourth Division, alongside the likes of Coventry City and Watford, teams that were to have illustrious futures. Less than a week after the last game of the season Spiers lost his job; the first casualty in the new Division. Like his four post-war predecessors, Spiers had had little success with Palace, who had averaged less than a point a game during his four-year stint in charge. Byrne had never rated Spiers as a tactician but saw him, along with Blore, as one of the men who gave him a start in the world he loved.

Britain and the world of football were shocked on 6 February 1958 when eight Manchester United players were among the 21 passengers killed in an air crash in Munich in West Germany. The United team had started their flight home to Manchester from Yugoslavia having fought out a draw with Red Star Belgrade to qualify for the last four of the European Cup. The aircraft struck a fence as it took off from Munich's Rhiem airport. England lost Roger Byrne, Duncan Edwards and Tommy Taylor. United's manager, Matt Busby, was seriously injured. What once had been a BEA Ambassador was reduced to a scrambled mass of shards and debris. The efforts of rescuers were made harder by the blizzard that blew across the airfield, whose name would forever mean sorrow in the annals of football.

In the same year, to its eternal shame, FIFA recognised the all-white SASF as the only governing soccer body in South Africa. Looking back it is hard to comprehend this decision. It could only have been motivated by entirely commercial considerations, the white establishment having the financial muscle that supported football in South Africa. That was and is nothing new, but the ramifications of the decision left an indelible blemish on the history of world football in the same way that apartheid stains the story of South Africa's development. That FIFA pronouncement in the last years of the 1950s, underwriting the barbarity of racial segregation, has left a sour taste in the mouth of every right-thinking supporter of the game, especially those of us who were alive at the time, that no amount of current rhetoric about anti-racism can remove. The one positive to come out of this abandonment of any sense of justice is that it demonstrates the fact that most lasting and profound forms of racism in football are not, as the media would have us believe, to be found in the support of football, but within the game as an institution. To confirm this one only has to look at the pathetic number of black managers and executives within the top echelons of the English Leagues and Football Association (relative to the numbers of black players that make the existence of these entities viable). Nearly 60 years on, FIFA has never apologised for or even tried to explain that despicable decision that dismissed as non-existent an entire footballing population.

The taller you become...

In June 1958 George Smith took over as manager of Crystal Palace. He immediately attracted attention by announcing that if he did not lead the team to promotion within two years he would resign. Smith, a former Charlton, Brentford and QPR centre-half, was an experienced coach and a hard disciplinarian. The first match Palace played under his leadership was the opening match of the club's first season in the Fourth Division. On 23 August 1959 Crewe Alexandra came to Selhurst Park to be greeted by a crowd of 13,551. The two clubs had never met in League competition and it was Crewe's first-ever visit to the home of the Glaziers. From the start Palace dominated the Railwaymen and the match became a personal triumph for Mike Deakin, who was making his first senior appearance for nine months after a major cartilage operation. He notched up a first-half hat-trick which was matched by Byrne, who at 19 was beginning to demonstrate the kind of insight that would become his trademark. Crewe replied with the only two goals centre-forward David Pearson would score for Alexandra. It was the best of starts for Palace and Smith, but only four points came from the next six games, and although Palace were often on the fringe of honours they finished badly in a crowded April programme. Smith's side were in seventh place at the end of the term. Deakin, although dropped three times, scored 27 goals in League and Cup games, the best post-war return by a Palace player up to that point, while Byrne claimed 20 and two newcomers, Tony Collins (whom John would encounter again during his first years in South Africa) from Watford and Roy Summersby from Millwall, both scored nine. The total of 99 goals in all competitive matches was a great improvement on the previous season.

However, there was little good news for South African blacks in 1959. New laws extended racial segregation by creating separate Bantustans, or homelands, for the largest black groups. It seemed that freedom was becoming less and less feasible for the majority of South Africans. In football the legislation did much to pave the way for the creation of a white professional league, the National Football League (NFL).

Byrne's mixture of natural balance, rare genius and ability to learn and practice took him into the England Under-23 side to become the first-ever Fourth Division player to win an England cap at that level. He was to make seven appearances for the Under-23s, scoring six goals. However, his international recognition opened Johnny's eyes and he saw that Selhurst Park, under the leadership of George Smith, had taken him as far as it could; he asked to be placed on the transfer list. But John was still in the Army and Palace put a price of £20,000 on his head. Not surprisingly there were no takers, so he was obliged to bite the bullet and play. And play he did. The arrival of the former West Ham and Brighton player Dave Sexton at Selhurst Park did much to expose the ineptitude of Smith. Sexton, who would go on to manage a number of top-flight sides, including the great Chelsea team of the late 1960s and early 1970s, and would remain influential within the English international game, was one of the founders of the Upton Park 'Academy', the informal think-tank that laid the ground for a new model of English football that would rule the world after 1966. During his brief spell with Palace during the 1959 season, Sexton appeared in only about half of Palace's games due to injury, but he did much to help the young Byrne hone his game and tactical awareness; at times he influenced the whole side. One such occasion was when Barrow visited Selhurst Park on 10 October 1959. Smith's men had lost the four matches leading up to this game and were occupying 10th place in the League, so no one really expected what was to come.

Ray Colfar, a clever left-winger who had joined Palace from Sutton United in 1958, scored the first goal of the match. It was achieved midway through the first half, via a long, sweeping, deadly accurate pass from Sexton, followed by an accomplished shot that Colfar unleashed from 20 yards out. Fifteen minutes later right-winger Johnny Gavin scored directly from a corner. Gavin had been in the glorious Tottenham side of the early 1950s, managed by Arthur Rowe, and was a seven-time Republic of Ireland international. This was followed by a swift brace from Lambeth boy Roy Summersby. The second half was still young when Colfar claimed his second and it seemed that Barrow had capitulated when on the hour Summersby hit them with two more strikes in quick succession; the first went in off an upright and was followed by a penalty, the punishment for a Barrow handball. With four goals from the match Summersby became the first Palace player since World War Two to have achieved such a feat. Byrne had a goal disallowed before he converted a pass from Colfar and with a minute to play it was left to Johnny to deliver the final blow with a shot that skimmed the very tips of the blades of grass that lay in its path. This became and remained Palace's biggest-ever win in any major competition. The team were: Rouse, Long, Noakes, Truett, Evans, McNichol, Gavin, Summersby, Sexton, Byrne and Colfar.

Palace reached the third round of the FA Cup for the third year running and goalkeeper Vic Rouse, having won a Welsh cap at Under-23 level, made his first and last full international outing in April 1959, becoming the first player from a Fourth Division club to gain full international recognition. However, his side lost 4–1 to Northern Ireland in Belfast. For all this, Byrne had little time for George Smith, who had continued the habit his predecessor had of playing Byrne wide rather than at centre-forward, the position John saw himself as being best suited for. As such he wasn't satisfied with the opportunities he was getting, seeing his 17 goals in 45 games in the 1958–59 term as evidence that his potential was being inhibited, although he was starting to draw the attention of bigger clubs. Their interest grew after he scored a goal of rare quality in the final of the Southern Floodlit Cup in 1959 in front of a crowd of 32,000. The goal is still talked about by older Palace fans to this day: it was a culmination of speed, shooting accuracy, poise and sheer exuberance.

If Smith was to achieve his ambition of promotion, Palace had to improve in 1959–60. On their day they played like champions, yet several seemingly safe points were lost. Byrne finished as top scorer with 19 League and Cup goals, and he hit a hat-trick against Chelmsford in the first round of the Cup. After Margate had been beaten at the second attempt, Palace saw their hopes of going beyond round three crushed yet again, this time at Scunthorpe. A run of 10 games without defeat followed the FA Cup exit, but this scorching period was succeeded by nine matches that yielded only eight points. Another bad finishing spell meant that Smith's side could only manage eighth position, one lower than the previous term. Smith, keeping his word, promptly resigned. In April 1961 he turned up at Portsmouth in the Second Division (Pompey had been relegated after the 1960–61 season). He led Pompey to the Third Division Championship in 1961–62 but probably gained most notoriety in 1965 when he became the first League manager to scrap reserve and youth games. Portsmouth missed relegation by a point and the reserve and youth teams were promptly restored.

Sharpeville

As the new decade opened the Cold War was in full swing, and many people thought a nuclear confrontation with the Soviet Union was an imminent threat. On 21 March 1960, South Africa saw a day of mass demonstrations across the country against the white government's hated pass laws, which obliged people of colour to carry identity passes at all times. The campaign was organised by the Pan-African Congress, a breakaway group from the African National Congress. It involved black people all over the country breaking the law by refusing to carry the passes with them and giving themselves up at their nearest police station to be arrested. Thousands took part in the protests, which were peaceful in the majority of places, but what had begun as a peaceful demonstration ended in calamity in the township of Sharpeville, five miles north of Vereeniging; police, without warning, opened fire on a crowd of black protesters, murdering 69 people and wounding 186. The marchers carried no weapons, save a few umbrellas and a handful of walking sticks. Their intent was to burn their passes in front of the police station to show their feelings about the apartheid law.

Official statements claimed that the shootings took place in self-defence when the crowd of 20,000 tried to storm the station. Black witnesses at the subsequent inquiry said that only 5,000 people were involved and that they had gone peacefully to the police station to discuss the pass laws. A medical expert testified that around 70 per cent of the victims had been shot from behind. One of the organisers of the protests said a few days after the shooting, 'The tree of freedom is watered with blood'.

In the second half of the 20th century football was always intermixed with politics in South Africa, and it was the same energy for freedom that enthused the mass pass law protests, and in particular Sharpeville, that, in 1960, motivated rebel officials within SASF to form the 'non-racial' professional South African Soccer League (SASL) and the South African Soccer Federation (SASF).

Arthur Sidney Rowe

The new manager of Crystal Palace was Arthur Rowe. He took up his responsibilities in April 1960. The board had sought Rowe's services in 1958, but his health had prevented him taking on the manager's role. By Fourth Division standards Rowe (a friend of Smith) inherited a good team and, in Rowe, the supporters and players at Palace acquired a rare footballing mind.

Arthur Sidney Rowe was born in Tottenham on 1 September 1906. As a boy he played for Cheshunt and Hertfordshire Schools before signing amateur forms for Tottenham Hotspur in 1923. Like youngsters before and after him (including future Tottenham manager Bill Nicholson) he was sent to the Spurs nursery club, Northfleet, before turning professional in May 1929 and making his debut the same year.

Rowe was an uncommonly sophisticated centre-half at a time when the position had been taken over by burly, uncompromising stoppers who stood mountain-like at the heart of defensive play. Unlike most of his contemporaries,

Rowe was able to convert his stance from defence to attack through accurate distribution and a good positional sense. As the 1930s progressed Rowe became club captain at Tottenham. Although only 5ft 9in and 12 stone 8lbs, he made 201 appearances over eight seasons as centre-half and at the age of 27 won his only England cap in the 4–1 defeat of France during the 1933–34 season, the first full international to be played at White Hart Lane.

However, the following season he sustained what was to be a long-term injury, and the wound would ultimately bring a premature end to his playing career. Rowe's prolonged absence from the side was seen as one of the main factors in his club's slide into the Second Division.

Arthur was obliged to retire in 1939 following a cartilage operation but he was to become one of a number of British players and coaches to first take modern football to the world in the 1930s. He was coaching in Hungary as the threat of war loomed, dispensing the ideas that would, after World War Two, influence the development of the Continental football that would challenge the complacency at the heart of the English game, which had set in after the blanket adoption of Arsenal manager Herbert Chapman's ideas in the late 1920s.

Just before the outbreak of World War Two Rowe returned home and, like many other post-war football managers, including Joe Mercer, Matt Busby and West Ham's Ted Fenton, became a physical training instructor in the Army. During the war Rowe managed the British Army football team and when he was released from military duties in July 1945, he joined non-league club Chelmsford City (Fenton was just down the road at Colchester) and guided them to victory in the Southern League Cup Trophy. His success motivated Spurs to bring their former centre-half back to White Hart Lane in May 1949 after the dismissal of Joe Hulme.

With signings like Alf Ramsey from Southampton, Rowe built a magnificent, attractive and sometimes erratic Spurs team around the fundamental principle of 'Keep it simple, make it quick'. He brought the Second Division Championship to White Hart Lane in 1950 and led the club to their first Division One Championship title the following year. Rowe almost made it two consecutive titles for Tottenham in 1952 when the club finished runners-up to Manchester United. In the same season Spurs reached the last four of the FA Cup. This was an unprecedented success story. Within the space of 20 months Tottenham Hotspur had gone from being something less than an ordinary Second Division side to one of the leading clubs in the most powerful footballing nation under the sun.

Spurs' success had been founded on Rowe's insistence that his team create a web of passes, each one a building block of progression and attack. These interchanges were swift and short and occurred, for the most part, along the ground. They were facilitated by players not holding on to the ball, running into space to receive a return pass, or outwitting an opposing defender. The whole plan of play depended on the ability and striking power of the forward line. Rowe would later use this same system with Palace. It came to be known as the 'push and run' game (a term Rowe detested), and Rowe claimed it made good players out of ordinary ones, but actually it required a team with a high level of fitness and skill to make it work effectively. It needed much more stamina than the game that revolved around the centre-half for instance, as all the players in the side were constantly on the move, including the goalkeeper, with whom, according to Rowe, every attack started. Rowe explained the other necessary ingredient that was often missed by those who sought to replicate this system:

> Although the basis of our game was quick, accurate, short passes and continuous movement, we needed variety. Len Duquemin was the perfect target man. Alf Ramsey, for instance, could drive long balls at his chest and we could then build up from an advanced position. Geoff Hurst did much the same thing with Johnny Byrne at West Ham. Johnny could kill a ball with almost any part of his body. That was a big feature of his game.

Alf Ramsey had an immensely fruitful relationship with Rowe. In Alf, though Rowe did not make him captain of his side, the job going to Ron Burgess, Arthur had found the perfect player to exert a benign, constructive influence over a lively team and Alf became Rowe's foremost lieutenant at Tottenham. Ramsey appeared taciturn, but although he was outwardly inhibited, internally he was as passionate and vulnerable as the ebullient cockney Rowe. Ramsey was a constructive full-back *par excellence*, although some said that Bill Nicholson, then the Spurs right-half, did his tackling for him and Sonny Walters, the right-winger, did his running, but Spurs never looked the same without Ramsey. His kicking, practiced for hours on end, was superb, while his use of the ball was splendidly intelligent and all the time he learnt from Rowe.

Hungry Alf

It was on the basis of his club's success that Alf Ramsey consolidated his place in the England team and played in the 1950 World Cup. He was part of the

1953 England defence that was comprehensively defeated by Hungary, which was a memorable moment for the player. Ramsey did score a penalty against the mighty Magyars, but the final score told the story: 6–3 to the visitors. It was the first time England had been beaten at home by a non-British side.

England's blinkered attitude to world football had allowed the Hungarians, the Olympic champions, who had not been beaten for 25 games over three years, to surprise them. The land that had invented the game had isolated itself from new ideas. After the match it was clear that the Hungarians, while remaining true to the basic principles of defensive play as laid down by Chapman, had modified traditional attacking strategies. Hidegkuti, the great centre-forward, dropped off into the middle of the field, leaving Puskas and Kocsis to make through passes and cut into the very heart of England's defence. The wingers, too, came deep, adding to the confusion of players who had become complacent. England's centre-half, Harry Johnston of Blackpool, was never sure whether he should follow Hidegkuti or stay in the middle of the defence. While covering full-backs, swinging round to give the defence depth, he merely created space into which the Hungarians could punt passes without fear of being caught offside. In the end the English side were a perplexed rabble, the disorientation having spread like an epidemic.

However complete and salutary the lesson, English football simply would not learn or see the true reason for the shattering defeat. It was blamed on poor selection. The critics, at least, were true to form. As such, the eventual return, England's visit to Budapest, was an even bigger disaster and they went home on the end of a 7–1 thrashing. Rowe was to recall:

> Before the 1950s there was no hint of what the Hungarians would later achieve. They were little more than apprentices at that time. And yet in 1953 they had the finest team in the world. They didn't have any secret. They were a great team because they had something like six world-class players and it was as simple as that. When they murdered England at Wembley in 1953 there were still people who looked at the wrong things. Skill, thought and mobility didn't take much recognising.

In the final analysis the situation was put down to Hungarian genius and the myth persists today. The Hungarians did indeed have rare skills and supreme fitness, but the England side of 1953 were, above all, tactically defeated, although the recent League Champions Spurs had been using a brand of the same strategy that had put England to the sword to dominate the English First

Division. And it was not only Rowe and Spurs! As Rowe was breaking new ground at White Hart Lane, Vic Buckingham, who had played at Tottenham with Rowe, set up a similar playing regime with Oxford and Cambridge side Pegasus, guiding them to victory in the 1951 Amateur Cup (by six clear goals) in front of a crowd of 100,000 at Wembley.

In 1953 Buckingham adapted the push and run strategy at West Bromwich Albion, winning the FA Cup in 1954, when, as runners-up, the team were just

BILL NICHOLSON (Spurs)

five points away from completing the first League Championship/FA Cup double of the 20th century. Buckingham was another thinker and a man receptive to new ideas. Under him Albion played a simple game, in a quick and intelligent manner. They were able to adapt and approached their football as a thoughtful exercise. The ball was used with respect but it was made to do most of the work. Possession was all-important. It was understood that without the ball an opponent was powerless – and error was less likely if passing was undertaken over shorter distances. Under Buckingham West Bromwich were a consistently good side and in 1959 he took over at Ajax of Amsterdam, where he was to discover and nurture the young Johann Cruyff and lead Ajax to dominate Dutch football, while sowing the seeds of what became known as 'total football'.

The truth of the matter was that Arthur Rowe had unwittingly paved the way for England's defeat 14 years before 1953. He had brought ideas back from Hungary of course, but both the Hungarian and Tottenham teams of the early 1950s showed major similarities to the attitude and style that Rowe had developed and exhibited in the Spurs side of the 1930s.

The defeat at the hands of Ferenc Puskas and his compatriots was to have a profound effect on professional football in England. Indeed England, as a footballing nation, carried that Wembley result like an albatross until the World Cup in 1966 when Arthur Rowe's disciple, Alf Ramsey, exorcised the ghosts of '53.

Think simplicity

Rowe was a thinker, a man with an unyielding conviction that the game was all about simplicity and movement. He gave Spurs subtlety and bite, encouraging his side to work with shrewdness and flair. He inspired his players with an idea of how to play, offering them a vision and philosophy of a football aesthetic. He was involved in coaching clinics and influenced young men like Malcolm Allison when the then West Ham defender was attending courses at Lilleshall, the national coaching centre. Allison was to work hard to merge Rowe's ideas with his own theories of play and this was to have a lasting effect at Upton Park, starting with the Hammers' Second Division Championship win in 1958, the year when Avon ladies first came knocking at British doors.

MAINE ROAD HEROES

Malcolm Allison

Allison, Rowe and later Greenwood and Nicholson, were men desperately looking for answers. It was a disaster and a waste that there was no major role for Rowe in English football after the early 1970s and certainly no input from Allison.

However, by the mid-fifties the successful Tottenham squad were starting to show their age and were beginning to have trouble maintaining the speed demanded by Rowe's methods, while other clubs were beginning to understand how to defend against the push and run system, running with the man and not after the ball. At the same time the club's youth system had been bettered by the likes of Manchester United, Chelsea and West Ham. Consequently, results started to dip, as did Rowe's health, as the pressure of keeping Spurs out of the relegation zone and the backbiting within the corridors of White Hart Lane took its toll. In 1954 Arthur suffered the breakdown which resulted in him being advised to stay away from football for a few years. When Rowe fell ill Jimmy Anderson was made acting manager and he eventually took over as full-time manager when Arthur resigned in 1955. Rowe's record shows the type of style he fostered:

Arthur Rowe						
Managerial Record at Tottenham Hotspur	Played	Won	Drew	Lost	For	Against
Football League	249	119	50	80	453	343
Cup Competitions & Other matches	34	16	9	9	64	44
Total	283	135	59	89	517	387

Rowe took up the less demanding job of coach to Pegasus, where his integrity, intelligence and humour were much appreciated, but he returned to the professional game as chief scout at West Bromwich Albion in August 1957 and arrived at Selhurst Park in October 1958 as assistant manager to George Smith, taking over as manager in April 1960. Rowe later became a director at Palace and continued to work on the Selhurst Park staff until May 1971. He was then employed by Football's Hall of Fame (a London exhibition) for six months after leaving Palace before he joined Orient as a consultant in January 1972. He took on a similar role at Millwall in 1978. Arthur passed away in 1993.

VIC
BUCKINGHAM
(MANAGER)
(W.B.A.)

When Alf Ramsey finished playing he managed Ipswich Town, who became the Second Division Champions in 1961. He guided the East Anglian club to the First Division Championship the following year. No side had done that since Rowe's Tottenham and no manager achieved this after Ramsey. Johnny Byrne would work with Ramsey later in the 1960s.

Rowe and his flaming 'kerfluffer'

It was Arthur Rowe who persuaded Byrne to become a centre-forward. He recalled:

> He was playing at inside-forward, a midfield 'kerfluffer' I called him. He'd had two great seasons for Palace. I said to him one day, 'Why don't you play up the front?' He said, 'I'm not big enough.' I told him that all the players I ever had trouble with in my career were little guys. He said he'd try it.
>
> It worked, and afterwards he said, 'It's not bad up there, I like it'. He was like Alan Ball, Eddie Bailey, all those small guys with bandy legs. He had a spark that could light fires! He had this tremendous skill. This ability to take people on. John was pigeon-toed, and it gave him four ways of dealing with a ball; the inside and outside of both feet. No ball ever gave him a problem.
>
> He was great at playing it away first time and moving off to a new position. He was so quick the defenders couldn't get near him. I would put him in the top four centre-forwards I ever came across. For two or three seasons he was fantastic.

With Byrne now being referred to as a 'genius' in some quarters, Palace, with their decent-sized ground and seasoned manager, were raising expectations. John instantly respected his new boss; he recognised Rowe's understanding of football and was to think of him as:

> ...one hell of a good guy... one of the greatest. Arthur Rowe was football. He was everybody's friend. I rated him as one of the kindest and most sincere men I met in the game. He was good with tactics and was able to show you by example on the training pitch. Arthur was always approachable and helpful. Whatever the problem players felt they could take it to him. I trusted the man completely. If it hadn't have been for his health letting him down Arthur would have been one of the great managers.

Rowe and Byrne were, in a number of ways, very much alike. Rowe was a jovial, working-class Londoner, while John was a bubbly, outgoing, second-generation Dublin Irishman. By 1963 Rowe had left Selhurst Park but he and Byrne corresponded long after John's playing days and Rowe's time as a scout for Orient were over. This relationship was to shape Byrne's football outlook and says much about his attitude to the game and the style of play he adopted and propagated.

From his first hours as manager at Selhurst Park Rowe began to make Palace work as a team, but without stifling Byrne's natural abilities. The side opened the 1960–61 season with a Selhurst Park match against Accrington Stanley. Rowe had said that the season would be one of 'expectation' and 15,653 expectant fans turned out to see how their club would be affected by the new manager and his several signings, perhaps in particular the blond, fleet-footed winger from South London rivals Millwall, Ron Heckman. This was to be the first appearance Stanley made at Selhurst Park.

Johnny Byrne scored the first Palace goal of the season – in fact it was the first goal of the entire football League season, as it took just 50 seconds to get – and he went on to score four that day. Centre-forward George Hudson equalised soon after, but eight minutes into the game Palace were 3–1 up. The former England Youth and Blackburn striker Jack Swindells made a second reply for Stanley, however at half-time the score stood at 5–2 to the Glaziers. In the second half Rowe's side hit four more without further response from Accrington. Alongside Byrne's quartet, Alan Woan scored a hat-trick and Heckman grabbed himself a couple of goals. Rowe called the 9–2 win 'a promising start'.

This was followed by three more victories in a row, and by mid-October Palace were clear Divisional leaders. Alan Woan, who had come from Northampton the previous season, helped Byrne and Summersby make up the most effective inside trio in the Division. The defence was strengthened by former West Ham player George Petchey, who came to Selhurst Park from Queen's Park Rangers and presented a solid front to almost every attack. But even alongside the new personnel, at times Byrne looked like someone from another dimension at Selhurst Park. One autumnal evening in late September, the ball, swirling on the edge of a penetrating wind, curled across the penalty area towards two men, a burly Southport defender and a neat, slight, Crystal Palace forward. While the centre was still airborne the forward feignted, seeming to move, but checking: instinctively the defender veered away. In the fraction of time before he swung back into the tackle, the young Palace player had taken the ball down from his chest and had hit it, full volley, high into the net, a shot of thunderbolt power, leaving no time for the green-jerseyed custodian to leap across the turf. It was a flash of pure intellect which would have graced any First Division game: in a Fourth Division match it stood out like a blazing beacon. In that match Byrne scored four times, taking each goal with the calm assurance of a man who knew he had no peer on the field that evening.

Proud Palace promptly promoted, Pongos play prodigiously

Woan left Palace suddenly, for Aldershot, but the introduction of the former Tottenham centre-forward Dennis Uphill from Watford early in October 1960 kept the attack sharp. Rowe saw the presence of Uphill, a robust, lumbering tank of a striker, but with a good brain and capable of some subtle moves, as having the potential to liberate the skills of Byrne and Summersby from the rugged tackles of Fourth Division defenders. Uphill did draw a lot of attrition, allowing the more artistic members of the team to express themselves to the full, and thus by early December, Palace were top of the League table, a point clear of Peterborough. So the visit to Bootham Crescent on 10 December, the only ground in the Division that had not tasted defeat so far that season, seemed like something of a test, especially as Posh looked certain of taking two points at Barrow. York were just behind the Division's leading pack and as such had ambitions of their own. They were a strong, grim foe and from the start the game was not for the faint of heart. The deadlock was broken by an Alf Noakes corner. Ron Heckman played a short pass to Byrne who brought

THE CRYSTAL PALACE FOOTBALL CLUB LIMITED

DIRECTORS

A. J. WAIT (Chairman)   J. R. H. DUNSTER, J.P. (Vice-Chairman)
V. A. ERCOLANI   R. SHRAGER

Manager : A. ROWE   Secretary : Miss M. E. MONTAGUE
Trainer : T. BROLLY
Medical Officer : P. SOMMERVILLE M.B., Ch.B.

Programme Price Fourpence

No. 25   Saturday, 29th April, 1961
Crystal Palace v. York City
Kick-Off 3.0 p.m.

CLUB NOTES
by
" GLAZIER "

" THAT'S YOUR LOT "

And with that goes the thanks of the Directors, Manager and staff for the truly wonderful support the club has received this season.

Maybe we can all agree that the best football was seen before Christmas, but taking it by and large not much fault

Noakes back into the move. Alf sent a square ball to George Petchey who played a thoughtful and glorious chip to score. With Summersby and Byrne making some inspired moves, Palace gradually took control in the second half, but the Minstermen reminded their guests that they were still dangerous by hitting the crossbar. With 15 minutes to play a fracturing Byrne pass released Uphill to power his way to the far flank and deliver a meaningful cross for Heckman to volley home.

The game at York (who would finish in fifth place in the Division) was probably the best away performance of that Palace campaign and, with Peterborough slipping up at Barrow, they were a point clear at the top of the Fourth Division. However, a surprising slump brought four successive defeats and enabled Posh, in their first League season, to begin their charge for the championship. Palace won six of their last seven games without being able to overhaul the newcomers, but they finished just two points behind and second place ensured promotion, with 110 League goals and 64 points from 46 games. Byrne was top scorer with 30 goals, while Summersby claimed 25. Together with Heckman, who had helped make many of Palace's goals, but also scored 14 in 42 outings, they had paved their team's way into the Third Division. It was Palace's first promotion in 40 years. The triumph had been achieved through attractive and polished play and the club's reliance on skill rather than strength had not only brought results, but also drew an average attendance of 19,020, which was the 25th highest of the 92 League clubs that season. The game against Millwall at Easter had attracted a crowd of 37,774. Rowe and the club rewarded the players with a summer trip to Bermuda.

This period saw Byrne complete his National Service. Like many players pulled into the forces during the decades of conscription, it had an effect on his career, but John was talented and disciplined enough to minimise any long-term detriment. He was stationed within three hours commuting distance from London and had plenty of time to develop his game. He played for 29 Company RAOC and helped his side win the Army Cup in the 1960–61 season, although the team had no credible form. John was always proud of this achievement: 'It was amazing really. Probably equivalent to a Third or Fourth Division side winning the FA Cup.'

Byrne skippered the British Army side in 1960–61 that included English internationals Alan Hodgkinson (Sheffield United) and Bill Foulkes (Manchester United). In one of his games for the Pongos John scored six goals.

When Byrne came out of the Army, Palace faced a problem. The maximum wage was a thing of the past. How much would their new star want? Could they afford to pay?

Arthur Rowe recollected:

> We'd talked about this and were a bit worried how much he'd ask for. When he came in I said, 'How much are you willing to sign for?'
>
> He said, 'I don't know, you tell me.' I said, 'All right, I'll tell you what I'll do, I'll give you twice what the other players are making.' He said, 'All right, that suits me.'
>
> In effect we got him cheap because he was worth far more than that!

Palace fielded three new players when they started their first campaign in the

Third Division in August 1961; centre-forward/winger Ronnie Allen, full-back Roy Little and Andy Smillie from West Ham. Andy was an exceptionally intelligent attacking player who modelled his game on Ferenc Puskas. He was to finish the season as top marksman in the League at Palace with 16 goals. Allen had turned out for West Bromwich Albion and England. While at the Hawthorns he had played alongside the Palace assistant manager Dick Graham. Little came to Selhurst Park from Brighton. He had played for Manchester City in the 1955 and 1956 FA Cup finals.

Palace continued to play the stylish push and run game in their Third Division incarnation. The club's first game of the season took them to Torquay, who had finished the previous term in mid-table. The Glaziers' attack blended well from the first minutes of the match. Palace looked the better side and they got better as half-time approached. Byrne struck the woodwork early on but put his side ahead with 15 minutes of play expended. He rounded the centre-half as one might a statue and with a measure of suave competence lashed the ball past the lost 'keeper. The ball seemed magnetically attracted to the back of the Gulls' net twice more before the break but offside decisions made the sojourns meaningless. The home side pulled themselves together in the second half, and managed to trouble the Palace defence, but 'keeper Vic Rouse was resilient while George Petchey was resplendent in defence and together they held off a 30-minute assault on the Palace goal. Out of these rearguard actions Byrne emerged and combined with Smillie to craft out a collusion with Summersby, who put the South Londoners two up. To their credit the hosts fought on and their close-season signing, outside-right and former Birmingham Blue, Gordon Astall, finally foiled the formerly indefatigable Rouse with a well-placed header.

As August turned into September proud Palace were atop the table and they would stay in the top six throughout the autumn.

The future was looking brighter and brighter for Johnny Byrne and in South Africa, against the odds, it seemed that things were also improving. In 1961 FIFA reversed its position on the South African segregation of football by suspending the FASA. In response NFL/FASA established the National Professional Soccer League for its SABFA clubs ('establishment' Africans).

'Budgie' for England!

John started the 1961–62 term as he had finished the previous season and in November 1961 he became the first Crystal Palace player to be capped by

England since 1923 and one of the very few Third Division players to be picked for full England honours. Indeed there were only two before him during the post-Second World War era: centre-forward Tommy Lawton (Notts County, 1947) and goalkeeper Reg Matthews (Coventry City, 1956). Coincidently the next player from the old Third Division to win an England cap was another Crystal Palace man, Peter Taylor (1976). Steve Bull (Wolverhampton Wanderers, 1989) was the last of the few. The equivalent of the old Third Division is the current Championship One. No player from a club in that Division has played for England.

It was during his first days with England that Byrne picked up the nickname that would stay with him the rest of his days. Johnny Haynes recalled his first encounter with Byrne:

> The first time I met him was on an England tour – I was the captain at the time and Budgie stuck to me like a leech. Wherever I went Budgie was snapping at my heels, night-clubs, restaurants, boxing tournaments. He never stopped talking and it was then that I nicknamed him 'Budgie'.

The epithet stuck to the extent that later John even signed his name as 'Budgie Byrne'. Budgie's first cap was awarded for his role in a hard match with Northern Ireland.

Date:	22 November 1961
Location:	Wembley
Competition:	Home Championship
Fixture:	England v Northern Ireland
Result:	1–1 (1–0)
England scorer:	R. Charlton
Northern Ireland scorer:	J. McIlroy
Team:	Springett, R.D.G. (Sheffield Wednesday), Armfield, J.C. (Blackpool), Wilson, R. (Huddersfield Town), Robson, R.W. (West Bromwich Albion), Swan, P. (Sheffield Wednesday), Flowers, R. (Wolverhampton Wanderers), Byrne, J.J. (Crystal Palace), Douglas, B. (Blackburn Rovers), Crawford, R. (Ipswich Town), Haynes, J.N. (Fulham) captain, Charlton, R. (Manchester United).

The Irish team that day was skippered by Danny Blanchflower. Byrne recalled that the 1–1 draw had been hard to get and that it was not a great English performance. It was a dull, grey occasion, with Wembley only a third full and England fighting to find some sort of rhythm against an Irish side imbued with fanatical enthusiasm seemingly built into every green shirt. Byrne, almost as much an Irishman as any of the opposition, stood out, confident enough to hold the ball, dribbling neatly and economically, passing precisely, with his customary sense of pace and timing. It was a typical Byrne performance. Given his almost faultless display his omission from the party to go to Chile for the World Cup was inexplicable.

Walter Winterbottom was Byrne's first international manager. Winterbottom struck John as being 'very intellectual' and John immediately understood that the man knew more about the game than all his players put together. Winterbottom's ability to analyze opposing teams and the ease with which he was able to assess Continental sides impressed the young centre-forward. However, Byrne also saw that Winterbottom was unfortunate to be part of an era wherein the England team was chosen by a panel of six selectors. Later, John understood that he had been disadvantaged by this regime and even at the time he resented the fact that his future lay in the hands of people who to him seemed ignorant of the modern professional game. This was exemplified for Byrne by one particular incident. John had been involved in an 'up and downer' with Don Howe, then a tough full-back playing for West Bromwich Albion. A selector witnessed the encounter and made it known that Byrne would not play for England again. He didn't play again during Winterbottom's tenure and the reign of the panel of selectors, even though the England coach thought highly of him:

> John Byrne was the best young player of his generation. He had learnt a lot from Arthur Rowe, but the fact that he was an intelligent young man made this possible. There were few of his age that could match his talent, both to think about what he wanted to do and do it. Really, Byrne should have ended his career with a few dozen, maybe 50 English caps.

Villa's villainy pops Palace

Palace had managed to reach the third round of the FA Cup on two occasions as a Fourth Division club, although both times they had been defeated away from home at the hands of unfashionable sides. But in early January 1962, on the first Saturday of the playing year, the Glaziers reached new heights in the Cup, producing what was seen by many as their best performance under Arthur Rowe. Palace had been drawn to face Aston Villa, who were then, as now, one of the elite sides of the English game. The tie was to be contested at Villa Park, a daunting prospect for any club, but particularly so for a team from the lower reaches of the League structure.

That cold day saw the Villains start the game with great confidence that was reinforced when Harry Burrows put the Midlanders in front, although many a neutral and all but the most myopic of Palace fans would argue that Burrows had been as offside as a cow in a field of love-starved bulls. Yet the decision by Mr Callaghan, the esteemed if visually challenged referee, seemed to inspire the Londoners and it was not long before Johnny Byrne made their reply when he bothered, bedazzled and bettered Villa keeper Nigel Sims. Dennis Uphill silenced the 39,011 crowd when, riding a tackle, he galloped on to stab Palace ahead. Winger Peter McParland, Aston Villa's Republic of Ireland international, dragged his side back to level terms with a glancing header. In the second 45 minutes Palace continued to play at a lightning pace, applying great dollops of skill in the process, and began to bewilder their hosts. It was just a matter of time before the inevitable happened; Byrne got his head on the end of a Ron Heckman cross and put his side back in front. Villa, in a kind of controlled panic, forced equality making it 3–3 by way of the legendary Northern Ireland international Derek Dougan.

Deep into time added on, Palace had matched and bettered Villa on every front. In the dying seconds a ball wafted high in the gathering mist of the cold January dusk. It was a bastard thing; between a cross and a centre. Burrows had launched it into the air and it fell out of the vapours, evading Vic Rouse's flailing hands to end up in the far reaches of the net. The game was restarted but there was no time for a rejoinder.

Goodbye Johnny, goodbye

The sequel to Johnny's success was, inevitably, his departure from Selhurst Park. In the words of Chairman Arthur Wait, the loss of Budgie was 'one of the saddest moments in Palace history'. The club had been unable to retain its greatest asset. Even today Johnny stands high in the list of Palace marksmen. Until Ian Wright, Byrne was the highest post-World War Two goalscorer for Crystal Palace and was only pushed into third by Mark Bright in the early 1990s:

Crystal Palace all-time top goalscorers

Peter Simpson	166
Ian Wright	117
Mark Bright	113
George Clark	105
Johnny Byrne	101
Albert Dawes	92
Dave Swindlehurst	81
Percy Cherret	65
Roy Summersby	60
Chris Armstrong	58
Cecil Blackmore	56
Jack Blackman	55
Andy Gray	51
George Whitworth	50

Byrne gave Palace a touch of class and personality that few clubs in such lowly ranks could muster. Quick to move, even quicker to react to a change of situation, Budgie was genuinely two-footed, gifted with balance and ball control, capable of instinctive genius yet well aware of the need for tactics and method. He could play anywhere in a forward line and, according to his mood, could create or score goals; he twice hit four for Palace. His career at Selhurst Park had been one of triumph and development. His gifts were rare and real and it is likely that no better player has worn the claret and blue of Crystal Palace, but a new dawn beckoned in a very different part of old London town.

CHAPTER 2

Sunrise

T HE 1961–62 season was to be West Ham's fourth in top flight of English football after a 26-year absence. In their first term back among the elite the East Enders had finished in a very creditable sixth place, but positions of 14th and 16th in the previous two campaigns made them very much part of the 'also rans' of the old Division One. Ron Greenwood had taken over as the Hammers manager in April 1961, replacing Ted Fenton, the ex-player who had led the Irons back to the First Division. Greenwood was the first West Ham manager not to have any previous links with the Boleyn Ground, but he did have strong credentials, moving to Upton Park from the assistant manager's post with Arsenal and with a good record working with the England Youth and Under-23 teams. Ron's father had worked at Wembley Stadium and Greenwood had been exposed to the best of football strategy from an early age. Ron had witnessed, first hand, the Hungarian demolition of England in 1953. At the time he was playing for Chelsea; he been exposed to the coaching of Arthur Rowe, having, as a teenager, seen him play for Spurs and of course Greenwood the centre-half (the same position as Rowe played) knew the Tottenham side of the early fifties well. Ron had also worked with Walter Winterbottom, having turned out for the England 'B' side, and had benefited from that great tactician's insight into the Hungarian style, although Greenwood had been one of the few who recognised the way the East Europeans played that day in 1953. In fact that November game, the last Harry Johnston (another centre-half) would play for England, had been something of a dream for Greenwood. Puskas and his men were working according to his own vision of the game; seeing his personal insight literally played out in front of his eyes proved to be a motivating influence that would guide the rest of Greenwood's career in football.

Being cautious by nature, although groundbreaking in his tactical awareness, Greenwood did not make wholesale personnel changes in the first part of his reign at Upton Park, but when the Irons were put out of the League Cup in early October, beaten in the second round by the holders, Aston Villa, and suffered a 4–0 League defeat at St Andrews, he was concerned enough to alter his schedule to go to Wembley on 22 November to see England achieve a 1–1 draw with Northern Ireland and Johnny Byrne gain his first full cap.

The New Year started badly for the Hammers. They crashed out of the FA Cup at the hands of Plymouth and were beaten 3–0 in the First Division by Nottingham Forest. Two good wins – revenge against Villa at Upton Park and completion of a League double at Stamford Bridge – were followed by four games without a win. It was clear that something had to be done to prevent the season from turning into a mediocre affair.

Johnny the Hammer

When the West Ham club secretary Eddie Chapman was questioned by the press about the rumour that the Hammers were about to make a bid of £70,000 for Johnny Byrne, he scoffed at the idea and asked: 'What do people think we are going to do for that sort of money, sell the ground?' However, there had been pressure on the board for some time to provide tangible evidence of its confidence in Greenwood. At the same time attendances were falling so the club bureaucrats needed to show they were prepared to invest and match other clubs in the top flight in terms of financing the playing side.

Greenwood's knowledge of the young players available to England meant that Johnny Byrne had, for some time, certainly since Ron had became assistant manager at Highbury, been established in his mind as a potentially great player. Greenwood had been manager of the England Under-23 side that had beaten West Germany 4–1 at White Hart Lane in front of almost 16,000 spectators in May 1961. Amid the chaotic administration that seemed to be the order of the day for representative teams at that time, Greenwood had been advised late by Football Association staff that he was short of players. In desperation he had called up winger Mike Harrison just after he had concluded a full day's training at Chelsea. Bobby Moore was in the side that evening (as were Freddie Hill of Bolton, Southampton's Terry Paine and Gunner John Barnwell) and he and Byrne, working together, tore the heart out of the Germans, but Johnny was almost unbelievable. Years later Moore said: 'Budgie must have had a hundred touches of the ball, 75 of them from my passes, most of that one-touch, all down to Ron's organisation.' In fact the Football Association had analysed that game, which included counting the number of balls that came from Moore to Byrne. John collected no fewer than 108 passes from Bobby over the 90 minutes.

From the moment he took over at West Ham Greenwood meant to bring Byrne to Upton Park. He wanted Johnny more than any other player and it was just a matter of finding the right moment. March 1962 seemed like the appropriate point.

Arthur Rowe didn't want to lose Byrne, but Palace were not in the best of situations financially so, knowing that a number of Italian clubs had looked at John, and feeling that West Ham would be a much better option for his young star, Rowe, aware of Greenwood's interest, let the Hammers' manager know that Byrne was available – at a price. Rowe knew Geoff Hurst's father Charlie from their days together at Chelmsford City (Hurst's father had been a professional footballer who had also played for Oldham Athletic) and Rowe had wanted Hurst to make up about 10 percent of the fee that would send Byrne to Upton Park. Greenwood talked the matter over with his chairman Reg Pratt, telling him what he thought Byrne could do for the West Ham side and saying that he would like to keep Hurst (who, in any case, had refused to move to Selhurst Park) as he had plans for the burly youngster to work alongside Johnny.

There wasn't much time. At least two Italian clubs had sent scouts to look at Byrne. Pratt handled the negotiations and it was agreed that West Ham would pay £58,000 plus centre-forward Ronnie Brett, who had come to the Boleyn Ground from Crystal Palace in 1959 and was valued at £7,500. Ronnie had netted four times in his 13 appearances for the Hammers, including home and away goals against Manchester United in 1960. It was agreed that part of the fee would be paid immediately, then the rest at the rate of £1,000 a week. This was the first and last time in Greenwood's tenure at the club that West Ham bought a player in any other way than by paying the full price up front. It was a record signing for West Ham and the biggest deal ever done between two English clubs. Byrne's starting salary was £40 a week. Sadly Brett was killed in a car crash in September 1962. His friend, Brian Rhodes, a West Ham goalkeeper at the time, came away from the same accident unhurt.

It was Greenwood who was to dub Byrne the 'Di Stefano of British football', and the similarities between Johnny and the Argentinian 'White Arrow' of Real Madrid were repeated in the press. Johnny, like Di Stefano, was short for a centre-forward, but able to play in any of the central attacking positions. Byrne also had an impressive turn of pace, tight ball control, a scorching shot and was a great passer. He wasn't yet 23 years of age but it was clear to anyone who watched him on the ball that he was an extremely skilful and artistic player. In a television interview shortly after the move John modestly stated that he hoped the move would benefit his own career as well as the future of his new club and that First Division soccer with the Hammers would enable him to achieve the highest honours in the game.

Byrne would often work deeper than a conventional striker and lay on as many goals for others as he scored himself. He added flair to a West Ham team already blessed with Moore and players like Ronnie Boyce and Hurst, who was breaking into the side, and Martin Peters and John Sissons developing behind the scenes.

Political football

As Budgie took the next step in his football life, soccer in South Africa continued to be part of the overall political struggle in 1962. In response to FIFA sanctions and internal threats from SASF, the FASA proposed unity with SASF. However the SASF rejected the proposal as it would have meant the adoption of apartheid principles, but in the same year an inter-racial soccer match was played in front of 10,000 spectators in Maseru, Basutoland (Lesotho) between (white) Germiston Callies and (African) Black Pirates.

Looking back on the situation South Africa seemed to be living in a kind of twilight world. Its football, like the rest of its society, was becoming increasingly isolated from the rest of the world, and the reaction within white South African soccer was not dissimilar to that of the English controllers of the game before Hungary destroyed all the illusions. There was an unspoken idea that development could take place in seclusion, which of course goes against everything we understand about how things grow and improve. However, South Africa, like English football after the trouncing of 1953, refused to see the obvious; the system was archaic, having little resemblance to the reality of things. It is particularly noticeable in terms of football and sport in general that every time the world rejected the South African regime it begrudgingly gave a little ground. But the result was always a kind of neurotic compromise that kept the principal of segregation hobbling along, tended by the white South African political and commercial establishment.

Where there's smoke...

At first it looked as if Byrne wasn't making much of a difference to the

Hammers. His first match, on 17 March 1962, was a goalless draw at Hillsborough. He made little impact on the game and West Ham never troubled England international goalkeeper Ron Springett. It was all the Hammers could do to keep Wednesday out, with England Under-23 striker Colin Dobson hitting an Irons post and West Ham's 'Hammer of Scotland', Laurie Leslie, playing like a man inspired between the sticks. However, it took two goal-line clearances from Joe Kirkup to give West Ham a point. Byrne's Upton Park debut saw Manchester City come away having thrashed the Irons 4–0. By the time John was in a winning West Ham side the Hammers had gone seven games and eight weeks without a victory. Byrne's first two-pointer came from an encounter at the Hawthorns with West Bromwich Albion. Malcolm Musgrove scored the only goal of the game.

Byrne's second appearance in front of the booing Boleyn Ground fans included a scolding by referee Collinge after a run-in with Birmingham defender Jimmy Bloomfield during a 2–2 draw with the Blues. But at last Budgie scored his first goal for the Hammers, the third in a 4–1 Upton Park defeat of Cardiff City on Good Friday, when 18-year-old Martin Peters, at the time seen as not much more than a good squad player, made his debut as Greenwood gave Bobby Moore the captaincy and dropped half-a-dozen players, including Phil Woosnam, Geoff Hurst and John Bond.

The Welsh were abysmal from the start. John hit the Cardiff crossbar in the 53rd minute, to see Alan Sealey slot home, and as the game moved towards its conclusion it seemed like 20 April was not going to be that good a Friday for Budgie. But with seven minutes of the match remaining Johnny hit the back of the net from a tight angle. He recalled:

> It was a great relief. But I wouldn't have said it at the time. The crowd at Upton Park were right on top of you, the pitch went right up to the front of the stands and the fans, although they were great supporters, were always honest about their feelings. It's understandable, but we were trying something new for most of us. The way Ron wanted us to play did take a bit of getting used to... more for some than others though. And there were a few who expressed their doubts in no uncertain terms. But Ron's way was if you didn't want to play his way, you didn't have to and you got dropped. He was a gentle, calm man, but he could be ruthless if pushed. He wasn't one to do his nut and as far as I was concerned you kind of knew what he was going to do as far as the team was

concerned. But if you didn't understand his ways he sometimes came across like a bit of an assassin.

According to West Ham manager-to-be John Lyall, who was then still playing the occasional first-team game in the Hammers defence:

Budgie was like Jimmy Greaves, being confident, bright, full of humour and able to improvise, but in his first days at Upton Park he was trying too hard, attempting to take the lace out of the ball every time he got into the penalty area. He had to be taught to do the simple things. I watched Budgie wriggle past defenders, walk around the goalkeeper and then miss an empty net.

Derek Woodley, another young and promising striker at Upton Park at the time of Byrne's arrival, recalled:

At first, in matches, nothing seemed to work out for Budgie. He had a difficult first few months where not much went right. He didn't let it get him down though and tried to work it out. He had some bad luck, but I don't think he had his head quite right. He had bags of character, but you've still got to settle in when you go to a new club and West Ham was very different to Palace in those days. Some people said he was trying too hard, having to justify his fee, but I don't know about that. The crowd might have got on his back a bit and truthfully, no one likes that, some say it don't bother them, but it does.

I think Greenwood said that he hit the ball a bit hard when shooting. But there was always a bit of an informal competition around who could strike the ball hardest, I think that came from John Bond, who had a kick like a donkey and a lot to do with the younger players who were at the club in the late fifties, along with Malcolm Allison and Noel Cantwell. Most of us liked to hit the ball when we had a chance; see what we could do.

I know a lot of people began saying that Greenwood spent loads of money on a player who hadn't done much more than play in the Third and Fourth Divisions. But no one at the club really doubted that Ron had got a good 'un in Johnny. You only had to see him in training to tell that. He could do things in a way no one else could. He had loads of balance and bags of vision. He had the ability to do the simple things in an extraordinary way I suppose.

Greenwood told his young striker to go back to basics, and concentrate on getting the foundations right while allowing his game to come together; giving his natural equilibrium and instinct room to mature. It took Byrne a year of hard work on the training ground before his new club began to get the best out of him and, according to Lyall, 'There's no doubt that once Ron got the message across Budgie became an outstanding striker'. At first things didn't go altogether smoothly off the field either. Former West Ham Boys player Charlie Green told me:

> When we signed Budgie Byrne, the 'grease monkey', he had Brylcreem everywhere; we used to go in Ed's café over the road, after training on a Wednesday night. It was six, seven o'clock at night. Everybody used to go in there, bacon sandwiches, sausage sandwiches, egg and chips. You all had to queue up, no matter if you played in the first team or the juniors or the 'A' team, or the reserves. Well, we're all lining up, there was a fair old queue that night and Budgie came in and went straight to the front of the queue! Well, that upset Johnnie Charles, he was skipper of the Youth side that won the FA Cup in '63 remember, and he gave Budgie a mouthful and that put Byrne right to the back of the queue. Charlo was only a junior or a colt then with us. There was a big round of applause. Raaay!!! That's the only time I ever see Charlo really angry.

However, Budgie and Charles were soon to become firm friends, and, unfortunately, notorious drinking companions.

While it would be unfair to say that Byrne was struggling during his early days at West Ham – he was supported by the manager, the coaching staff and his fellow players who were conscious of his talent – the initial period at Upton Park was not easy for Budgie. His friend and mentor, Johnny Haynes, recalled:

> I remember him going through a tough time in his early days with West Ham. The supporters wanted to see him scoring goals but Budgie wasn't a goalscorer, and he took a bit of stick from the crowds. But his uncanny ability to flick a pass through to Hurst or Peters nearly always resulted in a goal and eventually the West Ham supporters realised his worth.

Perhaps Budgie never really forgot the initial response to him at Upton Park. He always said that one of the biggest disappointments in his footballing career came when he left Crystal Palace, although John's actions always showed a deep affection for the Boleyn Ground. In later life he expressed the wish that

Crystal Palace
F.C.

Real Madrid
C. de F.

after his death he wanted his ashes spread over the turf of the home of the Hammers.

Real hot

Budgie showed his undoubted class when he kept a promise to return to Palace to face the mighty Spanish League and European Champions, Real Madrid, and the player that Greenwood had likened him to: Alfredo Di Stefano. It was 18 April 1962 when Byrne once again pulled on a Palace shirt and joined his former teammates for a friendly game with the great Spanish side that had won the first European Cup tournament in 1956 and had retained the title until 1960 when they became the first World Club Champions, beating Penarol of Uruguay 5–1. Real wanted to use their first visit to London as a warm-up match for their European Cup final game against Benfica, while Palace were celebrating the installation of their new floodlighting system.

At the start of 1962 the Palace board had discussed which side they might invite to mark the improvements in their stadium. A number of big English clubs were approached but asked for immense guarantees and expenses. Arthur Rowe then suggested that if the club were going to spend that much money they might as well bring the very best to the home of the Glaziers, and that meant Real Madrid. Somehow the Palace chairman, Arthur Wait, persuaded the Spanish giants to make the trip for a fee of £10,000.

Referee Kitabdjian of France called Johnny McNichol and Francisco Gento to exchange pennants and pleasantries and then signalled the start of the match. Johnny Byrne made it immediately clear that he was going to be nothing less than inspirational in what was to be the biggest single-club match ever contested at Selhurst Park in terms of the relative value of the men who played in it.

On that cold evening Real fielded the side that had beaten Standard Liège in the semi-final of the European Cup the week before and they almost ambled into a 2–0 lead after just eight minutes via Di Stefano and Gento. But Ron Heckman then collided with Byrne's left-foot cross to head his side back into the game. Real did not dwell on the shock but replied with wicked predictability two minutes later through a Puskas free-kick. The captain of the Magyars blasted home from 30 yards. Sanchez made it 4–1, finishing off a giddying mélange of passes put together by Puskas and Di Stefano.

But this was not the end of things. After the break, looking the part in their claret and blue striped shirts and claret shorts, Palace took their lead from the immaculate Byrne and matched the flair of their opponents. Andy Smillie, amazed to be facing his inspiration Puskas, jabbed a Roy Summersby pass beyond Vicente and Terry Long banged a 25-yard strike home that all but equalled Puskas's thunderbolt.

Palace keeper Vic Rouse let in four goals in the first half, but the aptly named Bill Glazier, perhaps the best goalie ever to wear Crystal Palace colours, kept a clean sheet in the second 45 minutes. However, the most impressive performance of the night came from the young London Irishman, who held his own against one of the greatest football teams in history. After that match Di Stefano hailed Byrne as a world-class player and Ferenc Puskas was to remark: 'Smillie was very good. He is very wise for a young man and Byrne is outstanding. He must be a prospect in England. He would not be in the wrong place with Real Madrid, but he talks more than I do!'

In spite of inflated prices to cover the Spanish fee and the torrential rain that had been falling for 18 hours before the match, nearly 25,000 people turned up to see the game. The gate generated receipts of £15,000, easily a Palace record and a profit of something like £3,000 on the night. If looked at relative to today's football salaries that was equivalent to well over £1,000,000 today. However, the warm-up they had wanted didn't help Real: despite a hat-trick by the great Hungarian Puskas, scourge of the English, they lost the European Cup Final 5–3 to the Eagles of Lisbon in Amsterdam. The immortal Eusebio scored the final two goals of the game for the Portuguese side in the 65th and 68th minutes of the match.

The world opens up

There was to be only one more win for the Hammers in that 1961–62 season, when the final game of the League schedule saw Fulham beaten 4–2 at Upton Park. John had made 11 appearances for the Irons by the end of his first season at Upton Park, which had seen his side score 10 and concede 17. Many were saying that the side had fared better when he had been absent from the starting 11, but since Byrne's arrival attendance at the Boleyn Ground had risen by an average of 4,000 and good early season form meant that the fans could point to a top-10 finish, just two points behind Aston Villa in seventh place, putting West Bromwich Albion below them on goal average and bettering Arsenal by one point and two places. In Greenwood's first complete term West Ham had made an improvement of eight places on their First Division position of the previous season.

JOHNNY BYRNE
CENTRE-FORWARD

JOHNNY COST VEST HAM £65,000 LAST SPRING HAS REPRESENTED ENGLAND AND ENGLAND UNDER 23's

★ Bazooka ★
THE CHEW OF CHAMPIONS

Apart from Byrne, all the other big names of the campaign were already at the club when Ron arrived. However, Greenwood had brought a crop of youngsters into the first-team squad, including Martin Peters, Alan Dickie, Jack Burkett and Ronnie Boyce, who, like Peters and Bobby Moore, was an East End boy. In fact, most of the young men that were vying for first-team positions were from the local area, lads who had grown up in the youth team together and knew each other well.

Although not performing as well as he might have wanted, Johnny, with his manager's backing, kept positive. For Byrne: 'Ron had enough faith in me to pay a lot of money for my contract. He never stopped believing in me as a player and I always believed in him as a manager.'

Despite his relatively poor form, in May Byrne was called up for a young England squad along with two other Hammers, Joe Kirkup and Bobby Moore. However, only Moore made Walter Winterbottom's squad for the Chile World Cup.

Greenwood and West Ham began to open up Byrne's world and in later life John was always conscious that football had allowed him to see the world. He relished his trips with West Ham to Belgium, Greece, Spain, the US and Africa, and these experiences were to stand him in good stead in future years. Groups of young men abroad will always have fun as they are educated! John recalled: 'When you were in other countries, as an England or West Ham player, you would stay in the best hotels, visit the best night clubs, meet the most beautiful girls in the world.' All the temptations were available and Budgie succumbed to more than a few.

West Ham's 1962 tour of what was then Southern Rhodesia (now Zimbabwe), Nyasaland and Ghana was among the most memorable for John. The first leg of the trip went well and the whole team enjoyed every minute. It was only after they had left Nyasaland and Southern Rhodesia and arrived in Ghana that things started to go wrong. The army had taken over and the country appeared to be in total chaos. Nobody met the side at Accra airport: the excuse, given later, was that it was thought the West Ham party were on another plane, although there was only one flight a day from Johannesburg (the Hammers' point of departure) to Accra at that time. The team then found themselves being shown into a hotel that was nothing more than, in Ron Greenwood's words, 'a doss-house'. The blankets seemed to be alive and nobody slept except striker John Dick, who had a reputation for being able to sleep literally anywhere.

Everything was foreign to the London boys. They couldn't eat the food or drink the water. John remembered some of his teammates, many of whom had never been out of Britain, breaking down and crying because of the conditions. Eventually some representatives from the Ghana FA turned up and another hotel was found for the next morning. When the West Ham party arrived at their alternative accommodation, although it was a new building, they found it to be damp, cold and apparently only three-quarters built. However, the Hammers stoically made their way to the stadium where they were scheduled to play their first match in Ghana, but when they got there they found that the changing room showers had seemingly been used as a urinal. It was all a far cry from Budgie's Caribbean experience with Palace.

It was in the face of these traumatic events that Byrne proved his worth as a team member off the field. His continual banter and leg-pulling did much to bolster team morale, helping them laugh at themselves and the situation. However, he had used his own method of acclimatisation:

> When we were in Africa, Ghana, Ken Brown and me were the only
> ones who managed to get away without having 'stomach problems'.
> It was because we drank nothing but beer; it poisoned the bugs you
> see.

At the same time John's young colleagues began to warm to him and looked to him to raise their spirits. This was the unexpected bonus of the tour. Through all the adversity the team spirit grew. The problems shared welded the side together. It also taught Greenwood a lot about the character of his players and Byrne in particular. He saw his good sense of humour and counted him among those he could rely on when things weren't going right. He also noted those who looked for problems and those who either would not or could not work to overcome difficulties.

As the Hammers plied their trade in Africa they encountered all sorts of strategies deployed to undermine the Englishmen's poise and break their concentration, including determined efforts (with mixed results) to get some members of the team into the nightclubs and meeting the local girls. After a while Greenwood weighed up matters and saw that there was little to gain from completing the tour. However, the British Embassy pleaded with him to see the schedule through and after the whole party discussed the matter West Ham went on to win their remaining games convincingly, scoring 20 goals and conceding just two in their six matches. However, as the tour was coming to an end they were informed that visiting sides were supposed to settle for honourable draws. For all that, the press had been generous in their reports about the tour:

> The best touring side seen in recent years... with so much to admire in their ball control/quick short passes and general timing... a happy high-spirited bunch; they dress and act like true ambassadors of professional soccer... West Ham and England are lucky to have such players as John Byrne. He was the shining star of the forward line.

Pass and move

While preparing for his second season at Upton Park, it was clear to Byrne that Greenwood's emphasis on passing and holding the ball would suit him. Ron, like Arthur Rowe, encouraged players to use space and move off the ball. Most of the West Ham professionals had been playing this way since their earliest days at the Boleyn Ground, under the influence of Malcolm Allison, but Greenwood had organised and developed the West Ham game and made it work in the 4–2–4 system. John fitted in well with this way of playing; it was natural to him, both physically and in temperament. He was a master of the first-time pass and his accuracy was phenomenal. John was the final piece in a pattern that would give West Ham so much. At its best it would work on a variation of this theme:

1 – Goalkeeper Standen, an accurate distributor of the ball, would clear up the centre.

2 – Byrne would volley it first time out to Peter Brabrook on the right wing.

3 – Brabrook would make ground and cross it to Hurst.

4 – Hurst would head home.

It was amazing how many times West Ham would score in this way. On this foundation the Hammers imposed a new and exciting style on English football and a whole new breed of managers came out of its success, men in the Greenwood mould. But you only had to look at the other influential players in the West Ham squad to see that the West Ham manager was, in essence, building a team that could play an advanced form of the game Arthur Rowe had pioneered in Britain. For example, Greenwood, talking about Ronnie Boyce, said: 'In other people's eyes he was a most underrated player, but to us he was invaluable. The thing that most impressed me about his play was his ability to do the simple things quickly and efficiently.' Byrne himself confirmed that Boyce was the type of player who, like him, fitted well into the Rowe/Spurs strategic model: 'Ronnie was a player's player. He had a very high work rate and would find space and get the ball to you when you had made space.'

The foundations of West Ham's 1960s side were laid. Now, like the world, the future was opening up for Budgie Byrne.

CHAPTER 3

The Flame Matures

JOHNNY Byrne scored West Ham's first goal after 78 minutes of the 1962–63 season, in the opening game at Villa Park. It was just a pity that the Villains had knocked in three long before his strike. Budgie was to play in the first 19 matches of West Ham's League and FA Cup schedule, which included his side's first away win of the season at Maine Road on 1 August. The two points lifted West Ham from the bottom of the table and dumped the Manchester Blues at the foot of the pile. Less than 30 minutes into the game the sides were deadlocked at 1–1. Goals from Scott, Byrne, Martin Peters, and a brace from the boot of Malcolm Musgrove buried City. After Musgrove's second, Bert Trautmann, the City 'keeper, accused the West Ham man of being offside and kicked the ball at the referee. It struck Mr Stokes in the back and that meant that the huge German went for an early bath (the second sending-off of his career). Alan Oakes had to go in goal for City for the final 20 minutes of the match, during which time Geoff Hurst made it a round half-dozen for the Hammers.

In mid-September at Anfield, Liverpool gained revenge for their defeat at Upton Park a few days previously. Jim Furnell, the Liverpool 'keeper, set up Ian St John with a long throw. The Scottish international put his side ahead. Furnell was made to pay for his creative instincts by Byrne, being unable to hold John's shot as Budgie emerged from a deep lying position. However, in the last five minutes of the match the big Aberdeen-born, Liverpool centre-half Ron Yeats sent a header crashing into Leslie's bar and St John snatched up the rebound to give the points to Shankly's men.

West Ham's third victory of the season came at Ewood Park. At the start of the game both sides had identical form, but after the then England Under-23 international Fred Pickering almost made the most of Blackburn's early charge, the Hammers sent Rovers to the very root of the League. Budgie and Martin Peters hit home in the last two minutes of the match, taking advantage of Rovers' desperate efforts to reply to earlier goals scored by Hurst and Musgrove.

In September John snatched a 20-minute Boleyn Ground League Cup hat-trick (his first for West Ham and the Hammers' only one that season). Following an early goal by Peters, Budgie hit two headers and, after Plymouth defender Bryce Fulton punched a Tony Scott lob over the bar, a penalty. This was the third Cup meeting between West Ham and Plymouth in two seasons and honours were even at the start of the game. But the Home Park side were weakened by injuries and before the hour was up Musgrove and Hurst had made it six for the Irons. The visitors had no effective response.

West Ham squeezed into the top half of the table at the start of October when Birmingham came to visit. The Blues had not won a match in the seven they had played away from St Andrews, letting in 21 goals without reply. Walter Winterbottom saw Johnny grab a double for the Hammers. Hurst, Malcolm Musgrove and Ken Brown made it 5–0 to the home side. This was West Ham's biggest-ever victory over Birmingham.

The centre-forward

Byrne had now scored five goals in six games and was becoming an influential team member. Greenwood was, in the main, using him as a deep lying centre-forward, although it is probably incorrect to label Byrne as a centre-forward, as at that time they tended to be tank-like players; big battering rams, used to smash their way into defences. The relatively diminutive Budgie was deployed in order to link the side together by bringing wingers and attacking midfielders into the game. Over his career both as a player and a manager Johnny Byrne constantly analysed the role of the centre-forward. According to John:

> I was accurate in my passing and as such I was a good link man. I was quick and could think fast. I was decent with both feet, that's very rare now. A 'swinger', a one-footed player, despite what Puskas said about a player who kicks with both feet falling on his arse, is limited in what he can do. So, if you think of it, I would have been wasted as an out-and-out attacking player. I wouldn't have been very good at it either. Not big enough!
>
> Games can depend on what happens between the centre-forward and the opponent's centre-half. If one gets the better of

the other it often decides a result. If the centre-forward is shut out of the game the entire forward line can just stop working. I always preferred playing at centre-forward. I'd played on the wing and inside-forward and in the middle but I liked that number nine shirt. Playing in other positions was helpful. I worked out on the wing at Palace, and that helped me learn how to make use of space and how I could, as a centre-forward, work with blokes playing wide. Playing inside-forward, especially for England, helped too; switching position, interplay. Trouble a half-back and he'll make a ricket. That's how me and Geoff Hurst played. You've got to have a bit of a brain to play in the way we did at West Ham. We kind of 'made' goals, crafted 'em if you like. I liked to pass the ball into the net. Playing centre-forward allows you to be more than just a striker.

By the end of 1962 the West Ham manager was asking Budgie to play in the same fashion as Nandor Hidegkuti, a key member of the great Hungarian side that took the football gold medal at the 1952 Helsinki Olympics and in November 1953 became the first non-British side to defeat England at Wembley. Hidegkuti had beaten England's Gil Merrick after just 90 seconds of that match and went on to beat the Birmingham City 'keeper two more times to claim a hat-trick in the 6–3 victory. The difference was that Budgie was a better player than Hidegkuti; he was faster, more mobile and certainly had greater overall vision. Geoff Hurst, who had worked hard with Greenwood to transform himself from an ineffectual wing-half into a deadly inside-left during the season, was Byrne's main point of focus, particularly for the near-post cross. This play, although not at all innovative, had become lost to English football. Byrne explained:

> In England everyone just used the far post as a target; almost not giving it a second thought, but this nearly always meant that the collecting attacker was faced with both the centre-half and the goalkeeper to beat. But, with Hurst practicing the late arrival into the box, the ball coming in to the near post often meant that he had a free pop at goal and given Geoff's power and accuracy this was often deadly. West Ham were playing a very modern game compared to most of their opponents. It was quite complicated, and not all the players really understood what was going on and this was perhaps why we were not the most consistent of sides. However,

when things fell together, when the team clicked and the system kicked in, we looked better than any side in Division One and could equal the best England and Europe had to offer and occasionally we'd beat them.

Right at the centre of all this was Johnny Byrne. Over the last few years there have been two books concerning themselves with the 'West Ham Dream Team'. Neither has included Budgie Byrne. As one of the many who saw him play, this oversight is more than ridiculous, it is a kind of blasphemy; an embarrassment that one, by instinct, wants to apologise to someone for. With all due respect, to include Joe Cole, Frank Lampard or Di Canio at the expense of Johnny Byrne is a gross betrayal of football intelligence, demonstrating at best paucity of historical awareness and at worst a kind of immoral act, the root of which is set in a brand of purposeful ignorance.

All roads lead to White Hart Lane
Two mid-October games were indicative of the Hammers' season (and perhaps their history). In front of nearly 50,000 supporters at Highbury, Billy Wright's side mimicked the 'route one' strategy and physicality of the former England skipper's playing days at Wolves and opened the scoring after 20 minutes when £70,000 man Joe Baker picked up on West Ham 'keeper Leslie's fumble of John McLeod's shot. However, just before the hour, it was Byrne's searing pass that allowed Tony Scott to equalise and deny the Gunners their first post-war win over West Ham. In the next game a trip to Millmoor saw the Hammers expelled from the League Cup by lowly Second Division Rotherham, by a 3–1 margin.

Just before Christmas the Hammers travelled to North London for what would be one of the finest London derbies Budgie was ever to be part of. At White Hart Lane over 44,000 had gathered to witness events. Tottenham, who were to finish as runners-up in the League that term, were hot favourites, sitting in second place at that point, lording it over West Ham who were languishing in 14th position.

Twenty minutes into the match things seemed to be following form with Spurs comfortably leading 2–0. One time Hammer John Smith, who had come in at right-half just before the game, scored in his first appearance of the season. The second had come from the hot left foot of Dave Mackay, a classic 20-yard slammer. To the surprise of many and the consternation of all Tottenham fans present, Martin Peters hit back for the Irons on the half-hour, banging home a Bobby Moore pass from close-range.

Following the break West Ham went for the jugular, and punched great holes in the formally impenetrable Spurs defence, which led to a quick equaliser from Joe Kirkup, who capitalised on the remnants of a Peters shot blocked by Tony Scott. Immediately following the kick-off Tottenham replied. A Jimmy Greaves cross fell at the feet of Jack Burkett and rebounded into the path of Mackay, who made no mistake in smacking the ball past Jim Standen.

West Ham drew level again in the 65th minute. A throw in from Alan Sealey was picked up by Byrne; with a kind of impish aplomb he lobbed the ball over his own head to the amazed Ronnie Boyce. Suspending speculation on how the ball got to him, 'Ticker' slipped the treasured globe past Spurs 'keeper Bill Brown. Eight minutes later Boyce supplied Burkett on the overlap. Jack's deep curling cross was pelted home by Scott to give West Ham the lead for the first time in the game. Now the Irons drove forward and it was left to Brown to deny both Scott and Sealey magnificently, but he was beaten by Moore although the goal was ruled offside.

Byrne and Boyce had been the start of everything that West Ham had done. Any neutrals at that match would have thought these men were the future of English football and they were only matched by the sheer will of Dave Mackay in the Tottenham ranks; he never stopped trying and with half a minute to play he smashed his way into the centre of the Hammers' penalty area to finish his hat-trick, powering a drive in from 10 yards with that lethal left foot.

West Ham had deserved a win but their fight back was no less astonishing. Although the match was drawn, it was the Hammers' attitude rather than the result that did much to compensate for the 6–1 thrashing West Ham had received from Bill Nicholson's Cup-holders in early August.

Elusive consistency

The Hammers' happy wandering continued with a visit to Nottingham Forest. The playing surface was buried beneath a covering of snow. Bob McKinlay's early own goal, knocking in Tony Scott's cross, was followed by Forest thrice foiling Jim Standen, and the game looked over with the second half hardly started, but Greenwood had instructed Byrne, who had played deep in the first half, to push forward. His response within a minute to Forest's third (Calvin Palmer's 49th-minute strike) was lethal; he went on sculpting out the space that allowed Ronnie Boyce to facilitate a Peter Brabrook double.

Johnny's final game of the season was West Ham's penultimate match at Bloomfield Road. Both the Hammers and Blackpool were floating in mid-table and the game symbolised the feeling of being in a no-man's land. Budgie did get the ball past England 'keeper-to-be Tony Waiters, only to see Barry Martin clear the line to save a point for the Seasiders and ensure the game remained goalless.

At the close of 1962 West Ham had been languishing at the foot of Division One. From the start of December John made 15 more starts for the Hammers and managed five goals, two of which were to help take the Irons to the quarter-final stage of the FA Cup, the side's best performance since 1955. The first came in a snowstorm at Craven Cottage after Fulham had forced a 0–0 draw at Upton Park (although the much-postponed game, which took place in sub-zero conditions, was nearly won by Byrne, who was thwarted by a fine save from Gibraltar-born England Under-23 international Tony Macedo). Ronnie Boyce was at his awesome best in winter-shrouded West London. Within a quarter of an hour he had slammed a 25-yard effort against a post, but the ball was going nowhere but in, despite the woodwork, and then as the clock ticked towards the last 20 minutes of the match, Boyce was floored as he was twisting round Eddie Lowe and Byrne's penalty kick went one way while Macedo went the other. Bobby Robson pulled the Cottagers back into the game and West Ham looked to have had victory snatched from them as England skipper Johnny Haynes closed in on the Hammers' penalty area, but Standen made an excellent save to send the Irons into a fourth round meeting with Swansea at Upton Park, where in early March, the corner flags marked out the only small areas of green on the pitch. Less than 10 minutes from half-time Budgie back-heeled in the mud to Peter Brabrook who, seeming to thrive in the conditions, sent a faultless cross to Boyce, who gave the Irons their first home win since early October. Later in the tie Budgie hit the post with a fair effort, but as he moved in for the rebound he found that it hadn't happened – the ball had been glued to the upright by cloying, adhesive sludge.

Five days later it was back to League business and West Ham were at Turf Moor facing a Burnley side that had lost at home just once since the start of the season. As such Greenwood went north with little more than defence on his mind. Just before the hour the former England striker Ray Pointer looked to have given the match to the Clarets, but fortune was with the East Londoners four minutes from time when Alan Sealey's cross was deflected past Scottish international keeper Adam Blacklaw by Budgie, who knew little about it until his comrades came and congratulated him for being in the right place at the right time.

The next hurdle was Everton (who would be League Champions that term) at Upton Park in the fifth round of the Cup. West Ham were slaughtered in the first half, but managed to keep a clean sheet, although when Dennis Stevens handled the ball in a penalty-box tussle with Bobby Moore, Byrne beat Everton's fine goalkeeper, Gordon West, from the spot. The Everton fans didn't take this well. John recalled: 'Most of 'em were wearing daft blue paper hats distributed by one of the national newspapers I think. They threw bottles and stuff onto the pitch and a policeman was injured.'

However, West Ham were into the final eight and faced a tie against Liverpool at Anfield. The difference between the two sides was Roger Hunt, nine minutes from time.

As spring came to the East End of London England manager Alf Ramsey wended his way to Upton Park to watch a very deflated West Ham meet a very disorganised Sheffield Wednesday, a game epitomised by the performance of England centre-half Peter Swan, who messed up a clearance to allow Hurst to open West Ham's account in the 14th minute. Half way through the second half Swan handled the ball. Byrne tied the experienced Ron Springett in knots with the penalty kick.

In the end West Ham settled for 12th place in the League. It had turned out to be a rather pedestrian season for the Hammers, but nevertheless Byrne was called up for the England squad along with Bobby Moore for the close-season tour of Europe. At this stage in his career John was still to master the elusive gift of consistency. On days when little went right from the start, when the

Date:	5 June 1963
Location:	Basle
Competition:	Friendly
Fixture:	Switzerland v England
Result:	1–8 (1–3)
Switzerland scorer:	Bertschi
England scorers:	Charlton (3), Byrne (2), Douglas, Kay, Melia
Team:	Springett, R.D.G. (Sheffield Wednesday), Armfield, J.C. (Blackpool) captain, Wilson, R. (Huddersfield Town), Kay, A.H. (Everton), Flowers, R. (Wolverhampton Wanderers), Moore, R.F.C. (West Ham United), Douglas, B. (Blackburn Rovers), Byrne, J.J. (West Ham United), Melia, J.J. (Liverpool), Greaves, J.P. (Tottenham Hotspur), Charlton, R. (Manchester United).

going or the opposition was notably uncultured, Byrne too often became subdued, as if lacking faith in himself or his colleagues. This inability to keep his game at the highest pitch, week in, week out, probably cost Byrne several caps. Between his first and second international appearance England played 16 internationals. However, after watching the first two games of England's tour, John was drafted into the team for the final match against Switzerland. He made the most of the opportunity by scoring twice in Basle.

There is no doubt that Budgie played well against the Swiss, but when October came round he was ignored for the first match with Wales, and was passed over when something of a shadow England team was named for the prestige game with the 'Rest of the World'.

America ignited

Having completed their international duties John and Bobby Moore joined their West Ham teammates, who were part-way through the 'American Soccer League Tournament' in the United States. Fourteen teams took part in two groups. The Irons played their group games in New York, Chicago and Detroit. By the time Budgie got to the States the Hammers had played two games, managing just a single point, and were bottom of their league, which included sides from Scotland, Italy, France, West Germany, Mexico and Brazil. After less than a day in America Byrne found himself playing in a West Ham XI that was a goal down at half-time to the Mexican side Oro at New York's Randalls Island stadium, normally a baseball venue. The second 45 minutes started fast and furiously. With Moore back at the heart of defence and directing play the Hammers were a different side to the one that had started the tournament and it was a long pass from Bobby that turned the game. Byrne killed the ball on his chest, turning himself and the ball as he did so, and darted into the box. The Mexican defenders flew at him one after the other and it was the third tackle that cut him down. It was a clear penalty. Johnny got to his feet, picked up the ball and sauntered towards the spot. The crowd fell silent as Byrne placed the ball on the penalty spot, turned and walked a few steps back. He eyed the ball a moment, then looked up at the Mexican 'keeper. Budgie ran towards the ball, making the slightest of curves. He struck the ball low, but firm, with the inside of his right boot. The leather sphere turned in the air, seemingly arching slightly downwards and left towards the 'keeper, but just as it seemed the custodian had judged his dive well, the ball curled up and away from him, just out of his reach.

It was a magical strike that no one quite believed; even the West Ham players looked at one another in disbelief as the referee faltered, unsure whether or not to signal a score. But there was no doubt: the ball was still twirling and twisting in the back of the net as it was confirmed that the East Londoners had drawn level. Then Byrne really began to torment the Mexicans, who seemed to have no answer to his challenge. This was Johnny at his best. He skipped over or simply danced through tackles, pulling away from defenders with dazzling acceleration, while the accuracy of his distribution was devastating. A long lob, that seemed to hang, meandering dizzily in mid-air for endless seconds, fell to Hurst, who made no mistake with the resulting volley. Geoff's second was another gift from Byrne, who this time sent the ball in from two yards short of the left corner flag, after a turning duel with three members of the Oro rear guard, right on the line. John launched his rocket on a clear trajectory straight to the forehead of the diving Hurst. Before the looping, curling projectile had made contact with flesh the outcome was clear. The Hammers had got their first win of the tournament.

However, a sterner test awaited the Irons. In the powerful glow of Detroit's University Stadium floodlights, Preussen Munster of West Germany and 10,000 or so of Detroit's massive German/American community were the opponents in a match that was billed as a contest between England and Germany. Preussen were a dour, stolid side, built on precision and discipline. They were a redoubtable unit of Teutonic knights, without fear or compassion, and for 70 minutes they met West Ham's urbane football aesthetic with grim and focused athleticism set within an iron wall of defensive sobriety. It was a Moore to Byrne move that led to Hurst breaking the deadlock with 20 minutes of the game left. Martin Peters got West Ham's second following a sweet one-two with Johnny that totally wrong-footed the bedazzled German defence.

The next trial was an evening match, set in New York, where West Ham faced Valenciennes, a side that were the antithesis of Munster. It was in New York that Byrne went with Moore to a television studio. Budgie introduced himself to every doorman, secretary, guard and potted plant in the place, joking and smiling all the way. Bobby Moore was due to appear on the *What's My Line?* show as good publicity for the tournament. However, Bobby wasn't too keen on the job and was about to ask John to stand in for him, thinking that if Budgie said that he was Moore no one would be any the wiser. But it was not to be. Byrne had wandered off on a tour of self-promotion as Moore was dragged off to the set. However, when the programme was over one of the

American producers commented, looking at Budgie, who was laughing and joking with a group of technicians; 'What a pity Bobby hasn't got the personality of that little guy. He's a star; Bob Hope with attitude'. It seems that John narrowly missed out on the road to Hollywood that day.

On the evening of West Ham's next match the temperature was over 35 degrees in New York. From the start Byrne seemed to build an empire emanating from the centre circle. Every movement, including each constituent part of Hurst's hat-trick, seemed to start with John. West Ham and Johnny Byrne were shining and looked invincible, but they were playing an incredibly artistic brand of football. No one had seen anything quite like it before. It was all movement and speed, everything was measured and accurate. Timing was part of it, but so was instinct and will. One commentator, who had followed every West Ham game, in true sixties spirit saw these claret and blue prophets as practicing 'A kind of Zen. What these guys are doing is a sort of dance of attrition, but with purpose and direction rather than work-rate and aggression.' Such a stance must have been incomprehensible in the land of the ball-park and grid-iron.

West Ham now needed just one point in their last game against the Brazilians, Recife, to give them the championship. But the hellishly hot conditions of the Randalls Island pitch suited the boys from Brazil better. For all that, West Ham went in to the break a goal up from another Byrne classic. John had picked the ball up some 20 yards from goal. He jinked around the Recife centre-half, 'out Brazilian-ing' the Brazilians, before releasing the ball to Peters who, with his back to the goal, knocked a simple pass back to the now charging Byrne, who lashed it home from 10 yards.

But the Samba men were not going to lie down. Five minutes into the second half, Jose Matos brought his side back into the game. With the heat taking its toll, Moore and Byrne drew closer together, pulling the Irons into a compact defending system. They were rewarded with the necessary draw. This was all the more impressive given that Alan Sealey had been sent off during the game, seemingly for allowing himself to be kicked to the ground by the Brazilians. He was treated for his injuries before the referee ordered him to leave the field of play.

West Ham came back to England as 'International Soccer League Champions', but this had qualified them for the American Challenge Cup (ACC), so after just a few weeks back home, the Hammers were again making a return journey to the 'Home of the Brave'.

Polish pyre

The ACC tournament consisted of two ties over two legs. In the first West Ham would play the tough Poles of Gornik, who had won another league that had been played out at the same time as the Hammers had been contesting the ISL Cup. The tie game, which would decide the destination of the Cup, would be between the winners of the Gornik/West Ham match and the American Challenge Cup winners of the previous year. The Gornik side were tough and skilful. They had defeated Spurs 4–2 in their home leg of the European Cup and included a future World Cup player, Lubanski, in their starting eleven.

The two games against Gornik were staged at Randalls Island. In the first match, a midweek, floodlit event that took place in front of a relatively big crowd of 10,000, Byrne looked very close to the complete article; a sleek, insidiously artful striker. He twinkled in his deep-lying centre-forward role; he was a dancing, lethal moth, elegantly weaving his way through one of the most brilliant games of his career. West Ham were always faster and more intelligent than their opponents, their solid defence treating the big Polish forwards as if they were harmless midgets. Byrne's dribble past four Gornik defenders that evening deserved a goal and he was only stopped by the Polish 'keeper's last-minute lunge of blind desperation. But Budgie was not to go unrewarded for his efforts. John scored the vital goal that gave West Ham a 1–1 draw. It came from a really juicy drive, hit from a central position just inside the goal area.

The second match against Gornik was contested on a steamy Sunday afternoon. Geoff Hurst's first-half goal (his ninth in the US), which was wrought out of nothing by Byrne, coupled with two disallowed Gornik goals in the second 45 minutes, caused tempers among the watching Poles to boil over. A pitch invasion caused injury to the referee and a hold-up of 30 minutes that almost led to the abandonment of the match. But the game was finally concluded and West Ham made for Chicago and the first leg of the final against Dukla of Czechoslovakia, who were looking for a hat-trick of American Challenge Cup wins.

Dukla

The men from Prague came to the 'Windy City' with Josef Masopust, European Footballer of the year in 1962 and Svatopluk Pluskal, who had turned out in all six of his country's World Cup games in Chile. Indeed, more than half of the Czech national side that had played in that World Cup were in the Dukla ranks.

However, under the dazzling floodlights in the huge, 110,000-seater Soldier Field, wherein the 11,000 crowd looked lost, the chiselled Czechs seemed intimidated by the West Ham side, enough to retreat into defence after scoring the only goal of the first leg.

In the second leg on the following Sunday afternoon, which was played before a crowd of 15,000, the largest of the tournament, back at Randalls Island, it took a fantastic display by Czech international goalkeeper Pavel Kouba to keep Hurst, liberally supplied by the feet of Byrne, from netting a hatful. But claret and blue pressure told when Tony Scott put West Ham ahead. Against the run of play, 59-cap Josef Masopust's goal meant that Dukla escaped defeat and retained the Cup.

West Ham's American expeditions had taught the Hammers a lot. The young Irons, with an average age of just 23, had given the experienced Czechs a close run and had matched some of the strongest club teams in the world. Masopust said of West Ham: 'They are very good. I predict they will be a world-class team within two years… They are young and in Moore and Byrne they have two generals; one of defence and one of attack.'

Geoff Hurst came back to England as the tournament's top scorer with nine goals and Bobby Moore was awarded the 'Eisenhower Trophy' as the Player of the Series. Later Ron Greenwood was to declare:

> Our second game against Dukla was the most perfect technical display I have seen from any British team I have been connected with… The team gained more experience in 10 matches against teams from other nations than the average League player at home gains in 15 years. We learnt more that summer about how the game was evolving around the world than we would have done in five European campaigns.

The Hammers had seen how well they could play as a unit and match teams and players that would have tested the very best of British sides. They had matured, maybe come of age in America, none more so than Johnny Byrne.

CHAPTER 4

Glowing Amity

BOBBY Moore is a name synonymous with football, England and West Ham. He was and remains the best-loved of all English sportspeople, but in the East End of London and east of the capital into Essex, 'Mooro' is a legend that is growing with time: he has come to embody a style, an ethic and a way of living; a secular saint who at once has glory and modesty, sexuality and sensitivity, nobility and the common touch – forever a majestic blond hero. It is not unusual to hear Pelé referred to as 'the greatest footballer of all time.' However, this is often said by people who know little of the game. Yes, Pelé was a great attacking player, one of the greatest, but could he be compared to Puskas or Johann Cruyff, Stanley Matthews or Eusebio?

Dave McKay was another great player, no Pelé, but he would, if the need had ever arisen, have done a good job stopping the remarkable Brazilian from playing, something Bobby Moore was certainly able to do. There was one particular moment that demonstrated this to me. It was the most graceful and poetic tackle I have ever seen. One sublime moment, in the group game between England and Brazil in the 1970 World Cup final in Mexico, saw Pelé confronted by Moore; there was a moment when they stood like duellists, but Bobby never took his eyes off of the ball. The England captain made the first move (the defender attacked – observing the old East End proverb 'Get in first!') and pushed his left shoulder towards Pelé and waited, a long second, before almost placing, but with some trajectory and force, the outside of his left foot along the equator of the ball. Like a fencer, Bobby stabbed the ball between the attacker's legs, letting his weight push the orb clear of and behind Pelé, dropping nearly onto his right knee in the process. At that point Moore was in a sort of half splits, but his upper body was upright. The Brazilian, in amazement, although still on his feet, found that his own momentum had taken him behind Moore and yards away from the ball, but by the time he had discovered this Moore had recovered and turned Pelé's attrition into an England attack: who was the best footballer then? That move, the manner in which it was executed, the timing and the subtlety, summed up Bobby Moore, surely the most efficient and sublime defender ever to draw breath. But how could he be called a defender when nearly every act of defence was transformed into attack?

Moore, like Johnny Byrne, was a superb distributor of the ball: he passed accurately with both feet, long and short distances, and he was a master reader of the game. It was this that enabled him so often to spot and break down attacks. Coolness under pressure allowed him to make the best possible use of the ball – you never saw Bobby making a desperate pass. He was able to dispossess a player and in that moment switch his whole game from defence into attack, making a spell out of the constructive use of the ball within his own half. According to Byrne, Moore's influence ran right through the West Ham side:

> Wherever you were Bobby could get the ball to you. Like Johnny Haynes, Bobby led by example and people learnt from playing with him. Also like Haynes, Mooro was a great leader. Haynes led by word of mouth but Bobby was calmer. When we first started playing together Bobby was a wing-half but he didn't quite have the pace for that position. As a double centre-half he was the best I had ever saw, better than even Franz Beckenbauer. Bobby's greatest asset was his reading of the game, but the way he made use of the ball from the defence marked him out as a player.
>
> There should have been more West Ham players in the World Cup side. I think if it hadn't have been for my injury I'd have made it. Jack Burkett certainly should have been, but he chose to go to America with West Ham instead of playing an Under-23 game and Alf didn't like that. Ronnie Boyce might also have been in the running. Other players that might have played for England were John Sissons, John Bond, Peter Brabrook and Johnny Charles. Ken Brown might have had more games too. Sometimes it's about luck, being in the right place at the right time. But we all benefited from playing and training with Bobby. He was great at the quiet word of encouragement, and that, just coming from him, was enough to give players a confidence boost.

For John, Moore was one of the true greats of English soccer and Bobby's opinion of Budgie pretty much mirrored John's thoughts about Moore. Indeed, he saw the fact that West Ham failed to replace Byrne as being a key factor in the Hammers' decline after 1966.

Byrne had played against Bobby when Moore was 16 and John was 17. They moved almost simultaneously into the England Under-23 side. After defeating Wales 2–0 at Goodison Park in February 1961, using a modified 4–2–4 system devised by Ron Greenwood, the English Under-23 side were beaten by their Scottish counterparts in March. It was Scotland's first win over England since the Under-23 games started in 1955. Denis Law had run riot and it was his header that Gordon Banks only managed to push to Johnny McLeod (then of Hibs, he was to move to Arsenal and then Aston Villa) who sent it back into the goalmouth. The 'Law-man' was waiting, marauder-like, to score the killer goal.

Any England manager hates being beaten by a Scottish side and as a result of this defeat only four of the team kept their places for the game against West Germany at White Hart Lane: Fulham's George Cohen, Bobby Moore, Mike O'Grady of Huddersfield and Johnny Byrne. Michael McNeil of Middlesbrough, who had been the captain, was out of the team and Ron Greenwood told Moore that he was to take over the captaincy.

Byrne, the only full international in the side, played with tremendous grace, judgement and athleticism, showing his fantastic positional sense as, time after time, when Moore moved forward to make a pass, he found that John was ideally placed to receive the ball. The Crystal Palace prodigy seemed to have an innate ability to exploit space, but it was Moore who was getting the ball to him. For long periods during the match it looked as if Moore and Byrne were taking on the Germans single-handedly and it was not a surprise when Greenwood kept them together for the next Under-23 outing against the Dutch the following season, nor that the team manager was so keen to bring Bobby and John together at Upton Park.

By the time John had played his first season at the Boleyn Ground he and Moore had forged an almost telepathic link on the field. The former West Ham defender, coach and manager John Lyall was always impressed by the Moore/Byrne partnership. He said of Budgie: 'He took up such marvellous positions that Bobby Moore could find him in the dark.'

It would have been difficult to have had the kind of understanding Moore and Budgie had without a solid friendship and they had almost a brotherly relationship right up until Bobby's death in 1993. Off the field of play Bobby's relaxed, cool demeanour was the perfect fit with Byrne's exuberance; they complimented each other as players and as social companions and together made a kind of whole, although they were also bound by a deal of mutual affection and respect, sharing a taste for the pleasures that living and working close to London's West End could offer. Budgie recalled:

> We'd go to the 21 Club in Great Chesterfield Street, the White Elephant in Curzon Street. At the Churchill Hotel, where we'd sometimes meet up, the piano player always played 'Bubbles' as he came in. Bob liked Langan's restaurant too.
>
> When we went away, either with West Ham or England, Mooro's suitcase would be tidier coming home than mine was going out. He was always more disciplined than everyone else in terms of the way he looked, trained and applied himself. That discipline was there in other parts of his personality. For instance, he never slagged anyone off and no one said a bad word about him. But people never knew how naughty he could be. His death was a tragedy. He was a very private man, but when he knew you well he was a lovely feller and a real laugh.

Like Bobby Moore, Byrne saw Greenwood as the ideal England manager, but one evening during a summer in the early 1970s, Moore was in South Africa, combining guest appearances for Hellenic, the Cape Town club that Budgie managed for the best part of the last third of the 20th century, with a vacation. The two began to talk about coaching. Together, standing on the long summit of Signal Hill, the former Hammers drank together as they had done so often. The great African sun was slowly gliding into the waters that ebb around Cape Town's rocks and beaches. As dusk gave way to night, the ocean was flowing red, a liquid fire lapping at the sky. They mused on how the England side had benefited from having Ramsey as its manager and how he had looked to Moore for advice on set pieces and confirmation of tactics, in much the same way that Greenwood had looked to Byrne while Budgie had been at Upton Park. They shared a smile when recalling how Alf had hardly ever modified his modest team talks. Ramsey nearly always said something about the way the opposition played, their strong points and their flaws, and would then repeat what was almost a mantra: 'They're more worried about us than we are about them. You're the best players in the world. The fittest. The strongest. Go out and win it!'

Budgie put it to Bobby that Ron Greenwood had far more knowledge of the game, and that if the West Ham manager had displayed some of Ramsey's gifts of 'man management' he would have made the perfect England manager. The Cape Town sky was dark blue and studded with silver stars that watched over Africa as Moore told his friend that together, John and himself could have done a better job than either Ramsey or Greenwood or even the combination of the two that Byrne had proposed. The sad fact is that England's golden skipper was probably right, but instead of that 'dream team' the English national game has, over the last 30 years, been led by a succession of men who have failed to take the game to the lofty heights that all fans of English football crave.

CHAPTER 5

Spark

—————

B Y THE late summer of 1963 Johnny Byrne began to shine, playing deep in the heart of the West Ham attack. With Bobby Moore now ensconced as sweeper, together they inspired and drove the whole side. At Stamford Bridge it was clear that West Ham's American adventure had a cost. The Hammers looked jaded against newly promoted Chelsea and Ron 'Chopper' Harris blotted Budgie out of the match. However, a victory at the Boleyn Ground over Blackpool helped lift the side. Boyce and Scott worked together to open up the visitors' defence for Peters to net the opener. The second came from Boyce himself after he had jinked through four floundering defenders, while Brabrook scored with a shot that swerved in the air. A late goal from Ray Charnley belied the fact that Blackpool had been massacred and that Byrne had played like a god. This game was a prime demonstration that the 4–2–4 formation was light years ahead of the traditional British game that the Blackpool side of the time exemplified so well (or badly, depending how you look at it). West Ham's opponents that day were out-played and out-manoeuvred in every facet of play. The Hammers were generally swifter, but also, as a team, they were much more intelligent than their opponents.

The next day it was Moore who received the plaudits in the press but Byrne's swerving run past four Blackpool defenders that evening was one of the outstanding highlights of a phenomenal demonstration of his skill and developing insight. He had two shots cleared off the line and at times he single-handedly distracted the entire Seasiders' defence and much of their midfield. It was now obvious to most Hammers supporters that Budgie was quite special. No one had seen his like before; his ability was obvious to even the dimmest spectator (including the ones who had booed him when he was new to Upton Park). Byrne was managing to consistently merge his natural subtlety with his innate speed and this, together with his swift mind and instinct for reading play, gave him a perception and awareness comparable to those of his teammates, Bobby Moore and Martin Peters. He darted around the field with the grace and litheness of a hunting dog. With his dark hair and cheeky good looks, he had massive confidence in his own ability that was rarely misplaced.

Four days after the match with Blackpool, Budgie netted the first goal of the game against Ipswich at Upton Park. The East Anglia Blues would finish bottom of Division One that season. Tony Scott crossed to the 18-yard line from the left flank. Byrne, hovering on one leg like a heron, struck a fantastic right-footed volley into the roof of the net past the hapless Roy Bailey (father of Gary, who would play for Manchester United between the sticks after his time with Witts University in South Africa). If the Hammers had held on to the lead that they had taken twice during the game they would have sat atop the First Division that evening, but as it was the match ended with the sides sharing the four goals.

At Bloomfield Road Byrne scored the only goal of the game from the penalty spot and headed his side's first goal in the 3–2 Upton Park defeat at the hands of Sheffield United. In September West Ham started a fine League Cup campaign. They beat Second Division Leyton Orient at the Boleyn Ground, despite the fact that Orient's Gordon Bolland ran rings around Dave Bickles and put the O's ahead before 10 minutes of the game had been played. The former Chelsea inside-forward, who would also play for Norwich, Charlton and Millwall, rounded the West Ham 'keeper Jim Standen with a stunning move. Scott put the Hammers level less than a quarter of an hour later. Budgie scored what turned out to be the match-winner on his fourth attempt, bamboozling 'keeper Reg Davies just before half-time.

Having been forced into defence during a visit to the City Ground, Byrne hit the net in the last 10 minutes to give the Hammers a consolation after Forest had put three past Standen (who'd had a tremendous game) and he headed home the equaliser to give West Ham a 1–1 draw with Wolves at Upton Park. Byrne missed West Ham's 3–0 defeat at Hillsborough a few days before the third round League Cup game at Villa Park as he was being treated for injuries sustained in a car crash. His condition was not serious, but he was not fit when the time came for the Hammers to journey to Birmingham and face Aston Villa. Given that West Ham had only won four games in 14 outings it was a surprise that Villa were beaten 2–0 on their own turf. In the absence of Byrne, defender John Bond and Martin Britt did the damage.

Budgie was still sidelined at the start of October and was unable to make the trip to the County Ground for the fourth round of the League Cup. West Ham had to fight to achieve a 3–3 draw with Second Division Swindon Town, but Byrne was back in the West Ham ranks for the League match at Highbury and it took him just 12 seconds to head past Bob Wilson. Arsenal hadn't beaten West Ham at Highbury since the start of World War Two and that was not going to change on 9 November 1963 as the sides equally divided the six goals that were scored.

In the fourth-round League Cup replay against Swindon John was close to being back to his best. With the score standing at 1–1 a Byrne header that hit the bar allowed Brabrook to score and the Robins were finally broken. Budgie made it 3–1 just over a quarter of an hour later when Brabrook paid Budgie back with a perfect cross that Byrne converted faultlessly, forcing the home side to push forward. The game ended with an 84th-minute goal from Tony Scott and Swindon were humbled. However, the Swindon manager, the dour West Countryman Bert Head, was not to forgive or forget the humiliating defeat, made worse by the behaviour of the cheeky Londoner Johnny Byrne, who represented much of what Head, who had never really lost the rural values of his birthplace, Midsomer Norton, despised in the modern game.

At the end of November Greenwood experimented with using Byrne as a winger during Fulham's visit to Upton Park. Budgie looked disorientated for most of the match under the critical gaze of Alf Ramsey. After 10 minutes the Hammers were a goal down from a shot by Scottish international winger Graham Leggat. Hurst hit the post twice before Bobby Moore equalised with nine minutes left on the clock after a mix-up in the Fulham defence dealing with a West Ham corner.

Johnny produced two goals in two minutes to give the Irons a draw against Chelsea at Upton Park just two days before West Ham welcomed Fourth Division Workington to the Boleyn Ground for the quarter-final of the League Cup. Budgie wasted little time in making an impact, tucking away a Hurst cross in the 12th minute. Byrne claimed his second West Ham hat-trick. Boyce, Hurst and Scott made it 6–0 as the crowd began to cheer the rare Workington forays into Hammers territory. West Ham had qualified for the semi-final stage of a major competition for the first time in 32 years.

Geoffrey Charles Hurst
Ron Greenwood's successor and disciple John Lyall saw that Budgie:

...had a great influence on the development of Geoff Hurst as a central striker. They formed a magnificent goalscoring partnership. I think Geoff first realised the full value of controlling the ball with the chest, a hallmark of his game, when he watched Budgie doing it. Budgie would take the ball on his chest and, before it reached the ground, volley it out to the wings. Johnny had a wonderful sense of timing that enabled him to out-jump taller defenders and although Hurst was much taller, Budgie helped Geoff appreciate the importance of timing your jump.

From the moment John had joined the Hammers there had been signs that a partnership was developing between Hurst and Byrne. Within a year they both knew where each other would be on the pitch at any given time. Hurst recalled Byrne as being:

Needle sharp and an incessant talker, he'd drive you mad in the dressing-room but, once on the pitch, you just stood back and admired a rare talent. In the penalty box he was as clever and cute as the Artful Dodger. He'd score goals and you'd scratch your head, wondering how he did it.

In their first season together as West Ham's striking partnership they divided 29 goals in first-team games. In the 1963–64 term the two men shared 59 goals. The next season saw them accumulate 48, and in 1965–66 they amassed 57 goals. In their first four seasons working in tandem Hurst scored a total of 100 goals in 191 first-team games while Budgie netted 93 in 163 matches.

There was a less well-known third element in this set up. Peter Brabrook's arrival at West Ham had coincided with the start of the Hurst/Byrne partnership and his contribution to the success of West Ham's twin strikers was critical. His incisive right-wing raids provided an element of service that cannot be underestimated. Peter recalled:

Ron was far in advance of anyone else as a manager and when I came from Chelsea it was an entirely different ball game. The coaching at Chelsea was nowhere near the same quality as that at West Ham... he baffled me a little bit because he was so far advanced. It was unbelievable really and things he used to do back then are even being done at West Ham now. That's how far-sighted he was. Geoff scored a lot of goals and Budgie, who was a tremendous player, got his fair share too. I'd get 10–12 a season, which was quite good for a winger, and we were a very exciting side to watch.

Budgie was a good player, very underrated really. I thought he was tremendous and he ended up getting capped by England, which was fully deserved. He was only small but, technically, he was brilliant and he'd bring other people into games. He was a good player to play with and you'd get good service off him. He'd take balls on his chest and ping them left or right with either foot. He had good movement and Ron's coaching got the best out of all of us.

Of course, after 1966 Hurst would be world famous, but in 1963 it was Budgie who was the star and Hurst the supporting act. Greenwood likened the collaboration to Byrne being the salmon and Hurst the chips, but Geoff always acknowledged that playing alongside Budgie was one of the best things that could have happened to him.

What Hurst gleaned from Byrne made Geoff a more complete, more modern striker. He commented: 'Playing behind Budgie and then playing up alongside him must have helped. That man was magic. Real touch, real class.'

But Hurst has to be given an awful lot of credit for being an exceptionally good learner: that, perhaps, was his main strength. He had learnt from Greenwood and, to a great extent, Budgie took over his education. However, Hurst was also an exceptionally hard worker and willing to practice endlessly to make this learning useful. There were a number of facets of Byrne's game that Hurst particularly respected and he worked to add them to his own inventory of skills. Hurst laboured to replicate Byrne's outstanding volleying ability. He trained to gain something of the close control that Budgie was so adept at and toiled to copy the way John cushioned passes on his chest and had the ball at his feet within fractions of a second, regardless of how hard it hit him. If ever you see recorded games involving Hurst, in the World Cup or any England game, you will see how well he adopted these skills; but they were hallmarks of Johnny Byrne's tuition.

For all this the two men were poles apart. In appearance Hurst was a strapping figure of a man, filled with potential power; Byrne was shorter, elegant and mischievous with the gift of instant control and a burst of pace that left defenders in his wake. As in so many successful partnerships, in football and elsewhere, it was perhaps the contrast that brought success; the combined talents of Hurst and Byrne created a formidable challenge to any defence in the world. What makes such dualities work? In Hurst and Byrne's case certainly a willing learner and a person who could teach, but both required ability. Budgie and Geoff were a partnership, a collaboration, they were colluding elements within a greater whole. It was not a relationship in the way that the association, the affiliation, the connection between Moore and Byrne was. The latter was a real meeting of minds, a type of unity.

A partnership has to be made to work; it is the product of effort and will, probably requiring a goal to facilitate its creation. Byrne and Hurst tapped into such potential in themselves and their context, but it must be true that the immortal hat-trick of '66 was something of a tribute to Johnny Byrne; if it hadn't been for him and by association Arthur Rowe, it is likely that there would have been no West Ham FA Cup, no Hammers European glory and no 1966 and all that. On the other hand, Moore and Byrne, well they 'just were'.

Goals, balls, cups

A penalty at Portman, which didn't stop West Ham losing 3–2 to rock-bottom Ipswich, brought Budgie's goal haul to 10 in 18 League outings by Christmas 1963. However, the first part of West Ham's League season had not been impressive. The Hammers, sitting in the bottom third of the First Division, had only managed six wins in 23 matches in Division One and had gone seven games without a single victory. But things got worse on Boxing Day when Blackburn came to Upton Park for an 11am kick-off.

Rovers, undefeated in 10 games and atop the First Division, arrived at the Boleyn Ground. The pitch was heavy and from the start it was clear that West Ham were uncomfortable on their home surface and Blackburn were adapting better. Bryan Douglas, the England winger, ripped the West Ham defence to shreds. Within a few minutes Fred Pickering had scored from 20 yards out, but Byrne's equaliser was a much more impressive goal. Budgie turned and swivelled passed a trio of Blackburn wardens to 'pass' the ball round Fred Else, the mesmerised Rovers 'keeper.

The goal seemed to inspire the Irons and a short time later Byrne was again threatening, blasting a perfectly struck shot against the Blackburn bar. Budgie did get a second goal just after the hour, but by then Blackburn had increased their tally to five by way of goals from Andy McEvoy, Mike Ferguson and Pickering. Three more were to follow as McEvoy and Pickering completed their hat-tricks. This was to be a record defeat for West Ham, the biggest away win in Division One for eight years and Rovers' best-ever victory away from their home ground.

There was some revenge two days later when on a sodden Ewood Park (in those days it was customary to play the same team twice over the holiday period) Greenwood replaced Martin Peters with hard man Eddie Bovington, to draw in the full-backs, forcing play out wide and restricting Douglas with a concentrated exercise in man-marking. The strategy broke West Ham's run of bad results by enabling the first defeat of Rovers in 11 matches. Looking back Budgie commented:

> At the time Eddie Bov was one of the best close markers in the game – he developed this side of his game under Greenwood. After the first game with Blackburn I think if Ron could have dropped the lot of us he would have done. We had a long meeting at our hotel the night before the match at Blackburn. Bov was a great tackler and he came in at wing-half for Martin Peters. Sissons went on the left wing.

> Although he wasn't keen on man-marking, Ron used Bovington that way. Bryan Douglas told Eddie after the match that he'd stopped him from getting a sniff of the ball.

The midfield doyen Douglas had been at the centre of Blackburn's glory at the Boleyn Ground on that fatal Boxing Day. On the heavy pitch he jigged and manoeuvered in the most confined spaces and fluttered over every tackle the Hammers tried. He stood out like a star in a dark sky. Before the return match the press were speculating not about who would win or lose, but about whether Blackburn could make double figures. The payback started early. After 16 minutes, Peter Brabrook dribbled around the left side of the Blackburn defence before sending an impeccably weighted ball to Hurst, who moved two paces forward before cracking the ball into the back of the net. The Irons' attack then proceeded to smash the home defence to pieces. As Douglas had been the architect of his side's victory two days before, it was now Byrne's turn to taunt, tease and tempt the Rovers back line. He should have scored when a shot was cleared off the line and Brabrook had his effort deflected the wrong side of a post by a matter of inches. Andy McEvoy made things even just after the half hour, totally against the run of play. For once Douglas slipped the 'Bov imposed' shackles to make the pass to McEvoy, who netted with a powerful drive.

Byrne brought his personal seasonal goal account against Blackburn to four in the second half. John Sissons drew his marker to send Hurst away, he centred to Budgie, who gained greater altitude than his towering sentinel, Welsh international Mike England (who would one day make 300 appearances at the heart of the Spurs defence), to head home after 58 minutes. Seven minutes later Byrne struck again to seal the win as the hardworking Boyce cut open the home defence with a wonderful through ball which Johnny flicked into the net, almost in passing, after he had rounded the Blackburn 'keeper. This was to be the turning point for West Ham, the revival in a season that would prove to be one of the most profound periods in the club's history. Greenwood's plan had worked and Bovington had done what few wing-half backs had accomplished that season, reducing Douglas to a frustrated member of what had become, after Eddie's demolition job, a weak Blackburn attack. Moore was dominant at left-half and seemed to be at the root of everything West Ham did.

The strange pendulum of West Ham form continued to swing positively when, in the eerie yellow gloom of January at Upton Park, Johnny Byrne's skills completely bemused Second Division Charlton Athletic. One of Byrne's gifts was a razor-sharp mind. His vast encyclopaedia of jokes seemed inexhaustible and, on the pitch, Byrne's ability to exploit the vulnerability of those blessed with brawn but little brain was devastating. In that third round FA Cup match West Ham pumped long balls down the wings for Brabrook and Sissons – the teenager was playing in his first FA Cup tie – to collect. It took 10 minutes for the Hammers to grab the lead. Moore slid an elegant pass to Sissons, who cut in and sent the ball to Hurst, who scored with his first touch. Another West Ham goal after 25 minutes was instigated by Byrne.

After a devastating burst down the middle he found himself hemmed in by former Manchester Red Frank Haydock. Budgie rolled the ball across to Brabrook, who bored in and beat Mike Rose with a shot that the South Londoners' 'keeper should have blocked. Sissons finished things in the final minute of the game when he scored from 25 yards. Budgie was man-of-the-match.

The momentum continued as Byrne scored the only goal in an Upton Park contest against third-placed Liverpool. The event went totally against the run of play; Ian Callaghan hit the post and, in the dying seconds, Roger Hunt provoked a miracle save from Jim Standen.

Next stop was Brisbane Road and another Cup hurdle in front of a record crowd for the stadium (34,345 – which stands to the present day). But West Ham's form stuttered as the O's forced a replay with a well deserved 1–1 draw. Norman Deeley nodded home the former England youth midfielder Gordon Gregory's corner after just two minutes and the feisty Orienteers had their

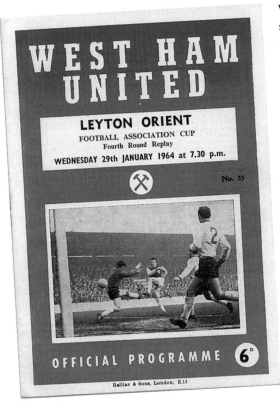

visitors on the defensive for quite some time, but not long after half-time Sissons slipped by the one-time England amateur international centre-half Stan Charlton to facilitate Brabrook's equaliser. The match at Upton Park was something of a one-way street, with three goals in the first 15 minutes – two from Hurst and the third from Budgie – that killed the match. Hurst had a penalty saved by another former England amateur cap, goalkeeper Mike Pinner, in the 51st minute. Pinner's brilliant form deprived both Hurst and Byrne of hat-tricks.

For all this, the Hammers seemed to have emptied their luck account when they visited Filbert Street for the first leg of the League Cup semi-final at the start of February. Before the first 20 minutes were up West Ham had let in three goals without reply. The Foxes had scored their second and third efforts with 10 men on the park; Frank McLintock was taken off with a gashed ankle. Although Geoff Hurst pulled one back on the half-hour, with little more than 20 minutes to play the Hammers were trailing 4–1. But the Irons weren't finished and started to play a more direct game which resulted in Byrne laying on Hurst's sixth goal in three games, running right through the Filberts' centre-half John King's challenge and crashing past the indomitable Gordon Banks in goal. This gave Mooro's men hope, and Sealey's determination to improve his side's chances paid off when he banged West Ham's third home, having picked up one of Moore's insightful passes with just eight minutes of the leg to go. Banks was again bypassed by Byrne but King blocked his effort on the goal line and Leicester took the game 4–3, but hopes were still high given that the Upton Park leg was still to come. Things looked even better when Spurs were trounced at the Boleyn Ground a few days later.

Although they came to the East End as leaders of Division One, the rare 4–0 drubbing of Bill Nicolson's men more or less ended Tottenham's hopes of the League Championship. It was a League double for West Ham over Spurs. Hurst, Sissons and Boyce engulfed the White Hart Lane brigade and Johnny Byrne finished them off, netting the final goal in front of a claret and blue horde

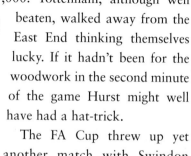

of nearly 37,000. Tottenham, although well beaten, walked away from the East End thinking themselves lucky. If it hadn't been for the woodwork in the second minute of the game Hurst might well have had a hat-trick.

The FA Cup threw up yet another match with Swindon Town. A club record crowd of 28,582 (7,000 of them West Ham travellers) saw Byrne again torment Head's team and complete the torture by converting a Brabrook cross to add to Hurst's previous brace and send the Hammers fans home happy with the 3–1 result.

West Ham got a day off and then it was up to the Midlands on the Monday to face Wolves. Hurst's goal, a second bite of the cherry after Fred Davies, the Wolverhampton 'keeper, had parried the initial shot, put him into double figures over six games. It was his 20th of the season. John Sissons set up Budgie for the second. Although the West Ham attack had done its job, Wolves were always hopeful as they had a talented attack that included the rising star Peter Knowles. But the Hammers' defence was really solid, playing with a 'funnel' system, and any energy from the old gold strike-line was all but snuffed out.

Budgie's 1964 goal total had ticked up to five before his hat-trick against Sheffield Wednesday in a 4–3 Upton Park Hammers victory. The thriller of a game had nearly been thrown away. The Londoners were leading 4–1 going into the last quarter-of-an-hour, following Byrne's first League threesome of the season. This was followed by Burnley's visit to Upton Park in the quarter-final of the FA Cup; West Ham's seventh game in February.

Burnley were 11th in the League, three places above the Hammers, and were an accomplished side. Two seasons earlier they had finished as runners-up in the championship and the FA Cup. An all-ticket crowd of 36,651, including England manager Alf Ramsey, saw the Irons lag a goal behind for nearly half the game, John Connelly having dodged three challenges over 35 yards before putting Burnley in front after 13 minutes. Just before the hour the worries of the Irons' followers were eased when Burnley's Northern Ireland defender, Alex Elder, could only help a Johnny Sissons effort, hit from an acute angle, over the line. Then West Ham turned on the pressure and just three minutes later, on the hour, Budgie hit a tasty right-foot volley from a Brabrook cross to put his side in front. Reporting for the *Newham Recorder* Trevor Smith wrote of this goal:

> Brabrook's centre into the vacant space was latched onto with telepathic
> accuracy by Byrne and volleyed joyfully high over Blacklaw to give West
> Ham the lead and Byrne a new post-war scoring record of 28 goals.

Budgie was now officially the best striker the Hammers had fielded since World War Two and, as if to confirm the event, when Burnley had hardly pulled themselves together, eight minutes after his first hit, Byrne struck again. Making the most of a defensive mistake by Brian Miller, Budgie dribbled around Scottish international 'keeper Adam Blacklaw and made scoring look easy. The Burnley side contested the goal with gusto. They really didn't think it had gone in, and in the fall-out Gordon Harris struck Hammers defender John Bond. For all that, it concentrated the Clarets' minds brilliantly. Pointer scored with 10 minutes left, but Budgie's gang held on to go through.

The League win at Ewood Park had been the season's seminal moment for the Hammers, but this match against Burnley marked the moment when the Irons matured. The side demonstrated a ruthless determination that had often been lacking in their make-up. Byrne had played wonderfully and his performance dominated the headlines of the morning papers the day after the match. He was, probably quite correctly, given the credit for taking West Ham

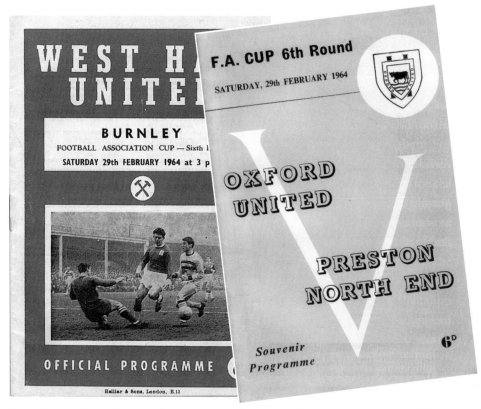

into the last four. His alacrity and control on a problematical surface had been the difference between the two sides.

Burnley got some recompense a few days later when in early March at Turf Moor they went into the break two up and made it three just after half-time. A Budgie special came too late to save the Irons from defeat and Hurst hit the post twice. However, Byrne had scored in six consecutive games and accrued nine goals in as many playing hours: a remarkable purple patch.

By an interesting turn of fate West Ham's last match before their FA Cup semi-final was a League game with Manchester United, the very side that now stood between the East Enders and Wembley. United were aiming for a League and FA Cup double and had qualified for the semis with a win over Sunderland. However, as a pre cup-tie indicator the match was a non-event. The Hammers' performance was so dire that it reminded spectators of the Boxing Day massacre. It looked as if the visitors would go away from Upton Park with the honours even before John Bond's back pass was picked up by David Sadler in the 72nd minute. Four minutes from time David Herd made it 2–0 as the Hammers pressed forward looking for a draw.

Matt Busby had fielded five reserves and therefore won the psychological battle. But the semi-final was now the only real focus for West Ham's young

side. They had scored three goals against every club they had faced in the Cup, two First and two Second Division sides. The team they faced in the last four had, since World War Two, won the championship three times and been runners-up on five occasions; they would be runners-up again in 1964. In the 1962–63 season they had beaten both Tottenham Hotspur and Sporting Lisbon by a 4–1 margin in the European Cup-Winners' Cup. They were the FA Cup holders; they had got to the semi-final stage of the Cup half a dozen times since the end of World War Two and had been finalists on four occasions, winning the tournament in 1948. West Ham's post-war FA Cup record showed that they had made the sixth round twice, in 1956 and 1963. Guess who were the favourites to get to Wembley in 1964?

CHAPTER 6

Fire Water

J OHNNY Byrne was bold and brash. In his winkle-picker shoes and stylish
clothes he was the centre of attention at Upton Park and that's where he
liked to be. He was a snappy dresser before most footballers had begun to
spend serious money on their appearance. His black hair was smart and
Brylcreemed and his entire demeanour was never less than debonair, in the
finest traditions of the early/mid-1960s. But behind the trappings of success and
fame, John, alongside a number of his playing colleagues, was busy shortening
his career. There was a culture of drink at Upton Park in the 1960s and it was
never much more than a badly kept secret. At that time, the players mingled
with the supporters. They would use the same pubs and cafés. Most of them
lived in the same area of East London and West Essex. They were doing a bit
better than most of their fans though: after a raise in 1964 most got around £40
a week. However, I have spoken to dozens of former Hammers professionals
and they, on the whole, agree that the 1960s were the time to be at West Ham.
They were 'infectious' years.

Often on match days by 1.30pm the gates of Upton Park had to be closed,
the ground being full of people waiting for a 3pm kick-off. Eight or nine
thousand spectators could turn up for reserve matches. While football has
become richer in terms of finance, the game, as a live spectator sport, was much
'bigger' in the 1960s, and West Ham players were very much part, for better or
worse, of the 'swinging London' era.

In his autobiography Bobby Moore remembered being with the late John
Charles, the captain of West Ham's FA Youth Cup winning team of 1963 who
was to turn out 118 times for the Hammers, and his fellow defender John
Cushley in 1967 in the United States. According to Moore they were so drunk
at three in the afternoon that they were not even able to maintain contact with

the beds that they tried to collapse onto. They finally crashed to the floor in total inebriation.

John Charles's son Keith, who was a young boy in the mid-sixties, told me: 'Everything centred round pubs, booze, laughs, jokes and all that.'

His father, who was to suffer the worst effects of alcoholism after being forced to leave the game, told me:

> It was amazing. In them days, no one was really fit. You'd get the odd few but everyone liked a drink, it wasn't just West Ham. It was footballers' lives in the sixties. 'Win, draw or lose we're on the booze!' You didn't even think about it. It was second nature. When players get pulled up for drinking now it's nothing. I spilt more down me tie than they put away!
>
> We went to the Retreat after training at Chigwell. Greenwood never seemed to notice. We used to hide our cars round the back. Then we'd go to the Slater's Arms, a right old dive of a pub in Romford, but they did afters. We'd go to and from away matches to places like Newcastle by first-class train. By the end of the journey home the bottles of miniatures were piled up in a big heap and we'd thrown half out of the window.
>
> Maybe the team didn't build on their success in the sixties because we were always on the piss. We went from the club to the pub. I was part of a hard drinking crowd, Brian Dear, Bobby Moore, Eddie Bovington, and Budgie. Mooro was as good as gold on the field and off the field, but he was a piss-head. He liked a gin and tonic... He liked a lager too. You couldn't get him drunk! He was one of the best drinkers I knew. He was on a par with Oliver Reed! Gawd he could drink! He was a quiet bloke but entertaining. There are times when I've gone down the Retreat at Chigwell, and I've thought, 'Mooro's car's outside his house, I'll drop in and see him'. We'd pop in sometimes and he'd get the beers out of the fridge and we'd forget the Retreat. We'd sit and have a chat. Then the next morning he'd come in and say, 'Do you know we drank about a crate and half of them lagers last night?'

It is certain that a drinking tradition was well established at West Ham by the early sixties and that Byrne was part of it. It is true that alcohol was synonymous with the game at that time, but at Upton Park it seemed far more deeply entrenched than at other clubs in the top flight. Charlie Green, a former

West Ham Boys player and a close friend of many of the West Ham professionals of the sixties confirmed the kind of 'brotherhood of alcohol' that revolved around the West Ham team of the sixties:

Hursty was a good boozer, not so much Peters. Lampard was another good boozer. But it weren't every night of the week. It was weekends after a game. The Black Lion in Plaistow was another 'in' place. It used to be a laugh... We used to go to away games in groups, 8, 10-handed. We went for a reason. We'd stay in the same hotel as the players and after the game we'd go out for a jolly. We'd meet up with them at about midnight, they'd been out for a meal and you'd be up to 5, 6, 7 in the morning. Birds were like bees to a honey pot. The team were on the piss before and after games. It's the same now, look at it. The only manager who had any sort of control was Brian Clough. He put up curfews. He was the only manager in the First Division to try to install a rigorous regime. Even he was banging his head against a brick wall most of the time.

Friday nights down the Roding before matches were the thing. You never booked yer table till 10 o'clock at night. Beer, champagne, you'd be there to 3, 4, 5am. They were all there, Mooro and that. Pissed! Bobby had hollow legs... He liked getting to the Northern nightclubs, mixing with players from Leeds, Manchester and Liverpool.

West Ham were a fashionable club and the Hammers' main revellers, Budgie, Charles, Moore and Brian Dear, were often joined by the likes of Jimmy Tarbuck, Kenny Lynch, Max Bygraves and Eric Sykes. Of course Byrne knew all the great players of the sixties and occasionally took to the clubs with George Best. He recalled that George: '...was always inundated with phone calls from birds... it was no wonder he was unable to play properly at times.'

After George had been awarded the Footballer of the Year trophy John was among those who accompanied the Manchester United star to the Astor Club in London. George, as usual, had a host of women on his heels. Byrne recalled:

He clicked with one and I finished up with him and her in her flat.

I can remember this beautiful lady saying 'There is no way you're going to get me into bed, Mr George Best'. She was quite adamant and it was one of the few occasions that George got a knock-back.

Byrne was always quite frank about where he might have made mistakes. He reflected that although his career might seem:

> ...like too much wine, women and gambling, I did at some stage realise I was a professional footballer. This is the life I led. Money was 'an easy come and easy go' sort of thing. And it happened to me at a very early stage. I was hero worshipped and unfortunately when this happens some are not able to contain it... I kept telling myself 'you've got to knuckle down', but I never did for very long.

For all this, John was lucky to have Margaret in the background. She was the rock in his life, his stability and the person who was always there. John loved his family, his three children and Margaret and it was because he was a footballer, with a relatively high amount of free time on his hands, that he was able to maintain a family life, play the game and party, but something had to give and it wasn't going to be family or merrymaking. John's one-time manager, mentor and long-time friend, Arthur Rowe, reflected:

> John should have been around a lot longer than he was in the English game, but you know what happened. He didn't honour his potential. He got mixed up with the big boys off the field and that was it. Crystal Palace bought him back later when everyone knew he wasn't the same player. I begged them not to.

A former West Ham colleague recalled:

> Budgie was a funny man. But when he'd had a drink he could be bit acerbic, particularly with blokes he saw as not having as much talent as him – which was most of us. He lost it too early; it was a tragedy. He ought to have been England's centre-forward from 1961 right up to the mid-seventies. Budgie was the best in the country by 1965, that's for sure, but he chose to mess about and piss away all that ability. He let himself go. He had all the confidence in the world about his own ability, but he couldn't do what Bobby did. Mooro would come in after a night on the lager in a rubber suit and sweat it all off. Budgie wasn't going to have any of that! Greenwood loved him. Johnny got on better with Ron than anyone of us.
>
> Budgie was like George Best in that he could never say no. He didn't have the strength or the discipline that Bobby had; the ability to say 'not tonight'. If it hadn't been for the drink aggravating his weight problem Budgie would have been in the England side in the 1966 World Cup Final. It's true that a cartilage operation in the

mid-sixties nearly always left players slower and less mobile, but had he controlled himself a bit more, been just a bit fitter, that might never have happened. He knew that and always regretted it and to be fair he used it as a lesson to younger players later on. He was an exceptional player and, if he had watched his weight and what he ate, he would have been one of the all-time greats in the British game.

Always time for a drink

Moore and Byrne were as good at drinking as they were at playing together but Bobby thought that John did himself no favours with the booze. During the 1965–66 European Cup-Winners' Cup campaign West Ham travelled to Greece for a return match against Olympiakos. Budgie recalled:

Most of us were drinking on the plane to Greece. We had to make a stopover in Switzerland and before we took off again the pilot came through and asked me how much more champagne I was likely to want. I said: 'Just another crate.'

When we got to Greece they had to put me to bed for couple of days, but some of the blokes went straight out on the booze the night we arrived in Greece. They had all sorts of problems after that, stomachs mostly.

It was incredible, but I used to be able to get away with that sort of thing. It was a struggle to get out of bed on the day of that match, but I played well.

Gangster number one

Serious, committed drinking in London's East End during the 1960s could be a risky business in more ways than one. John Charles, West Ham's first black player and a good friend of Johnny Byrne and Bobby Moore told me of one very early morning encounter in a drinking club in Bethnal Green as the three were winding down from a night of concentrated boozing. Charlo (as Charles was known within the ranks of the Hammers) found himself talking to a well spoken man who claimed to be a High Court judge. In cultured tones he asked John 'Where do you come from?' In pure cockney John answered 'Cannin' Taan'. The regal looking gentleman looked confused. 'No,' he shook his grey head, 'I mean, where do you come from?' Charlo merely repeated his former response, 'Cannin' Taan'. The aged pin-striped toff tried again. 'From where do you originate?' John looked hard at his inquisitor. 'Cannin' Taan' he reiterated. 'I was born on a f*****' 'ot day!' The old boy didn't get it, but the surrounding throng were suitably amused. Charlo continued, nodding towards Budgie, 'and that's me twin bruvva. Our mum was from Ghana and our dad was an Irishman with a bike'. That was the end of the tale as told to me by Charlo, but Budgie remembered what happened next. As the laughter accompanied John's verbal crucifiction of the pompus old bigot a voice came through the crowd. 'I f****** hate the Irish'. Everyone knew the face that had growled his enmity and according to Budgie,

> I said, 'oh well, I was ready to go anyway' but Charlo was having none of it. 'That ain't nice' he said. 'I think you owe us an apology'. For the most part John was a good laugh sober or pissed, but if you upset him after a long session he could get the hump. But this was the wrong place to get the hump and the wrong person to get the hump with.

The Irons' tough-tackling, uncompromising full-back was apparently unperturbed and was staring hard at the verbose xenophobe who also happened to be the nearest thing East London had to Al Capone. Budgie speculated:

> It might have been the jibe about the twins that done it, but I really didn't care, it was all getting a bit too serious. I looked at Bobby and he looked at me, we both knew what one another were thinking: 'Oh dear!'. It was very tense. Bleedin' scary really.

Returning Charlo's fixed gaze the voice that had frozen the moment formed a wicked chuckle. 'Why don't you lads have a drink on me?' 'For half a second I thought John was going to tell hime to poke it', Budgie recalled, 'Which would not have been good. But he just said "Ta very much" and we were back having a laugh. But for a minute I thought we were going to end up propping up Bow flyover for the next 50 years.'

We went completely berserk

Johnny was to see the mid-sixties as West Ham's peak years but unfortunately the side were unable to sustain their success. For Byrne this was due to a combination of factors. The West Ham side were young and team spirit was tremendous but according to Byrne these boisterous, mostly East End boys could not be controlled by Ron Greenwood. He admitted:

> We needed someone a lot stronger who could keep us in check. He

could do nothing to stop us and we went completely berserk, living it up day in and day out. We went to dinners, functions and boxing tournaments. This was probably the downfall of myself and one or two others at West Ham.

But chasing players was not Greenwood's way. He wanted them to act like adults and thought the only way that would happen was if they were treated and trusted like adults. He believed that they had to take responsibility for themselves and deal with the consequences, and according to Ron, one of the consequences of John's behaviour was that he didn't get as many England caps as he should have. But Greenwood understood that Budgie's problems were of a deeper order than just the liking for a drink. For him Byrne was:

>...everybody's friend but his own worst enemy... I told him that he should play for England until he was past 30 but he was not a moderate man. By the time he was 28 his lifestyle was telling. He couldn't say 'No'. He lived life to the full but while he was young he recovered quickly and never gave a thought to the eventual cost. Nobody can have it both ways, and there is always a bill.

CHAPTER 7

Red Hot Irons

A S SOON as the draw was made for the semi-final of the FA Cup in 1963 and it was known that the two Second Division clubs, Swansea City and Preston North End, would meet for the right to face West Ham United or Manchester United at Wembley, the media agreed that West Ham would not be in the final. No one gave the East Enders a chance at Hillsborough, as the likes of Denis Law, Bobby Charlton and Pat Crerand were returning to the United side for the match after lay-offs. The fact that the game was played at Hillsborough, close to Manchester but a long journey for the East Londoners, served to increase the pessimism about the Hammers' chances.

THE FOOTBALL ASSOCIATION
CHALLENGE CUP

Semi-Final

Preston North End

v.

Swansea Town

SATURDAY, MARCH 14th, 1964
Kick-off 3-0 p.m.

Villa Park · Birmingham

Official Souvenir Programme
ONE SHILLING

However, following the West Ham club policy of studying opponents, Johnny Byrne and Bobby Moore were sent to watch United in their sixth-round replay against Sunderland, who would be promoted to Division One that year, and the two friends were not overly impressed by Matt Busby's side. According to the Irons' spies, the Manchester team only looked good when they were in front, and seemed to be a side that might find it very difficult to come back in a game if they were losing by a goal or two. But both Bobby and Budgie returned to London with a high regard for the ability of the young Irish winger, George Best: he had been the outstanding player on the park that evening. For all this, Byrne and Moore were clear that they knew how to beat the Manchester giants. Budgie recalled the analysis: 'Don't give em any space, cut off their ability to run the game, make them follow us.' He remembered the morning of the game:

> I used to room with Ken Brown and I told him when we got up that it had been chucking it down all night. In fact that was the start of the second day of solid rain. On the route from the hotel to Hillsborough we were thinking that the match might be called off, it was pissing down. On the way we saw loads of West Ham supporters, most looking like drowned rats, and you thought you had to do something for them. Seeing them motivated us.

In the League, United were in fifth place while the Hammers were nine positions adrift of them. This said, historically almost any United team is good, but this was one of the great sides to come out of Old Trafford. Their path to the last four had, on paper, been easier than West Ham's journey. Matt's men had disposed of two Second Division and two Third Division sides: Southampton, Bristol Rovers, Barnsley and Sunderland, although Sunderland took two replays to beat. United had scored 21 goals on the way to Hillsborough compared to West Ham's 19. The Manchester Reds that lined up to face the Hammers had an ominous look: Gaskell had England youth credentials, Seamus Brennan had been an Irish Under-19 defender, Tony Dunne was a full Irish international, Paddy Crerand was a regular in the Scottish side, Bill Foulkes had survived the Munich disaster and played for England, Maurice Setters had a string of England Under-23 appearances at wing-half under his belt, Scotsman David Herd was to represent his country five times, Phil

Chisnall was another English Under-23 international and of course there were Charlton, Law and Best. But the pre-match entertainment was provided by the Dagenham Girl Pipers, so the Hammers had at least some home advantage. John recalled:

> In the tunnel under the stand the United players were busy chatting up the girls and didn't seem to care much about the game. I think that might have fired one or two of us up; they didn't seem to be taking us seriously. They were, I think, 3/1 on to beat us and we were 3/1 against to win!

The rain that had been saturating Sheffield as Budgie had awoken that morning was still pelting down as the teams took to the field and, as the referee blew for the start of the game, the 65,000 supporters were thoroughly drenched, having paid between 5s and £1 10s a ticket for the privilege. This massive congregation included 20,000 who had made the pilgrimage from East London by car, train and 12 coaches that had left Upton Park at midnight the evening before the match. The coach convoy had arrived in Sheffield at 8am in the morning. The passengers had seen very little more than flooded fields as dawn had broken through the dark clouds before they were expelled from their transport to be wet through in the day-long deluge, wandering around the swampy 'Steel Town' streets. The rumour that persisted for years after that many returned to London with webbed feet has never been substantiated.

Budgie recalled running out onto the pitch and literally paddling in the liquid mud. Only a brief let-up in the weather just before the game had persuaded the referee, Mr Stokes, to allow the match to be played. Prior to games Bobby Moore had a habit of putting Vaseline on his forehead, just above his eyebrows, to stop sweat running into his eyes, but even before he and Denis Law had tossed up the water was running down Moore's face in small torrents. Just a few minutes into the match the 22 players on the Hillsborough pitch were covered in mud (it looked slightly worse on the Reds, who that day had started as the 'Whites' – the Hammers wore their light blue shirts with the two claret hoops around the chest). Manchester United, being a stronger and more physical side than the Irons, might have been thought to be favoured by the conditions; the midfield especially would have been demanding for even the hardiest. Yet from the moment West Ham kicked off, playing towards the Leppings Lane end, they worked together with a great deal of confidence, playing above themselves, depriving the opposition of the ball. According to Byrne:

We liked to play football, we were a footballing side; the mud didn't make much difference to that. Bovington marked Charlton and Ken Brown was on Denis Law. Jim Standen was solid in goal while me and Geoff worked well up front.

The Hammers certainly adapted to the muddy conditions much better than their counterparts in the Manchester team. Bobby Moore was dominating the field, marshalling Bond, Burkett, Bovington and Brown to generate a resilient defence. It was clear that the two teams were involved in the kind of game where it was vital to score the first goal and both sides came close. Sissons was doing a great job against the intimidating Crerand and Hurst brought a magnificent save from Dave Gaskell in the United goal. United also had their chances, the best coming from the 17-year-old George Best, who hit the West Ham crossbar from 20 yards. However, at half-time there was no score.

When the teams came out for the second 45 minutes every player on the park seemed determined to break the stalemate, but it was the Irons' 21-year-old inside-right Ron Boyce who scored when, just over 10 minutes into the second half, he looked up to see the United keeper off his line. Ron knew of Gaskell's propensity to do this and lofted in a 25-yarder, just inside the United half, past the stranded 'keeper into the top left-hand corner of the net. With Budgie looking like the best centre-forward in England, West Ham made it 2–0 when Sissons, seeing Jack Burkett running towards him, intended to cut a short corner back to the Hammers full-back. But he noted Pat Crerand making his way across the field to cover this ploy, so Sissons shaped up as if he was about to take a conventional corner. Seeing this Crerand moved back to the middle, at which point Sissons made the short pass to Burkett who sent in a curling, shoulder-high centre, which was met, on the six-yard line, central to the goal, by the head of Boyce, who had expertly timed his run. The glancing contact sent the ball just inside Gaskell's far post. The goal had 'made in Chadwell Heath' written all over it; it was a West Ham training-ground special that delighted Ron Greenwood. In a seven-minute period during the first 20 minutes of the second half, West Ham had taken control. As his teammates slapped Boyce's soggy shirt after the second goal, Wembley seemed a certainty, but it was far from over. United went into overdrive and laid siege to the West Ham goal. However, the cockney boys defended like demons until, with only 15 minutes to go, Jim Standen went face first into the mud as Law piled into the Hammers custodian with a two-footed tackle. The West Ham 'keeper was dizzy and completely blinded by mud. Johnny Sissons ran to the touchline and brought back a bucket of water and Standen washed the mud out of his eyes, but his vision hadn't cleared when play was restarted.

By this time the pitch was a sea of slime. Ken Brown put the ball on a mound for John Bond to take a free kick, to give the ailing Standen some recovery time. The mark was just outside the West Ham box and Bond kicked mud before ball. 'Muffin', as the Hammers' veteran defender was known, was, as his nickname indicated, one of the most powerful strikers of the ball in the game, but one is not allowed mistakes in FA Cup semi-finals against Manchester United and in a trice Best was in possession and passed to Phil Chisnall, who sent over a cross that connected with the head of Denis Law, for once free of Ken Brown's watchful presence. Law out-jumped the still-dazed Standen and, after 78 minutes, United were back in the game. Standen hadn't even seen the cross coming in. Budgie recalled:

Bondy had said 'leave it to me' and then gave the ball away. Poor old John got a right bollocking from everyone.

But just seconds later a ball broke loose on the left, inside West Ham's half. It was near enough to the touchline for Pat Crerand to decide that Moore couldn't reach it in time, or if he did that Bobby would have no room to go past him. With the mud making quick changes of direction almost impossible, Crerand was too late to move when Moore got to the ball and hit it past the tough Caledonian right-half on the outside. Bobby then ran past Crerand in a curve which took Moore over the touchline and back onto the field of play. Fending off two challenges, the Hammers' skipper somehow kept the ball in play and took it along the line for about 30 yards before hitting a perfect low pass into the gap vacated by the Manchester pivot, Bill Foulkes (who had moved wide to cover Moore's surge upfield), ahead of Geoff Hurst, who as usual had made himself space to run on to the ball. The big striker tore through the hole left by Foulkes to strike the ball low and hard, wide and right of Gaskell, from the edge of the penalty area. Practically the same move would be enacted in the World Cup final of 1966. It was still raining as Hurst was mobbed by his muddy colleagues. A minute later, with United putting everything into the attack, Hurst nearly grabbed a fourth goal, having beaten Gaskell to the ball, but could only watch the clinging mud check his net-bound effort.

At last the final whistle blew and West Ham had reached Wembley for the first time in 41 years. At the same time, they had belied their reputation for being a team that could only play football on the firm, flat pitches of autumn and spring. Moore had been central to the whole affair, fending off attack after attack. Boyce had motored over every inch of the field. He didn't score many, just 11 that season, and in all his 339 outings for West Ham he netted just 29 times, but he had chosen the right time to score two goals in a first-team match: he had never done it before and would never do it again. Eddie Bovington had shackled Charlton while Budgie had linked everything together and the West Ham fans, sodden in the uncovered Kop, went home delighted. John remembered: 'We hardly believed we'd won. It was a great feeling. We'd made the final!' After the match Greenwood paid tribute to his team:

> Look at them; this is the greatest day in their lives. I have been proud to be associated with this bunch of youngsters. Now the world and his friend will claim them. I accept that this must happen, but I will not let the leeches, hangers-on, glad-handers destroy what they have built for themselves. I will do everything I can to protect them from the wrong sort of reaction to this success.

That said, on the train back to London the West Ham party, who had been ensconced in their reserved dining carriage, celebrated hard and long with jubilant fans and officials. According to Johnny:

> The Cup meant more then I think. We were all in the restaurant car trying to eat, but it was packed with people. West Ham fans were always great. It wasn't about winning and losing. They laid into you at times, but they always gave you credit for trying.

This was their finest hour… and a half

That semi-final will always stand as one of West Ham's finest 90 minutes and among the best days in Budgie's career in England. Matt Busby was to say it was one of his greatest disappointments and biggest surprises. Beating Manchester United is a big event in the history of any team, but to knock them out of the FA Cup at the semi-final stage is a rare achievement for any English club and not many West Ham players thought that it was possible, but doubt had never entered Budgie's head:

> Most of the blokes thought that the draw against United was just the end of a good run, especially as they had beaten us the week before. In the bar after the Burnley match everyone was laughing and saying that it wasn't worth us turning up at Sheffield. I had a laugh too, but I never believed that we couldn't win. Greenwood has to take a lot of the credit. He'd tell us the obvious, like; 'When

you're on the ball and space is not in front of you, it's behind you', it seems a stupid thing to say, but it often takes a genius to see the simplest things. He was big on 'taking the ball on the half-turn'. If you could do that it gave you that split-second advantage. He liked to open sides up. He loved the game and was the best coach in England in his time – few have ever bettered him. He wasn't really like an English coach. He had much more in common with Continental managers. He liked his sides to play the European sides and learn from them and he'd go through things we picked up at Chadwell Heath. We were doing things then that clubs like Arsenal and Chelsea just started doing in the 1980s. Playing the 4–4–2 we were thought of as a European side. For Ron the most important things in his life was his family and football and that was part of the reason why I thought we could do United.

Everything after the Hillsborough triumph, maybe even the FA Cup final itself, was going to be an anticlimax for the Boleyn Boys. With the final looming, nerves ruled when Arsenal came to the home of the Hammers. Standen saved a George Eastman penalty and the lanky Scottish centre-half, Ian Ure, kicked Johnny Byrne all over the park, and once right out of it, over a barrier, during the 1–1 draw two days before the second leg of the League Cup final at Upton Park.

The West Ham side for the second League Cup semi-final match included Eddie Bovington and John Sissons, who came into the Irons XI in place of Peters and Sealey. Leicester used Graham Cross in place of Ken Keyworth, but it was Gordon Banks who denied the Hammers for the first half-hour. Then, against the run of play, McLintock struck a decisive blow 13 minutes before the interval, by which time the Irons should have been three up. Roberts sealed the East Enders fate after 70 minutes, despite a fine display of the 'keeper's art from Standen, and West Ham lost the opportunity to become the first side to win both the major English cup competitions in a single season. The goalkeeping legend-to-be Gordon Banks had returned to the side after five weeks of injury and played like a man with a point to prove. The Filberts went back to the Midlands with a 2–0 victory and went on to beat Stoke City in the final.

West Ham beat the other League Cup finalists, Stoke, 4–1 four days later; the goal of the match followed a four-player move that culminated in Byrne scoring after 14 minutes. It was the first time he had hit the back of the net for a month. His next was West Ham's second in Bolton's 3–2 win at Upton Park in early April. Byrne's final goal of the League season was the Hammers' final word in the 5–0 thrashing of their spring visitors Birmingham City. Budgie was absent for the final Division One game, a 1–0 defeat at Goodison. West Ham got to 14th place in the League, finishing just above Fulham. Liverpool (from whom the Hammers took the full four League points that term) won the Championship and Manchester United were runners-up, but of course the Irons had beaten them two times out of three that season (4–3 to the cockney boys!). Hurst and Byrne were West Ham's goal providers. Together they scored 58 of the 105 the Hammers scored in all competitions before the FA Cup Final. Budgie was top scorer at the club with 33 to his name. In a run of five games between 14 and 28 December Byrne had netted in every match and accrued 10 goals. In six matches from 5 February to 3 March he again got his name on the scoresheet of each encounter, amassing a total of nine goals. Unsurprisingly Johnny was named Hammer of the Year.

Both Byrne and Moore were picked for England's match against the Scots at Hampden. This was the first time for 41 years that two Hammers had played together for England at Hampden, Jack Tresadern and Vic Watson having helped fight out a 2–2 draw in 1923. Watson had scored in that 50th encounter with the 'auld enemy', but Tresadern, who would one day manage a Tottenham Hotspur team that included Arthur Rowe, had made a mistake that led to the first of the Scottish goals.

The game at Hampden in the spring of 1964 was the 101st played between England and Scotland. For the first time in 80 years the Scots completed a hat-trick of victories over their traditional rivals. When the victorious Scottish side gave in to the demands of the crowd for a lap of honour after the match, some of them were barefooted. It had been Allen Gilzean's head, then still dark, that had done the damage. He had soared high above the English centre-half Norman and nutted Wilson's corner beyond the groping hands of Gordon Banks. It was not a great game and both sides certainly played below their best in a swirling gale and driving rain, but Scotland were the better side on the day, looking better set to play the 4–2–4 formation with their greater flexibility and overall decisiveness. Indeed, if it hadn't been for their sturdy defence England might have taken much more of a beating. Moore, supported firmly by Norman, looked peerless in the sweeper's role, reading and meeting each Scottish attack with intelligence and, on several occasions, denying the capricious Law or the darting Henderson the goal that seemed imminent. However, both midfields looked fussy, especially the English section, and this led to a bias to move the ball across the pitch rather than in a forward direction. Budgie recalled:

> The fundamental difference between the teams was the superiority of Jim Baxter and Denis Law, the Scottish midfield link players. They just outplayed George Eastman and Gordon Milne. When Baxter and Law were involved they were just so effective and in the end it was only problems with the finishing that had a lot to do with Mooro, which kept the Scots on the one goal.

Date:	11 April 1964
Location:	Hampden Park, Glasgow
Competition:	Home Championship
Fixture:	Scotland v England
Result:	1–0 (HT 0–0)
Scotland scorer:	Gilzean (78 mins)
Team:	Banks, G. (Leicester City), Armfield, J.C. (Blackpool) captain, Wilson, R. (Huddersfield Town), Milne, G. (Liverpool), Norman, M. (Tottenham Hotspur), Moore, R.F.C. (West Ham United), Paine, T.L. (Southampton), Hunt, R. (Liverpool), Eastham, G.E (Arsenal), Byrne, J.J. (West Ham United), Charlton, R. (Manchester United).
Scotland:	Forsyth, C. (Kilmarnock), Hamilton, A. (Dundee), Kennedy (Celtic), Greig (Rangers), McNeill (Celtic), Baxter, J. (Rangers), Henderson (Rangers), White, J. (Tottenham Hotspur), Gilzean, A. (Dundee), Law, D. (Manchester United), Wilson, D. (Rangers).
Attendance:	133,245
Referee:	Leo Horn (Holland)

CHAPTER 8

Scorching Wembley

T HE FA Cup Final of 1964 was West Ham's first Wembley appearance since the War Cup final of 1940, and their first FA Cup Final since the famous 'White Horse' epic of 1923. Ron Greenwood's eleven for the game against Preston North End had played in every round of their FA Cup campaign. Greenwood used the same side that won in the League at Ewood Park where Bovington had come in for Martin Peters. Peters was always to feel frustrated about that decision, feeling that he had been singled out from the entire team that had conceded eight goals against Blackburn at Upton Park on Boxing Day 1963. The rationale was much more impersonal than this. If anything Peters was much more to Greenwood's footballing taste than the pugnacious Bovington, who himself owned up to being in the Andy Malcolm tradition at Upton Park; belligerent, uncompromising and focused on destruction. Malcolm had been among the first to be shipped out when Greenwood replaced Ted Fenton as West Ham manager: the 'way of the warrior' had never been part of Ron's philosophy. But Greenwood was also a pragmatic man and he knew that battles against lower division clubs and even the lesser lights of the First Division required the presence of a strongman. His side had to achieve a balance that could respond to the opposition. With Byrne, Sissons, Brabrook, Boyce, Moore and to a lesser extent Burkett, there was more than enough 'art' in the side. The skilled power came from Bond, Brown, Bovington and Hurst. Although Peters was often underestimated as a steely player, his selection would have compromised the Hammers' armour in the context of the English attrition that was the FA Cup in the 1960s. West Ham's European adventures, that were to require more craft, cunning and subtlety, would see Peters come into his own, but the warlike forwards of North End would have to face the menacing tackling persona, the intimidating, confrontational power of 'Eddie the Bov.'

As a Division One side West Ham were favourites to beat Preston, although the Lancastrians had finished third in the Second Division behind promoted sides Leeds and Sunderland. However, North End were weakened by the absence of left-half Ian Davidson, the Scotsman having been suspended, and the Hammers looked a quality side with Bobby Moore, Footballer of the Year, leading them and England striker Johnny Byrne (who came fourth in the same poll) sculpting their attack.

WEST HAM
1964

The Official Publication of the West Ham Players

Price **2/6**

John confessed that like most of the other West Ham players, he had, at times, thought that the Hammers would never win anything. But sometime during 1964:

> Suddenly everything altered. We had become more confident. We thought, 'This is going to be our year'. There was a lot more interest in European competition. Win the FA Cup and you were in on that.
>
> West Ham stayed in a hotel in North London the night before the match. There wasn't much sign of nerves. Ron had done his homework on Preston and we had all gone to see them play. Me and Kenny Brown kept the lads laughing.
>
> Our coach got to Empire Way about an hour before the kick-off. The West Ham fans were cheering, blowing horns and whirling rattles. Of course the Preston supporters were booing us.

North End

Preston, the Lilywhites, had reached Wembley by beating First Division Bolton Wanderers after a replay, and overcoming Carlisle United and Oxford United from Division Three. They had defeated Second Division Swansea Town (this was before the Swans became 'City') 2–1 at Villa Park in the semi-finals, with

JAMES MILNE,
Preston North End F.C.

goals from Alex Dawson and Andy Singleton. Preston North End: even their name suggested their character. Like Accrington Stanley, Barnsley and Easington Colliery, there was a tough pragmatism associated with them – they were from Preston, the North End. They were a hard side; hard to beat, hard to play, moulded in the image of their manager, a Lancashire legend: Jimmy Milne.

Jimmy Milne

Jimmy Milne joined Preston from Dundee United in 1932 for a fee of £900. He made his debut for the club on 29 October 1932 at Lincoln. Jimmy was one of the finest uncapped half-backs of the time and played for Preston during a period when North End were among the football elite of England. His defensive partnership with Bill Shankly, who would become immortalised as one of the finest managers in the history of Liverpool Football Club, became renowned. Other stars of that Preston side included Tom Smith, Bob and Andy Beattie and George Mutch.

Milne became a consistent performer, able to give his all in match after match. He had great composure on the ball but was a strong tackler and was soon to become a regular in North End's first team. Although his more illustrious teammates often pushed Jimmy into the background, in his second season with the club he helped Preston win promotion to Division One, shunting Bolton Wanderers into runners-up position by a single point.

Milne was a rock as North End made it through to the sixth round of the FA Cup in the 1934–35 term. They were only stopped by an excellent West Bromwich Albion side. But Jimmy went to the final in 1937. Preston were the underdogs against Sunderland, who had finished as League Champions the previous season and dominated the match, winning 3–1. However, 1937 had its compensations for Jimmy. His son Gordon was born in March of that year, and the boy would eventually follow his father into the Preston side as a stylish wing-half and win 14 England caps.

The following season Preston found themselves level on points with Arsenal at the top of the League. When the Gunners came to Deepdale great things were expected as Milne and his compatriots had knocked Arsenal out of the Cup at Highbury. However, Jimmy broke his collarbone early on in the match and Preston were beaten 3–1. With Milne out of the side Preston nose-dived and finished the season in third place. However, the Deepdale lads met Huddersfield in the Cup Final and Jimmy watched his side win 1–0 from a last-minute penalty.

GORDON MILNE
England

During World War Two Milne became a police officer. From time to time he played for Preston but in common with most players of the time his football career suffered. After the War Jimmy became player-manager of Wigan and later, in 1947, the first-ever manager of Morecambe FC (he was again player-manager), before taking up the role of trainer with Doncaster. He came back to Deepdale and served the club for 11 years as a trainer, again going to Wembley in 1954, this time to watch his side beaten by West Bromwich Albion. Milne took over as club manager in 1961, the year Preston fell out of the top flight. With the abolition of the maximum wage North End found it hard to hold on to their younger players and compete with the big clubs of the 1960s. One such loss was Jimmy's son

Gordon, who in August 1960 joined his father's former defensive partner Bill Shankly at Liverpool and in 1962 won a Second Division Championship medal with the Reds. However, just like his father, Gordon missed a Cup Final through injury when Liverpool beat Leeds in 1965 to record their first-ever win in the tournament. But his first England cap (against Brazil) in 1963, League Championship wins of 1964 and 1966, and inclusion in England's 1966 World Cup squad must have gone some way towards making up for his disappointing exclusion from the Cup Final of 1965.

Jimmy retired from management in 1968 and became Preston's chief scout. With North End he had gone to Wembley as a player, spectator, trainer and in 1964 as manager. He had only ever watched them win. Jimmy died on 13 December 1997 still attached to Deepdale and its cause. Gordon Milne, after finishing his playing career at Blackpool, went on, like his father, to manage Wigan, guiding them to the Northern Premier League title and an FA Cup run that ended with a narrow defeat at Maine Road. He later managed Coventry City, Leicester City, the England Youth side that won the European Youth Championships in 1972 and Besiktas of Turkey, taking the latter to three championship wins between 1990 and 1992 and two Turkish Cup wins in 1990 and 1992.

Team Preston
Jimmy Milne had chiselled his Cup Final side out of 1960s football. There was a completeness about them, a granite-like quality that said, simply, determinedly, ominously 'North'. The Preston goalkeeper, Alan Kelly, was an Irish international, who would, by 1975, play 447 games for Preston. The defence looked more than solid with Scotsman George Ross, who would turn out nearly 400 times for North End before moving to Southport in 1972 and the Preston skipper at Wembley, Norbert Lawton. Born in Newton Heath, Manchester, in 1940, Nobby had joined Preston in 1962 after spending three years with Manchester United. A probing, pushing right-half, he was a product of Manchester Schools football and was a member of the 1955 Manchester Schoolboys side that ended West Ham Schoolboys' nine-year unbeaten run and reached the final of the English Schools Shield only to lose 4–3 on aggregate over two legs to Swansea Schoolboys. Nobby was to represent Lancashire Schools and initially went to Old Trafford as an amateur, training two nights a week while working for a coal merchant. He turned professional at 18, just after the Munich disaster, and made his first League appearance late in the

1959–60 season. Lawton's best term at United was 1961–62 when, looking bright and creative in a transitional team, he played in 20 League matches and scored six goals, the highlight being his hat-trick, from inside-left, in the 6–3 win against Nottingham Forest at Old Trafford on Boxing Day 1961. In the following campaign, however, he was not able to gain a regular place in the side, and when United paid £55,000 for Paddy Crerand, Lawton was allowed to leave. He blossomed at Deepdale and his inspired captaincy did much to bring his club to Wembley in 1964. After Preston, Lawton had a two-year spell with Brighton and Hove Albion and he finished his career at Lincoln City. Having been obliged to leave football after a knee injury at the age of 32, Nobby worked as a sales director of an export packaging company.

Preston's protective carapace was completed by Jimmy Smith, who had played for Scotland as a schoolboy, and the hard, Preston-born centre-half Andy Singleton. The midfield included Howard Kendall and Alan Spavin. Seventeen-year-old (and 345 days) Kendall, at left-half, was to be the youngest player ever to appear in a Wembley final and the youngest Cup finalist of the century up to that point. He would gain half-a-dozen England Under-23 caps and spend the majority of his career with Everton, playing his part in the superb 1970 Championship-winning side, and he eventually became manager of the Liverpool Blues. The 22-year-old Spavin was the dynamo of the Preston side; he would play 414 games for the Lilywhites over the next 14 years, interrupted by four years playing in the US.

Another England Under-23 international in the Preston side was winger Davie Wilson, who would spend two years at Anfield from 1967. Inside-forward Alec Ashworth had been with Everton, Luton and Northampton Town; he had scored 25 goals in 30 games for the Cobblers in their Third Division championship campaign of 1962–63 before joining Preston. North End's Alex Dawson was a tall, strong and fearless man, seemingly designed for aerial combat. As Preston's top marksman, he was one of a dying breed of battleship forwards in the mould of Nat Lofthouse. Dawson was the son of a Grimsby trawlerman and although he was born in Scotland he played six times for England Schoolboys in 1954–55. Alex had been a member of Manchester United's FA Youth Cup-winning side in 1956 and was also in the team that beat West Ham 8–2 in the 1957 final. Dawson netted in each of the final three matches of that season, helping United clinch the League championship. Along with other Old Trafford youngsters Dawson came regularly into the side after Munich. He netted on his debut in the League, the League Cup and the FA Cup.

In that term he scored his memorable hat-trick in the semi-final replay against Fulham at Highbury on 26 March 1958. This took him and his side to Wembley. That made him the youngest post-war player to score a hat-trick (he was 18 years and 33 days) in the FA Cup. Dawson played outside-right in the final, which was won 2–0 by Bolton Wanderers. Strong and robust, with a direct approach, Dawson began to be pushed aside with the arrival of David Herd at Old Trafford and moved to Preston in October 1961 for £18,000. Manchester United and England hard man Nobby Stiles called him 'a wrecking ball of a player'. His menacing demeanour, dark hair and complexion earned him the moniker of 'The Black Prince of Preston'. During his five years at Old Trafford he put away 45 goals in 80 games and would by 1966 score 114 goals in just under 200 outings for Preston. Towards the end of his League career he was loaned to Brentford. In typical style he scored six goals in 10 matches, but the Bees could not afford his transfer fee. Dawson was on target 212 times in League games during 394 games. He was a centre-forward of the English tradition and the main threat to the West Ham defence at Wembley in 1964.

Doug Holden, who had said before the final 'I've not come to Wembley for a third time to lose', had joined North End from Bolton Wanderers at the age of 32. While at Burnden Park he had won five England caps in 1959, which included facing a powerful Italian side at Wembley and the then World Champions Brazil in Rio de Janeiro. Before 1964 Doug had played in two FA Cup Finals. In 1953 he went away with a loser's medal, Bolton having been narrowly beaten, 4–3, by Stanley Matthews's Blackpool. Five years later Holden had been part of the victorious Wanderers side that had beaten the Munich-ravaged Manchester United 2–0.

SOCCER GALLERY

ALEX DAWSON
Preston North End

Looking at North End's side it was clear that they were a strong team. They had a good combination of youth and experience. Yet for all this, it seemed that few people outside of Lancashire had any great hopes for Preston. Byrne recalled:

> We were the favourites and I suppose this might have added to the tension. The neutrals always go for the unfancied side and the newspapers love a shock result. But if you look at the sides they were fairly equally matched; perhaps we had a bit more skill, but

they had more experience in their side. Before the game Preston were being seen as 'brave underdogs', but we kept laughing.

Waiting

John gave a picture of the West Ham dressing room just before the final:

People had ways of dealing with stress. Some players always seemed to be ready ages before a game. Eddie Bovington and Ron Boyce were like that. Kenny Brown always had a back massage. I never changed until just before kick-off. It was a long walk out to the pitch so we had plenty of time to think about what Ron Greenwood told us before we left the changing rooms. He said, 'All you've got to do is play your normal game… Just play football.' He just wanted us to relax and do what we did best. Ron also told us to start the game with Eddie Bovington playing deep to give us an extra marker. Bobby started the match as a sweeper. This seemed a bit dangerous as Dawson was a threat in the air and that wasn't Mooro's strong point, but Ron was thinking that there was a good chance of there being plenty of knock downs as much as anything else.

The combined bands of the Coldstream and Irish Guards had been blowing away from 1.30pm and their repertoire was an indicator of the times. They knocked out *Gigi, Telstar, World Without Love* (originally sung by Peter and Gordon, two Oxbridge graduates with bobbed hair and tank-tops!), *Can't Buy Me Love* and, surreally, *Maigret*. *Bubbles* of course went down a treat but *I'm a Lassie from Lancashire* felt like an act of tokenism and was hard for many of the mostly male northern supporters to sing with any real conviction.

Wembley Hammers

John recalled: 'We lined up opposite Preston, sizing them up and being sized up as the Earl of Harewood, who looked like a James Bond villain, was introduced to the teams.'

Edmonton born Jim Standen was in goal for West Ham. He was playing for Rickmansworth Town when Arsenal signed him as a professional in April 1953, but he was always in the shadow of Jack Kelsey and went to Luton Town in 1960, where he almost moved to non-League Hereford United before he put on the gloves for West Ham. In November 1962 he rejoined his former Highbury coach Ron Greenwood at Upton Park when Scottish international Lawrie Leslie broke a leg. Jim was sure-handed and agile. He had more than one string to his sporting bow, being a fast bowler for Worcestershire County Cricket Club. He wasn't a big goalie at 5ft 11in and weighing 11 stone 4lbs, but he was a reliable goal guardian for West Ham for most of the sixties. John Bond was a 6ft 2in, 14 stone, claret and blue right-back. Born in Colchester, he was the longest-serving player in the West Ham side, having signed professional for the club in March 1950 after a spell as an amateur with the Irons and Colchester Casuals. John made the first of his more than 350 Cup and League appearances up to the FA Cup final of 1964 in the 1951–52 season. He toured South Africa with the FA in 1956 and had played for England B and Football League sides. Bond had a kick like a donkey and could hit a dead ball harder than any player one might care to nominate. He would, of course, give a lifetime of service to top-class football as a player, coach, manager and director, right up to the first years of the 21st century, when he worked with Wigan as they went into the First Division.

West Ham's left-back Jack Burkett played schoolboy soccer for Tottenham before joining the West Ham ground staff. Born in Bow but raised in Edmonton, North London, Jack played in the FA Youth Cup runners-up side in 1959 and for England Youth. Jack signed professional forms in October that year and made his League debut three years later. He had missed only three games in the season before his first Wembley final. Jack was a swift, studious defender, able to join the attack and combine with Sissons, which he did to lay on the second goal of West Ham's three in the semi-final defeat of Manchester United. Burkett would become one of England's leading coaches and the mentor of many top internationals in his role with the Professional Footballers' Association.

Right-half Eddie Bovington was another member of the 1959 West Ham FA Youth Cup runners-up side. At centre-half Ken Brown, alongside Bond, was a survivor of West Ham's Second Division Championship side of 1958. Ken represented London in the 1958 match with Barcelona and was elected 'Hammer of the Year' in 1959. He won his only England cap against Northern Ireland at Wembley in the same year. Ken was a big, rugged and dependable defender, who made up for any lack of mobility with his massive enthusiasm. Again, like Bond, Brown would become one of the best managers in Britain when he retired from playing.

West Ham's Wembley and all-time captain was left-half Bobby Moore. In 1964 he was already England's undisputed skipper. He was born in Barking, and played as an amateur for West Ham before turning professional in June

1958 after serving on the ground staff. He played for Essex and London Boys, and London and England Youth sides (he gained 18 caps at this level, more than any other player before him) and went on to represent his country as an Under-23 and play for the Football League. Bobby toured the Far East with the FA in 1961 and the following year made his senior England debut against Peru in Lima before going on to play in all four World Cup games in England's 1962 campaign. By 1964 he had twice been Hammer of the Year. Nothing adequate can be said about his career after the FA Cup Final, and much has been said since his tragic death in 1993 at the age of just 52. He would be West Ham's World Cup captain, the greatest Hammer of them all and by far and away the most impressive defender born... ever.

Peter Brabrook, the son of a London docker, played his schoolboy football for East Ham, Essex and London and might have come to Upton Park for a nominal signing-on fee, but he went to Chelsea and West Ham had to pay £35,000, a hefty fee in October 1962, to bring him to the Boleyn Ground. That said, he was one of the best buys the Irons would ever make. West Ham's outside-right at Wembley had won Youth and eight Under-23 caps. He played his debut senior international in a World Cup game against the USSR in 1958 and was called up again for his country to face Northern Ireland and Spain in the years before the FA Cup Final of 1964. Brabrook was fast, skilful and able to switch wings at will. He would stay with West Ham until his retirement in 2003. He was to coach three generations of Hammers. Inside-right Ronnie Boyce was born and bred in West Ham and played for England at every level up to Under-23, and was tremendously unlucky never to be selected for his country's senior side. Ron was the engine of West Ham, the kingpin of the side. He was never out of the Irons' first eleven after he broke into the team on the departure of Welsh international Phil Woosnam to Aston Villa in November 1962 until he was rested for one match before the final.

Johnny Byrne played as West Ham's centre-forward on 2 May 1964, presenting a powerful strike force alongside inside-left Geoff Hurst. Hurst had just six England Youth caps to his name when he walked out onto the Wembley pitch for the first time in Hammers colours. Even the most ardent Hammers fans would not have guessed that the Essex cricketer, converted wing-half and willing workhorse of the side would become a World Cup hero, one of the most feared and renowned strikers on the face of the earth and, eventually, a knight of the realm. Alongside Byrne Hurst's other main supply line was John Sissons. This young Hammer had scored four goals in his first England Boys

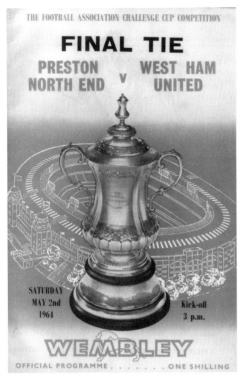

THE FOOTBALL ASSOCIATION CHALLENGE CUP COMPETITION

FINAL TIE

PRESTON NORTH END v WEST HAM UNITED

SATURDAY MAY 2nd 1964

Kick-off 3 p.m.

WEMBLEY

OFFICIAL PROGRAMME . . . . . . ONE SHILLING

appearance, coming to the side from Middlesex Boys. He played international football at Youth level (he was in England's Junior World Cup-winning side) and would go on to represent his country as an Under-23. The programme for the final (which cost 1s) named him as the youngest player on the pitch, but in reality Howard Kendall took that honour when he was named late for the Preston side. This was West Ham's second-ever FA Cup Final eleven. All except Jim Standen and Budgie had matured through the West Ham youth system. Standen would be the only member of the team not to gain international honours at some level. Most of the side were born or brought up within 10 miles of the Hammers East End Upton Park home; they were all claret and blue to the bone, and they were all English.

The contest for the Cup

In the first half the cultured Irons were unable to collect themselves, being disallowed any chance to establish their rhythm. Using long ball tactics Preston gave the Hammers a range of early problems. Within minutes of the kick-off Kendall justified his shock selection in the North End eleven. His ingenuity started the first attack that could have led to a Lancastrian lead. The youngster pushed the ball to his captain Lawton, who placed it between Bond and Moore, for Ashworth to pick up. Standen just saved the situation. According to Byrne:

> From the start we didn't play that well. I thought Jack Burkett was
> going to be sent off in the first 10 minutes; he fouled their winger,
> Wilson, about three times and the ref told him he'd kick him off if
> he kept kicking. We had lost four of our last five League games and
> I suppose we were a bit careful. That's hardly ever a good thing. We
> were a side that counter-attacked; we liked teams to come at us and

relied on moving fast out of defence and getting the ball up to players like myself, who could hold the ball up until someone else ran forward into the clear. At Wembley we couldn't get the counter-attacks going. The Preston skipper, their right-half Nobby Lawton, and their inside-left Alan Spavin, kept Preston pressing forward. That was really the way to play West Ham in those days.

This strategy bore fruit when after just nine minutes Ashworth shot wide from only six yards. A minute later Kendall passed to the powerful, muscular Dawson, who sent a left-foot shot from the edge of the penalty area with a not inconsiderable clout. Standen, whose nerves had been tested from the opening whistle, got down to the shot but was unable to hold on to the ball and Doug Holden took swift advantage, having to do no more than stroke the ball home. This was not a disaster, but it felt like it to the West Ham fans watching from the stands. The last thing any team wanted playing on the energy-sapping Wembley turf was to go a goal down early on in a game. It was now vital for the Hammers to respond.

Inevitably it was Moore who was to initiate a rejoinder for the Irons. The blond prince pushed his side forward and just 60 seconds after the goal West Ham had replied. Budgie remembered the moment:

> Bobby moved into Preston's half, changing position with me, and got the ball to Sissons who immediately sprinted down the wing. He passed it inside to me, and as John ran on I sent it back to him sharpish, he picked it up at about knee height. Johnny went past two of the four defenders in the Preston box and screwed the ball into the net, between Kelly and the post. It was a really tight angle.
>
> He was a lovely player, Johnny.

This made Sissons the youngest player ever to score in an FA Cup Final.

Kendall was back into things from the restart. Wilson, who had followed up a well-placed Kendall pass, lofted the ball in from the right wing. Watched by the horrified Standen, it rolled almost the length of the Hammers' crossbar before it fell harmlessly behind the goal.

It was clear that West Ham's close-passing play, founded on Byrne and Moore, was being read by Preston. The hard tackling of Singleton was taking its toll on Budgie while Lawton was making frequent sorties upfield, dragging Moore with him to leave gaping holes in the Irons' defence. Greenwood had seen this, but in the heat of battle, with Preston throwing themselves forward, the on-field Hammers were not given time to collectively build a counter strategy and were doing all they could do, thrown back on a primal fight-back response. Being cut off, Byrne had to draw on his individual skill, epitomised by the moment when he dribbled round three defenders and gave the hard grafting Geoff Hurst the opportunity to produce a great shot, which was brilliantly saved by Kelly in the 30th minute. The Preston goalie launched himself the full length of the goal to put the ball around the post; up to that point it was the best save of the match. However, Budgie recollected that:

> Our attacks were breaking down before we got within sight of the Preston goal. Lawton kept his strikers pressing forwards and Preston weren't looking like the underdogs. Five minutes before half-time they were in front again. Wilson, their right-left winger, took a corner. Ken Brown stumbled, trying to close in, and Jim Standen slipped as Dawson, using his strength to hurtle through our defence, headed it in with Standen and Johnny Bond rooted on the goal line.
>
> Preston's half-back line, Lawton, Kendall and Singleton, were making it hard for us to get through. I was doing okay when Bobby was sending up long balls, but Mooro couldn't risk too many runs upfield as Ken Brown had enough to do holding on to Dawson. Preston deserved to go in with the lead. Their distribution had been good. We were not getting on top of Dawson and their wingers, Wilson and Holden, were making good use of the space we had given them.

Space

At half-time the West Ham players knew they had been bettered in the first 45 minutes, but they probably looked a little fresher than their Preston counterparts. North End had been doing the majority of the running.

As the crowd were treated to more brass band delights and a marching display by the massed bands of the Brigade of Guards, there was a West Ham seminar going on. Budgie recalled:

> At half-time Ron Greenwood said that Preston had played well, having taken the lead twice, and that they deserved to be in front. He told us that we just had to play better than we had been. He told us to go back out and win the Cup even if it killed us. Yeah, fine. But how do you 'play better'? A lot of other managers would have left it at that, maybe after a bollocking. But Ron had a brilliant

football brain and told us that we had allowed Spavin and Lawton much too much time and space in midfield and this meant that play was bypassing Mooro, who hadn't done much at all in the first half. Wembley was so big that the usual marking systems were messed up.

Preston were running the midfield so Ron told Eddie Bovington to push into midfield to make an earlier impact and speed up the pace of the game, but also to keep an eye on Spavin while Lawton would be marked by Ronnie Boyce. Bobby would shift up alongside Kenny Brown to help him with Dawson and Ashworth who had got used to playing on the big pitch better than our attack and were giving Ken problems in the air. At the same time we were to switch to a flat back four, in a 4–2–4 formation. We basically reversed our tactics.

So we went out looking to make Preston play our way. Shutting down Lawton seemed to kill their attack and Greenwood's plan began to open the way to goal; we had a number of chances. Having said that about Ron's strategy, our equaliser was just a little bit lucky.

West Ham drew level in the 53rd minute. Peter Brabrook took a corner on the right that Brown headed to Hurst, who launched himself above everyone else. Kelly finger-tipped the ball on to the underside of the bar and it bounced about a foot off the goal line. Hurst was on his knees as Kelly made a grab for the ball and in so doing managed to knock it into the net. According to Budgie:

> At that point we all thought they were beaten. They had really dominated up to then but we had gained control of midfield and the attack was getting some service, all we had to do to score more goals was to hang on to this; keep things that way.

The match now started to move at break-neck pace, going backwards and forwards. Chances came and went at either end as Preston were now obliged to call on their most primitive reserves, producing forceful runs and battering hard into West Ham's midfield and defence, chasing the Irons' attack that had now coupled with the rest of the side. This all-out effort, drawn from the core of the Preston men's battling instincts, gave the stoic Lilywhites the majority of opportunities. One of the best was a potent Dawson drive that brought Standen to his knees, but it was costing them; they were expending energy and West Ham began to take advantage as Hurst beat the man of steel, Singleton, to bring a fine save from Kelly. Although it still seemed to be anybody's game,

Budgie was working hard to claim it for West Ham; as the match went into the last half-hour every time Byrne got the ball the Preston players sensed danger:

Not long after the goal, out on the left, I took the ball on my chest and turned at the same time to send it to Geoff at about waist height. The ball went across the goal but Hurst, with Singleton all over him, completely missed it, five yards out! Then Sissons nearly scored his second with a shot that beat Kelly but crawled past the far post.

Ashworth and Dawson continued to test Standen but their efforts were weakening. Like a raging bull that had for too long been fighting matadors and picadors in an Iberian ring of blood letting, Preston were faltering. Lawson kept coming forward, he never stopped trying, but a West Ham corner, that was almost converted by a pile-driver of a shot from Boyce, seemed to be the turning point. Kelly stood firm under his crossbar. A scrum followed and play was held up as the Preston 'keeper was treated for a back injury. John continued:

With 10 minutes of the match left Brabrook, taking advantage of the space created for him by our change in tactics, centred with Hurst waiting. However, Kelly was determined to reach the ball before him and 'keeper and striker collided as Geoff connected and the header went wide. As the game went into the second minute of injury time West Ham were still applying the pressure. But Preston weren't dead yet. Holden got past Bond and hit the ball into the side net.

I remember Peter Brabrook having his socks around his ankles at that point. You used see a lot of that at Wembley. It was a big pitch, but at least we were a bit prepared for that. I had told Ron about the central area at West Ham dog track. He had no idea what the inside of Custom House Stadium was like, but the middle of the track was almost as big as the Wembley playing area and we had trained on it. But Wembley's turf was thick and tended to bring on cramp. Anyway, Hurst picked up the ball from a goal kick and hurtled forward on a swerving run on the right, breaking through a barrage of challenges. At just the right second Geoff swept the ball to Brabrook and as Peter sent a high ball to Ronnie, Ticker had begun a run towards their goal. That was typical of Boycie. He had marvellous positional vision. He was still running when Peter's cross connected with his head and he kept on running as the ball went wide of Kelly. I was just behind him, just in case anything had gone wrong. The crowd seemed to take ages to react. I did a head-over-heels and as I jumped up they started cheering. Ronnie ran round the goal, I think that was the first time I'd seen a pro player do that. The last few minutes felt like about an hour.

Boyce, 'Ticker' to his teammates, as he was the heart of the side, the man with wonderful timing, the player who so often made the team 'tick'; made it work like clockwork, had executed a beautiful movement. His header had been part of a precise and coordinated forward motion of his body, his head and trunk had moved in unison.

Kelly, at that point, was suffering from an injured left leg, but like his North End comrades he dug deep and struggled on. The Lancashire men were not going to give in; they were not that kind of side; they would fight to and beyond the end. This Preston team were truly admirable; every one of them was a man of pride, proud to play for 'Proud Preston'. Their collective will to keep on running, to metaphorically stand and fight, not to let each other or their supporters down, caused even the most ardent West Ham fan to respect these men as, like a great and terminally holed battle cruiser, they went down with all guns blazing.

But in the end, for Byrne, the sides were divided not by skill but by preparation and tactics:

> In the end Preston played well, probably better than us, but it was the pitch that beat them as much as anything else. Those sessions at Custom House had paid off for us, and of course, we had Ron Greenwood.

With two or three seconds to go the Hammers had a nervous moment when North End were given a free-kick on the edge of the West Ham penalty area, but the fates were with the East Enders and the cup was in the hands of the Boleyn Boys.

The last Englishmen

The Hammers had come from behind to win what had proved to be a real battle. This West Ham side was the last all-English side to win the FA Cup. The winning West Ham team of 1975 nearly replicated the feat, but the big Bermudan Clyde Best had played in the fourth round and replay against Swindon. The Manchester City side built by ex-Hammer Malcolm Allison had also come close to being the last all-English side to win the FA Cup in 1969 but they had played Scotsman Arthur Mann in the third round match at Maine

Road against Luton. All-English sides had won before, but the Irons of 1964 would be the last all-English eleven to win the FA Cup.

As Budgie received his FA Cup medal from the Earl of Harewood he momentarily turned to look at the Hammers' fans:

> The thing that hit you was that they were so happy. I'm not sure I'd ever seen, or ever would see, so much joy in one place. I was well pleased we won, but I don't think I'd ever expected that a game I'd play, anything I would do, would cause so much pleasure. It was infectious. And when we got back to the pitch for the lap of honour we were all falling about laughing and passing round a great big Hammer that Bobby had got from someone in the crowd. It was about eight foot high; you'd never get it into an English ground these days! The noise our fans made was amazing.
>
> But as I was going back onto the pitch I spotted Nobby Lawton and couldn't help feeling sorry him. He'd played out of his skin and had brought his side within a hair's breadth of winning the Cup. But that said, we were so relieved we'd done what we went to Wembley to do and maybe the pressure being suddenly off explained the hysteria that followed the match, or perhaps it was just because we didn't totally deserve to win and had. But then, how many matches did West Ham play and deserve to win and didn't? I've heard it said that after the United game Wembley was an anticlimax, but it wasn't for me. Like everyone says, it is over too soon, but it was a great day. I never experienced anything like it again.

Wembley looked a sea of claret and blue after the game, but the Hammers and Preston had only been allocated 15,000 tickets each for the final. West Ham's share, which had been stored under club secretary Eddie Chapman's bed, were distributed at one match by way of 'lucky vouchers' (this had not been advertised) after season ticket holders were given their automatic allocation. However, given that after the final the Empire Stadium looked like Upton Park writ large, it seems that the good old East End 'bobbing and weaving, ducking and diving' had paid effective if nefarious dividends.

The official banquet at the Hilton after the match included the 69-year-old West Ham veteran Billy Moore (no relation to Bobby). Billy had played in the last Cup Final the Hammers had been involved in. That year, 1923, Bolton Wanderers defeated West Ham 2–0 in the very first at Wembley Final. However, for Budgie, the celebrations didn't quite live up to expectations:

West Ham had kept the guest list on the low side. There were a few hundred people kind of lost in a great big room. It was a bit gloomy and we enjoyed ourselves much more after it was finished.

The following day the newspapers portrayed Preston as the brave losers. Peter Wilson, the legendary sports journalist, who wrote under the aphorism, 'The Man They Can't Gag', was one of the few commentators overtly disappointed with the final. He apparently felt that the Hammers' performance had been something less than mediocre and asked rhetorically: 'How do you think this team will fare next season in the European Cup-Winners' Cup?'

Twelve months later he might have wished, just on that occasion maybe, that 'they' had managed to gag him.

Coming home

The next day the East End of London virtually came to a standstill as the Hammers brought the Cup home for the first time in West Ham's history. Byrne had told Greenwood that he didn't think anyone would be out on the streets to welcome the Cup into the Docklands, but the reality was quite the opposite, as Budgie remembered:

> First thing Peter Brabrook woke up Ken Brown and me in our room at the Hilton. We'd had a good night. From Aldgate to East Ham, through Whitechapel and the Mile End Road, the crowds lined the route our coach took. It was eight to 10 deep most of the way! Banners out on balconies and the sides of buildings; there must have been a million people out on the streets. It took us four hours to reach East Ham Town Hall, which was normally a 25-minute drive. We all loved it. The Cup, which had spent the night in Ron Greenwood's bed, was being passed round and held up for the half-a-dozen miles from Petticoat Lane to East Ham. This was the kind of thing you always dreamed of. It's not the money that motivates you in the end but the chance of glory, the kind of appreciation the supporters gave us that day. It was a nice feeling; kinda that you'd given the fans something.

For many of the tens of thousands applauding as the team coach slowly edged its way down the Barking Road the Wembley triumph was the realisation and culmination of deeply held hopes and long-standing dreams. It made West Ham something. That said, for most of the Hammers' side winning the Cup was a means to an end rather than and end in itself. Byrne said:

After the game we didn't say 'We've done it', we said 'We're there'. We had made it into Europe because that's where it was at for us. It might have been Ron's influence, but we wanted to play at the highest level, where the innovation was happening and that was what European football would offer us.

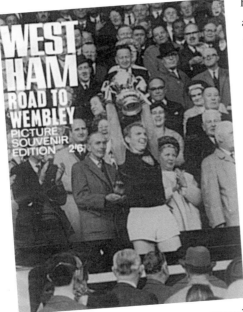

Greenwood confirmed Budgie's point of view: 'Winning at Wembley was the greatest moment in the life of this club, but it is only a stage in development.'

The West Ham team, being 'The Academy', the think-tank that produced a whole new generation of managers, men who thought about the game and looked to create the means to make sides play better, were always going to examine what they had done together. Players like Moore, Brown and Bond, who had been influenced by the analytical mind of West Ham's guerrilla leader of the late 1950s, Malcolm Allison, along with Byrne, who had worked alongside Arthur Rowe, Walter Winterbottom, Alf Ramsey and Greenwood, were disappointed in their Wembley performance. The game had been an exciting spectacle, some said the best Cup Final for a decade, and it is true that the final third of the match had enlivened the game as an event, but for Budgie:

We didn't play well. We didn't do what we had done against United and, having played so well in that game, felt a bit let down by our performance at Wembley. We were probably lucky to win against Preston. I think it says something that on the way home from Hillsborough Ron had cried. I think that was because he had seen his vision fulfilled, and that will always be a bitter sweet thing. The game against Preston wouldn't have given him the same sort of feeling.

Ron always said that coaching was nothing magical. It was about getting players to think for themselves and take responsibility.

Mistakes are never intentional, even the best of players make them; the trick is to learn from your mistakes. The truth is, despite the old saying, many of us don't learn; we make the same mistakes over and over again. The way to begin not making the same error twice is to admit to the gaffes you have made; then you can begin to do something about preventing them from happening again and that is part of responsibility taking. It was looking at the 8–2 defeat by Blackburn on Boxing Day 1963 and the FA Cup Final of 1964 in that way that I think led to the club winning the Cup-Winners' Cup in 1965.

Pathe Pictorial made an 8mm film of the 1964 FA Cup Final. A black and white silent edition cost £2 15s. It lasted 10 minutes so it didn't show the fact that Preston had 23 goal attempts, seven more than the Hammers, and that the Irons had spent long periods of the game chasing the match, but it has to be said that West Ham, having played relatively badly, had recovered. They had dealt with anxiety and fear by a belief in themselves. Such qualities would stand them in good stead over the next year. But more immediately Johnny Byrne, along with Moore, had to report directly for England duty while Ronnie Boyce married his life-long partner Dawn – 'Ticker' had had a good year.

England captain Billy Wright exchanging pennants with Hungary's Ferenc Puskas before the famous 6–3 reverse at Wembley in November 1953.

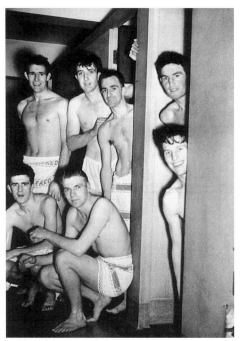

West Ham players take in the brine baths at Brighton during the 1955–56 FA Cup run.

A teenage Bobby Moore in his early Hammers days.

Johnny Byrne in his Crystal Palace days, pictured in 1960–61 when the Glaziers won promotion from Division Four and Byrne scored 30 League goals.

The promotion-winning Palace side of 1960–61. Back Row: Petchey, Long, Rouse, Barnett, Choules, Lunnis. Front Row: Byrne, Uphill, Summersby, McNichol, Colfar.

Action from a 3–3 draw at Highbury. West Ham left-back Burkett and 'keeper Jim Standen attempt to foil an Arsenal attack. Byrne scored twice for the Hammers in this match.

Johnny Byrne pictured in action for England against Uruguay on 6 May 1964 at Wembley. Budgie scored both the England goals in a 2–1 win.

Johnny Byrne tries to clear Taibo, the Uruguayan goalkeeper, during the match with England at Wembley in May 1966. He was unable to add to his two goals this time. Jimmy Greaves, later to play for West Ham, is also pictured (number 8).

The Hammers at Wembley in 1964. Budgie has the ball at his feet in the centre of the front row.

Bobby Moore shakes hands with the North End captain Nobby Lawton.

John Sissons scores the first West Ham goal in the 3–2 Cup Final win over Preston.

Victorious Hammers with Budgie third from left at the front.

Eddie Bovington and Jim Standen parade with the cup.

Sissons and Geoff Hurst take their turn to hold the famous trophy.

Budgie again takes centre stage as West Ham show off their silverware.

Pre-season roll call 1964–65.

*Bobby Moore,
captain of all
the Hammers.*

A turning point in Budgie's career as he hobbles out of England's Home Championship match with Scotland on 10 April 1965 with the aid of a St John's ambulanceman. Many believe he was never as effective again when he returned from his injury, by which time places in the 1966 World Cup team were being cemented.

Moore swaps pennants with the skipper of TSV Munich before the 1965 Cup-Winners' Cup final at Wembley.

CHAPTER 9

Hot Dogs

A S WELL as drinking conventions, West Ham also had an active gambling tradition and Johnny Byrne, along with several other professionals at the Boleyn Ground, including Peter Brabrook, Brian Dear and Alan Sealey, was a gambling man (although, as he himself admitted, he was never a winner). The fascination with pursuits of chance went back to immediate post-war days of the Hammers' history, and the faces of the likes of Malcolm Allison and John Dick were well known at the Custom House Stadium, home of West Ham greyhound racing. When Byrne came to Upton Park players would be involved in regular card schools that took place as the Irons journeyed around England and on tour. Many of the older professionals were long aficionados of greyhound racing and the turf accountants, and a major activity in the treatment room was the swapping of tips with Rob Jenkins, the club physiotherapist. According to former England youth international centre-half, Dave Bickles, who was with the Hammers from 1963 to 1966:

> Budgie and Sammy (Alan Sealey was known as 'Sammy', after the popular children's character of the time, 'Sammy the Seal') were two of the club's most well-known gamblers, but it was a big thing with a lot of players. Johnny and others would nearly always go to the dogs before a Saturday match anywhere they were playing, it was a way of relaxing I suppose and I don't think anyone really overdone it a lot. But if the lads were playing at St James' Park they might go to Gosforth Park; before a game against Manchester City or United it might be Salford. They'd always be card games to and from matches. It filled in time between playing, and thinking about gambling, going to the dogs, is a bit like thinking about and playing football.

As anyone who has been to the dogs and been a football supporter knows, there is a great deal in what Dave said. A typical week in life as part of the West

Ham United gambling fraternity was: Monday night, Wembley dogs; Tuesday afternoon, Dagenham dogs; Tuesday evening, Romford dogs; Wednesday evening, West Ham dogs; Thursday evening, Clapton dogs; Friday evening, West Ham dogs. Greyhound racing meetings were held at the West Ham venue from the earliest days of the sport in Britain until the beginning of the 1970s, when the stadium was sold to developers. Custom House Stadium was just a few minutes drive from Upton Park, it was the home of the cockney classic, the *Cesarewitch* and in its heyday Custom House had housed up to 85,000 cinder fans for its speedway events. This is where, on its vast central area, the Hammers, on the suggestion of Johnny Byrne, had trained in preparation for their 1964 FA Cup victory.

In the bright little houses that made up the tight streets that nestled around the easterly reaches of London's river, children had their tea and watched *The Lone Ranger* or *Lassie*, in glorious black and white of course. And, as the sea of sleep beckoned those who had to go to school the next day, the tens of thousands in the great Custom House Stadium quietened as the main lights of the huge arena were extinguished. Just the bright oval of the track was left illuminated. In the unreal stillness of that moment, a slow, mechanical wailing and winding could be heard, echoed by the canine noise of dogs keen to be released. The sound of automation speeded up to become a 'whoosh'... the hare was running. The ever-pursued creature flashed past the main stand and, to a cockney roar, the traps clanged open and the West Ham dogs bounded out.

Pennies, pounds, fortunes, hopes and dreams rested on those hounds. Seconds later, as they passed the finishing post, the canine troop was cheered, cursed, loved and hated. 'Told you so's' and 'never knews' were muttered, there was a tearing of slips and the smell of booze, and the whiff of fried onions filled the nose, blending with the aroma of cigarette, cigar and pipe tobacco. It was a heady mix and the excitement of those nights was a great draw for Byrne and his contemporaries.

Like Upton Park, the dog track offered the young Hammers another world; a world apart, a place often used to escape, but it was never escapism – it was always too real for that. But while they were there it was hard to think of anything else.

Find the Ball

Alan Sealey was perhaps Budgie's most consistent racing partner. John recalled: 'Sammy was a friend, colleague, gambling and social mate...a real comedian...

we had a lot in common.' Byrne looked back on one particular speculative venture that he and Sealey were involved in:

> I remember on one occasion we had been to Walthamstow dogs and unfortunately it was one of those days when we both backed too many 'also-rans'. We ended up going home with about two quid between us and decided to stop off for a drink, knowing full well that the couple of pounds we had would not get us very far, but I had been scheming and when we had knocked out the money we had, I 'went to work'. As we had some celebrity status, it did not take long to get an audience. In those days I was pretty adept at lining up half a dozen tanners (sixpenny pieces) on my sweaty forehead. Yours truly managed to win 20 quid for us and off we went with a tenner each and a good laugh before I dropped him off in Barking.

Budgie also liked a flutter on other sporting events. He recalled:

> Not long before I left West Ham, on a Wednesday in the April, we won the Wembley fives beating Arsenal in the final. We had been lucky to beat Charlton 2–1 to make the final and I was doing my nut all the way through as I had got 10 to one for us to win the tournament! That was a good bet because we had a strong team; Colin Mackleworth in goal, plus Mooro, Martin Peters, Geoff Hurst and John Sissons was substitute.

The celebrated horse racing meetings were also great attractions for Budgie, especially the big Cheltenham event. He recalled another outing with Alan Sealey:

> …we went to the Cheltenham Festival. Sammy and I were both very excited, as neither of us had been to Cheltenham races before. Somehow we managed to get the day off training and we were soon speeding through the countryside towards Cheltenham. We had a marvellous day and we actually won money. The champagne flowed. The one thing that people hadn't warned us about was that getting out of Cheltenham was a nightmare. I think I must have tried four or five times and each time we finished up in the champagne bar. We eventually got home around 10pm that evening after spending a wonderful day together.

Budgie eventually became an owner of greyhounds. The best was quite fittingly called 'Find the Ball', but Budgie always called it 'Bouncer'. It ran at

Catford and, having a liking for the rails, often came out of trap one. It was more than a fair pup. In fact the animal became something of a hero. It found the front and stayed there in 30 races. Another of Budgie's dogs was 'John the Nark', named in honour of Johnny Haynes. When asked about this Haynes's explanation was accompanied by a wry smile:

> My mate Budgie Byrne was betting mad, horses and dogs, it didn't
> matter. He called a dog John the Nark because he called me Narky.
> On the field, I used to ruck a bit. I'd rant and rave and put them in
> their place. I bollocked everyone.

Ownership made John someone 'in the know' around the tracks and the attention and gravitas that this brought him suited Budgie just fine.

Bonding

For all this, gambling, and particularly greyhound racing, was an asset to West Ham United in general and Budgie in particular, because it had the capacity to bring the youthful side together in a common pursuit outside the game, and it was a pastime that offered some chance of sheer fun, the reason why these young men took to football as children, which had been taken away from them on the serious professional field of play. For example, on one occasion, looking for a change from their usual racing schedule, Budgie and four of his teammates borrowed a very good greyhound and entered him in a race a Yarmouth, at that time a flapping track (these were racing venues that existed outside of the controls that governed the major stadiums). The conspirators knew the dog could win, as the opposition was relatively weak. Peter Brabrook and Geoff Hurst were part of the group. It was one of the few times Hurst spent money on gambling. Budgie recalled:

> We chipped in £20 each, a fair proportion of our weekly wage in
> those days, at odds of 2–1. It romped home by about 20 lengths. We
> collected our winnings and took off for the nearest casino. This was
> the start of two solid nights on the town that were to cost me two
> days training and the price of a fur coat as a peace offering to
> Margaret.

There was no doubt that the whole culture of gambling and greyhounds had become an important part of Budgie's life – and in many ways it is not surprising that this effervescent character was caught up in the whirl that accompanied life at the heart of this most exciting of sports.

CHAPTER 10

After Glow

T HE EARLY 1960s had been something of a political roundabout for world football in terms of the South African game. During 1963 the FIFA executive had, inexplicably, lifted FASA's suspension. This was swiftly followed by FASA announcing a typically mad example of apartheid reasoning masquerading as rational compromise by saying it would send an all-white team to the 1966 World Cup and an all-black team to the 1970 World Cup. The response to this was swift. FASA's suspension was reimposed in 1964 by the FIFA Congress. All this attention was not well met by the apartheid regime that persecuted, arrested, and/or banned the SASF leadership. This, in a perverse way, acted against the South African government in that it showed that they politicised sport, the very factor that would keep them out of the world sporting community.

One in the eye for Uruguay

Johnny Byrne also had some international footballing business. During the 1963–64 season Budgie led the Football League attack twice against League of Ireland and Scottish League and following the Hammers' victory at Wembley Byrne, alongside his skipper and friend Bobby Moore, went on to play for the England side at Hampden. Although the Scots won that match with a goal from Alan Gilzean, Johnny went on to play six more times for his country during May and June of 1964. The next match to be played at Wembley after West Ham's FA Cup Final win saw John score twice against Uruguay. You could have seen that game for 7s 6d and got the best seat in the stadium for £2 10s.

William Martinez, who gained 55 caps for Uruguay between 1950 and 1965, later remarked that Byrne had the potential to become a great player on the world stage and likened him to Omar Miguez, Uruguay's most prolific scorer of the post-World War Two period. John's goals against Uruguay were the first of his 1964 total for England that would give him an average of a goal a game for his country.

Date:	6 April 1964
Location:	Wembley
Competition:	Friendly
Fixture:	England v Uruguay
Result:	2–1 (HT 1–0)
England scorers:	Byrne (2)
Uruguay scorer:	Spencer
Team:	Banks, G. (Leicester City), Cohen, G.R. (Fulham), Wilson, R. (Huddersfield Town), Milne, G. (Liverpool), Norman, M. (Tottenham Hotspur), Moore, R.F.C. (West Ham United) captain, Paine, T.L. (Southampton), Greaves, J.P. (Tottenham Hotspur), Eastham, G.E. (Arsenal), Byrne, J.J. (West Ham United), Charlton, R. (Manchester United).

Who's a pretty boy then?

The pinnacle of Byrne's international career was a fabulous hat-trick in England's 4–3 win against a fine Portuguese side in Lisbon. For Budgie this match was:

> ...the best I played for England with the three sweetest goals I ever scored, including the winner, three minutes from time. That trip had allowed me to watch the likes of Puskas, Di Stefano and Gento up close and this had a real effect on my football education. It was only later that I realised that I had been the first West Ham player to score a hat-trick for England. The next would be Geoff Hurst in the World Cup final at Wembley in 1966.

John was in a mood of rare impudence that night. Perhaps the best example of his disposition was when he scored from an edge of the penalty area chip that floated over three defenders and the Portuguese goalkeeper. After that everyone wanted to know him and a number of phone calls from Italy and Spain went through the Upton Park switchboard. It was unthinkable that John would leave West Ham at that time, just when he was reaching the very peak of his powers. But for all that, if bringing foreign players into Britain hadn't been so problematic at that time, Byrne might well have been playing in the European Cup by 1965. As it was there was no player in the British game that could adequately replace John at the Boleyn Ground, so Budgie stayed with the Hammers.

Date:	17 April 1964
Location:	Lisbon
Competition:	Friendly
Fixture:	Portugal v England
Result:	3–4 (HT 1–0)
England scorers:	Byrne (3), Charlton
Portugal scorers:	Torres (2), Eusebio
Team:	Banks G. (Leicester City), Cohen G.R. (Fulham), Wilson R. (Huddersfield Town), Milne G. (Liverpool), Norman M. (Tottenham Hotspur), Moore R.F.C. (West Ham United) captain, Thompson P. (Liverpool), Greaves J.P. (Tottenham Hotspur), Eastham G.E. (Arsenal), Byrne J.J. (West Ham United), Charlton R. (Manchester United).

You ain't 'alf 'ard Alf

Four days before that game in Lisbon the England party assembled in London. The squad were due to fly to Portugal on Thursday and booked into White's Hotel near Lancaster Gate. Ramsey took training at the Bank of England sports ground at Roehampton, then bought his players a round in the club bar before ushering them back to the hotel for dinner. After the meal Moore and Budgie took a stroll along Bayswater Road before going on to spend the evening in Mayfair, not knowing that Ramsey had imposed a curfew. The players didn't return to the hotel until the small hours.

As Budgie entered the room he was sharing with Bobby he noticed that their passports were on their pillows. 'Bobby, we've been tumbled,' he said. Team officials normally kept the travel documents so it seemed that this was a sign that the two men were to be left behind in England as punishment for their carousing.

However, the next day Ramsey made no mention of the previous night and the squad flew to Lisbon with the impression that any misdemeanours had been forgotten, forgiven or had not been discovered. But on the eve of the match, before the final training session, Ramsey asked seven players to remain behind in the hotel. Budgie recalled:

> Gordon Banks, Ray Wilson, Bobby Charlton, George Eastham, Jimmy Greaves, Bobby Moore and me waited. We were asking each other what it might all be about when Alf, in his usual casual way said, 'Okay boys, what's going on? What's it all about? When you come away with me I don't expect to see you disappearing in the middle of the night!'
>
> George Eastham was the first to speak up. He said, 'Well, Alf. It's the normal thing. We normally go out and have a few drinks; after all the game was still three or four days away.'
>
> After a slight pause, in which his face turned white, Ramsey lost it and gave us a right bollocking saying that if he had seven replacements he would have willingly sent the lot of us home.

Byrne always remembered this Ramsey tirade as the most severe and punishing reprimand he was ever to experience. The net effect was that the seven bad boys were all in the eleven to face Portugal and they all played like tigers. Budgie was convinced that Alf understood that a harsh chiding, at the right moment, would bring out the best in the erring crew:

> Looking back, I think Alf was mucking us around a bit. He knew we went out and we weren't that late back. He had a dry sense of humour, but he liked the odd bit of psychology and exerting his authority. That said, it worked, so it's hard to knock it. It weren't funny at the time, but now I can see the joke was on us and you've got to hand it to Alf and laugh about it. He scared the shit out of most of us! But I'm not sure Bobby bought it. He could read Alf like a book. I'd still like to know who put Alf wise though…

It was quite a feature of Alf Ramsey's reign as England manager that he seemed to know what was going on most of the time among his players. As such most were quite wary of his gaze and that of Harold Sheperdson, his symbolic batman. There is little doubt that Alf had an informer within the squad and that he picked some players not only on merit but also because of their value as a resource to the squad. Although he shared a great deal in terms of tactics with Bobby Moore, discussing ideas and seeking advice, the two men never really trusted each other. They were born not too far from each other, on the borders of East London and Essex. Moore was, if anything, proud of his roots, but after his playing days Ramsey worked hard to lose his accent and modify the kind of 'colourful' language he had deployed as a full-back at White Hart Lane; he made a great effort to become 'respectable'. Alf came from humble origins, and grew up in an era where he probably suffered three levels of stigma. He was working class, he came from what was regarded as the rough East End of London and there were also rumours that his family had Gypsy connections. As such it would not have been surprising that when he started mixing with the Lancaster Gate elite he protected himself with a change of identity. Yet another Dagenham boy, Terry Venables, has a story that goes a long way towards summing up how Ramsey may have felt about his origins. Venables's father was a friend of a man called Sid, who had been the next-door neighbour of the Ramsey family when Alf was a boy. While Terry was playing with the England squad, Sid had asked Venables to give Ramsey his regards, which the young Chelsea player did during a break in training. On the mention of Sid there was a strained and protracted pause while a look of disgust spread across the Ramsey countenance. Alf then walked away from the bemused Venables without a word. After this uncomfortable encounter Venables found himself dropped from the England team and replaced by Johnny Byrne.

So, who was the Ramsey 'grass'? When one looks at the players Ramsey was most loyal to, many seem to be the ones closest to his own age and personality; the slightly introverted, less expressive emotionally, more self-conscious players. These very few were Alf's 'old guard', whom he stuck by through thick and thin, which was one reason why he was, in the end, sacked by the FA. And there was one in particular who kept a low profile in terms of character; he was renowned for being quiet and watchful.

'Who is Byrne?'

For all this, the eventual scoreline perhaps proved that the means justified the end, as did Budgie's hat-trick. The legendary Benfica striker, Eusebio, who scored Portugal's third goal on 17 May 1964, recalled his side's reaction to Byrne:

> Everybody was asking 'Who is Byrne? Where does he come from? Why does he keep talking?' That day he looked the most complete attacking player I had ever seen. He ran round tackles almost before they were made. His passing was brilliant, but he also seemed to be on the end of every pass coming out of the England defence. With his vision he was like an attacking Bobby Moore and the two of them seemed to have linked minds.

For all this, the most memorable part of the whole game for Budgie was Ramsey's reaction. Never the most demonstrative of men:

> When the game was over Alf ran on to the field cheering and picked
> me up. I was glad because it was showed that what had happened
> had been put down to experience. But maybe he was pleased as
> much with himself as us. Good luck to him!

John loved his time with the England squad. During his first tour with his country he impressed the quieter members of the party with the cool way he gambled in Estoril. He was the joker of the trip. In Vienna he shocked passers-by by suddenly going down on all fours and imitating an epileptic dog.

But it was spending time with some of the true characters of the English game that appealed to him most, men like East Ham's very own Jimmy Greaves. Budgie had almost been involved in drowning Greaves, who had never been able to swim, on one England trip. Budgie was relaxing by a swimming pool with some other players when Greaves arrived dressed in an expensive brown suit. Jim knelt down to feel the warmth of the water and, being unable to resist the target, Byrne came up behind him and pushed the amazed and terrified striker into the pool. Somebody pulled the gasping Tottenham man out after he had gone down for a second time.

During another trip the whole England side, the worse for wear after a night of imbibing the local delights, played a game of football at 3am on a beach in Spain against the staff of the hotel where they were staying. The English were well beaten but thankfully the press never picked up on that event.

There were also lessons about life outside of football to be learnt with the England squad. John remembered how:

> Bobby Charlton hated flying. He had, of course, been one of the few
> who survived the Munich air crash, which virtually wiped out the
> whole of the Manchester United side. He perspired constantly but I
> admired him for the courage he showed on those England flights.
> Although he was petrified he had made himself fly again. Whenever
> we shared a plane journey I could sense the agony he underwent, as
> he looked so uneasy.

After the Portugal game England flew to Budgie's ancestral home, Dublin, to play the Republic of Ireland. The consequent victory included a goal from John. Long-time Republic of Ireland international and former Hammers skipper Noel Cantwell said of Byrne's performance:

> He looked deadly. He was sharp and fast and really made the

difference to the England attack. A few days before we had beaten Norway 4–1 in Oslo and in the game after we played England we defeated Poland 3–2 in Dublin and so what was really an experimental English side did well. But we should have grabbed John for ourselves early on. Alongside Johnny Giles he would have been a revelation and of course he would not have got the injury that finished his career.

England took a VC10 from Shannon Airport to New York for a match against the US. From there the party would make for South America.

Date:	24 May 1964
Location:	Dublin
Competition:	Friendly
Fixture:	Republic of Ireland v England
Result:	1–3 (HT 1–2)
England scorers:	Eastham, Byrne, Greaves
Republic of Ireland scorer:	Strahan
Team:	Waiters, A.K. (Blackpool), Cohen, G.R. (Fulham), Wilson, R. (Huddersfield Town), Milne, G. (Liverpool), Flowers, R. (Wolverhampton Wanderers), Moore, R.F.C. (West Ham United) captain, Thompson, P. (Liverpool), Greaves, J.P. (Tottenham Hotspur), Eastham, G.E. (Arsenal), Byrne, J.J. (West Ham United), Charlton, R. (Manchester United).

The players were in good spirits and there was much laughing and joking as they climbed on board their winged chariot. They had six hours of flying ahead of them and Johnny, with one or two others, was thinking of the food and champagne en route. As they made their way to their seats Budgie found that he was next to Bobby Moore, but both of them were puzzled why there were two empty seats behind them. For all this the pair were quite pleased, as they wanted to keep clear of Ramsey. However, minutes before the plane was to take to the air Alf sat himself behind Budgie and Mooro. Budgie recalled Alf's words as he took up his station: 'You tried to get to the front so you could both have a nice piss-up.' In response Byrne looked back between the seats and said: 'No, Alf, not us. Don't be like that.'

Once in the air the steward came round with champagne and other delights, as the side were flying first class, but Ramsey ordered only fresh orange juice for his young Hammers. However, sleep eventually overcame Alf and while Harold Shepherdson was engrossed in his newspaper, the players, including Moore and Byrne, singly and in pairs, crept towards the first-class lounge to imbibe and as Budgie recalled '...talk soccer, there were no birds'.

On landing in New York Ramsey demonstrated his seeming omnipresence by imposing a curfew on the squad. However, the pressmen who had travelled with the team arranged for a party in one of the suites at the Waldorf Astoria. But Ramsey seemed to have eyes and ears everywhere and asked England's medical officer, Dr Allan Bass, to telephone the suite. This the good doctor did before the first glasses had been drained and counselled the gathering that he would be there in 15 minutes and didn't expect to find any members of the England team in attendance. John advised his fellows to, 'forget him,' and said that, 'if he comes in and finds us all here he can't send us all home'.

However, such was the fear that Alf inspired, that many of the players vanished. The party was on the 25th floor while the squad were accommodated some 20 floors below.

Players took to the stairs, and lifts like lemmings. Alf, in the meantime, had locked all the rooms, causing panic and in his mind teaching lessons about his authority. Typically Byrne was the last to leave the party. But he managed to get into his room with mystic aplomb. Nothing more was said of the incident but everyone had been reminded of 'the power of Alf'.

Byrne never quite came to terms with Ramsey. It took a long time before Johnny could say he got on with him. He admired Alf and respected him for the role he played in England winning the World Cup in 1966 but, as a manager, Byrne did not rate Alf as highly as Walter Winterbottom and Ron Greenwood.

There's an awful lot more than coffee in Brazil

Ramsey left Byrne out of England's 10–0 win over the United States but this and the successes against Portugal and Eire were put in perspective when Byrne and his England colleagues were brought back to earth with a bump in Rio de Janeiro in the Brazilian Jubilee Tournament. This event commemorated the Brazilian Football Association's 50th anniversary and was heralded as the 'Little World Cup'. In May Pelé was among the scorers in England's 5–1 defeat.

Date:	30 May 1964
Location:	Rio de Janerio
Competition:	Copa de las Naciones
Fixture:	Brazil v England
Result:	5–1 (HT 1–0)
England scorer:	Greaves
Brazil scorers:	Rinaldo (2), Pelé, Julinho Roberto Dias
Team:	Waiters, A.K. (Blackpool), Cohen, G.R. (Fulham), Wilson, R. (Huddersfield Town), Milne, G. (Liverpool), Moore, R.F.C. (West Ham United) captain, Norman, M. (Tottenham Hotspur), Thompson, P. (Liverpool), Greaves, J. P. (Tottenham Hotspur), Eastham, G.E. (Arsenal), Byrne, J.J. (West Ham United), Charlton, R. (Manchester United).

In the second match in the tournament Byrne found himself facing the Portuguese for the second time in a month. But Brazil did not prove a happy hunting ground for Budgie.

Date:	4 June 1964
Location:	Sao Paulo
Competition:	Copa de las Naciones
Fixture:	Portugal v England
Result:	1–1 (HT 1–0)
England scorer:	Hunt
Portugal scorer:	Peres
Team:	Banks, G. (Leicester City), Thomson, R.A. (Wolverhampton Wanderers), Wilson, R. (Huddersfield Town), Flowers, R. (Wolverhampton Wanderers), Moore, R.F.C. (West Ham United) captain, Norman, M. (Tottenham Hotspur), Thompson P. (Liverpool), Greaves, J.P. (Tottenham Hotspur), Paine, T.L. (Southampton), Byrne, J.J. (West Ham United), Hunt, R. (Liverpool).

In the last match of their Brazilian experience, against Argentina, England and Byrne were again obliged to learn some South American lessons.

Date:	6 June 1964
Location:	Rio de Janeiro
Competition:	Copa de las Naciones
Fixture:	Argentina v England
Result:	1–0 (HT 0–0)
Argentina scorer:	A. Rojas
Team:	Banks, G. (Leicester City), Thomson, R.A. (Wolverhampton Wanderers), Wilson, R. (Huddersfield Town), Milne, G. (Liverpool), Moore, R.F.C. (West Ham United) captain, Norman, M. (Tottenham Hotspur), Thompson, P. (Liverpool), Greaves, J.P. (Tottenham Hotspur), Eastham, G.E. (Arsenal), Byrne, J.J. (West Ham United), Charlton, R. (Manchester United).

The final table did not look good, but England had learnt a lot and would put the experience, and particularly the lessons of the Argentinian match, to good use during the World Cup finals in England in 1966. This of course was Ramsey's main reason for being in Brazil.

Taça das Nações [Nations' Cup] Tournament, Brazil, 1964

Team	P	W	D	L	F	A	GD	Pts
Argentina	3	3	0	0	6	0	+6	6
Brazil	3	2	0	1	9	5	+4	4
England	3	0	1	2	2	7	−5	1
Portugal	3	0	1	2	2	7	−5	1

Match	Venue	Attendance
Brazil v England	Estádio Maracanã, Rio de Janeiro	77,000
Argentina v Portugal	Estádio Maracanã, Rio de Janeiro	N.K.
Brazil v Argentina	Estádio Pacaembu, São Paulo	N.K.
England v Portugal	Estádio Pacaembu, São Paulo	25,000
Argentina v England	Estádio Maracanã, Rio de Janeiro	15,000
Brazil v Portugal	Estádio Maracanã, Rio de Janeiro	N.K.

NB: The attendance figures for England's three matches given in Mike Payne, *England: The Complete Post-War Record*, pp. 197–98 (1993) are Brazil 110,000, Portugal 70,000 and Argentina 95,000. These are much larger than those stated in Ron Hockings & Keir Radnedge, *Nations of Europe*, vol. 1, p. 194, vol. 2, p. 24 (1993) which are Brazil 77,000, Portugal 25,000 and Argentina 15,000.

On the day of the final between Brazil and Argentina Alf Ramsey told the England players that they could either watch the match or spend the day on the beach. The squad had all seen both teams play and had been playing, training and travelling without a break for a long time, so it was unanimously agreed to go to the beach. As the sun lashed down on Copacabana most of the young men made for the water. Budgie was diving, splashing, and, of course, talking when a large breaker crashed over him and he disappeared yelling for help. Johnny was constantly joking during England tours and most of what he did was taken by his teammates as being a joke and this 'drowning' activity was largely ignored, although Jimmy Greaves, remembering how Budgie had nearly consigned him to Davy Jones's Locker, called out from the beach, 'Drown, you bastard,' and Budgie almost obliged. In fact it was Jimmy's tongue-in-cheek (probably) remark that started the collective realisation that Budgie was in fact in difficulties. Bobby Charlton was the first to get to the floundering Byrne and as his comrades carried Budgie up on to the beach he was pale-faced, shocked and exhausted. He lay motionless for about an hour before he recovered. For the whole of those 60 minutes he could hardly speak. As Budgie recalled, 'that was the first time in my life I had been speechless.'

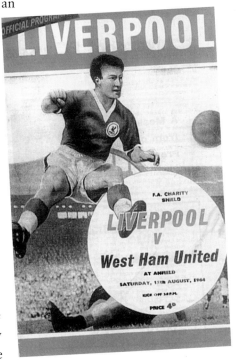

Charity begins… away

In the traditional curtain-raiser to the season West Ham's first game of the 1964–65 term took them to Anfield for a Charity Shield encounter with League Champions Liverpool. At the time it was the tradition to play the fixture at the club that had won the League. It was not until 10 years later that it was staged at Wembley. After a three-match pre-season tour of Germany, Greenwood and his side flew back to London on the Thursday morning before boarding another plane bound for Manchester, where they stayed before travelling to Liverpool by coach on Saturday 15 August. A crowd of almost 39,000 greeted them at the home of Bill Shankly's Reds.

The first half was little short of magnificent. Although substitutes had not yet been introduced in major competitions, Liverpool brought on Phil Chisnall for the injured Alf Arrowsmith, who had sustained damaged knee ligaments, after 12 minutes. Liverpool took the lead with just under half an hour played. Moore made an uncharacteristic mistake as he intercepted a seemingly harmless centre from Ian Callaghan. Looking to pass back to keeper Standen, Bobby played the ball into the path of Gordon Wallace, who darted in to send the ball onto a post: it banged into the opposite support as well before going in. The Irons had given as good as they had got until that moment, moving fluently and calmly. Budgie was proving slippery for his huge shadow, the gargantuan Ron Yeats. He interchanged passes with Hurst to make chances while Brabrook and Sissons were exposing the lack of pace in the Liverpool defence. Playing a subtle and effective form of 4–3–3 the Hammers pulled level with an archetypal example of their artistic best four minutes before half-time. The ball moved from Moore to Boyce to Hurst and then Bovington, who demonstrated his often overlooked skill by playing a long chip over Yeats into the Liverpool goalmouth. Byrne once more cut loose from his marker before slashing past three defenders to hook the ball, at chest height, past Tommy Lawrence, who had moved out from his goal line to confront the danger.

Liverpool took the lead for a second time before the second half was five minutes old, just after Byrne had brought a full-length save from Lawrence. Finding the right wing impassable, Ian Callaghan pushed the ball back to attacking defender Gerry Byrne. The 'other Byrne' (no relation) on the pitch hit a pumping 25-yard shot that was going nowhere but in the net. It seemed to be 'the Pool's' game, but just half a dozen crippling minutes before the final whistle, following efforts from Budgie and Hurst, Brabrook hit a hard drive that Lawrence just could not hold and Hurst stabbed the ball home to give the Irons a share of the Shield. West Ham won a post-match toss which entitled the Hammers to hold the trophy for the next six months before posting it on to Liverpool – a strange arrangement to say the least – but typical of West Ham's customary eccentricity. However, the sharing caught on as the following year Liverpool again divided the Shield with Manchester United; the Hammers were ever the trendsetters. But after the 1964 Charity Shield many West Ham fans, their team having been obliged to play the match on their opponent's home ground, saw the Boleyn Boys able to claim a moral victory. Sixteen seasons later the Hammers would once again meet Liverpool in the Charity Shield; then matters were decided at Wembley.

CHAPTER 11

The Heat Goes On

A FTER the Charity Shield game against Liverpool Brian Granville wrote:

> West Ham are a consistently interesting side to watch because they are consistently trying to do something interesting. They are, in the approved contemporary fashion, a counter-attacking team, playing the ball out of a massed defence to an inventive forward line.

But this is something of a misnomer. The physical nature of football in the 1960s would pin a side like West Ham down with long-ball oriented pressure, but when the Hammers made a break, usually through swift midfielders and forwards, the likes of Byrne, Sissons and Boyce, pundits like Granville would call it a 'counter-attacking style'. In fact West Ham's play was built on patience and calmness in the face of sustained pressure. At times it was intensely frustrating to watch and seemed that the Hammers allowed their opponents to take advantage of them; the seeming lack of panic could easily be mistaken for apathy. But when, as a spectator, one realised the effort being made one began to see the way West Ham waited as almost predatory.

The inaugural match of the League season gave West Ham a decent 2–1 away win over Fulham, who would just escape relegation that term. Budgie's friend and England mentor Johnny Haynes had a good game, as did Byrne himself. Johnny started the move that got him and West Ham their first League goal of 1964–65. Metchick grabbed the equaliser, lashing at the ball with thoughtless hope; he was more surprised than anyone else to see his effort go in off the post. The Hammers' match-winner came via Hurst's boot. Macedo blocked the shot, but the ball found its fateful way to Sissons, who finished with serene efficiency.

There's a hole in the North Bank

On the following Monday, the Irons kept up their domination of Manchester United. In four games against them West Ham had come away with three victories. The Hammers were two up with about 10 minutes to play at Upton Park. Johnny had put away the first after just four minutes, after Sissons had seen his shot blocked, then, with 19 minutes of the match played, Sissons scored with a well-timed lob, eclipsing George Best and giving some credibility to Greenwood's boast that the England Under-23 Hammer was at least as good as the Belfast boy. On the half-hour the Reds were left with 10 men (there were no substitutes in 1964) when Maurice Setters was carried off after Boyce had cut through one of Maurice's boots with his studs. The European Footballer of the Year, Denis Law, headed home to make it 2–1 and provide the crowd with a frantic finale that resulted in a goal by Hurst with just five minutes of the game left.

I was in the West Ham North Bank that day, in what was to be the biggest crowd of the season at Upton Park; they crammed in 37,070. During such a match, from the centre of the North Bank it took about 15 minutes to get to the toilet, which was usually necessary at some point before or after half-time given the tradition of the 'pre-match bevvy' and/or the 'half-time bevvy'. Of course, it took about the same time to return from ones ablutions to the place where ones comrades had congregated. With the time one took to 'do the business' it was possible that a call of nature would take somewhere between half and three quarters of an hour to reconcile. Those who reminisce about the 'days of the terraces' nearly always forget this intriguing facet of being crushed on the steps of the decaying football grounds of the 1960s. As a consequence of this situation it was not unusual, although not altogether common, for spectators to urinate where and when they could, sometimes where they stood. However, on this occasion there had been an emergency of a more solid kind on our beloved North Bank. To the tune of the popular song of the time

There's a hole in my bucket dear Liza the inhabitants of the Hammers' northerly stand sang as a gap widened in the midst of the crowd, around the offending turd:

There's a hole in the North Bank, the North Bank, the North Bank,

There's a hole in the North Bank, in the North Bank a hole...

No doubt the perpetrator had committed his crime in an act of desperation, but looking back I like to think it might also have been his way of saying, 'United are shit'.

Scoring form

Johnny kept up a goal a game average against Nottingham Forest at Upton Park in a Friday night thriller. It was a Budgie penalty that started things off, which Nottingham forward John Barnwell and the visiting Forest fans did not appreciate. The latter showered the pitch with bottles and other missiles and the former shoved the referee and was lucky not to be sent off. Ironically it was Barnwell who put Forest in front with two goals in the 36th and 58th minutes. Sissons pulled one back in the last quarter of the game but it was not enough to prevent West Ham from falling to their first defeat of the season as Hinton hit home just two minutes after Sissons had equalised. However, Byrne had scored in the first four games of 1964–65.

In the next nine League matches the Hammers managed to accrue nine points but Budgie was in scoring form, netting in all but one of these games. He got the Hammers goal in a 3–1 defeat at the Victoria Ground – his shot going in off the bar – and the third in a 5–0 thrashing of Wolves at Upton Park was his as well. In the 3–2 Boleyn Ground defeat of Spurs, although Budgie's penalty was saved by Pat Jennings after Jimmy Greaves had covertly told the Northern Ireland international keeper where Byrne would place the ball (the two had practiced penalties together during England training), he picked up the rebound. From that day on John promised himself that he would never aim a penalty in the same place on consecutive occasions. Budgie finished a fine hat-trick and won the game for West Ham when he juggled in the 87th-minute winner.

At Molineux a 61st-minute penalty put West Ham even after bottom club Wolves had dominated the first half, but the Midlanders won the game with a late winner from Peter Knowles. Although John pulled the Hammers level after 21 minutes, like Wolves, Burnley chalked up their first win of the season when the Irons came calling, taking the match 3–2. However, Budgie had scored in five consecutive matches collecting a total of seven goals.

Fifth-placed Sheffield United were beaten 3–1 in the East End. John celebrated the birth of his daughter Karen with two goals: the first was an equaliser 11 minutes into the game and the second came from a spot-kick after he had been waylaid by Brian Richardson. At Goodison, Budgie sent in a real rocket to put West Ham in front. England Under-23 keeper Andy Rankin got both hands to it, but the power of the ball's flight took it to the back of the net. Former England Youth player Brian Harris saved Everton's blushes in the last minute. The final goal in Byrne's magnificent scoring run was the first in West Ham's 3–0 win over Villa at Upton Park. Budgie netted, having been nicely set up by Hurst. By this time, the Hammers were eighth in the League, up from a low point of 17th in early September. The mini-recovery owed much to Byrne's form both in scoring and making goals.

Ghent, Wales, Prague and the rest

During this first part of their League campaign West Ham had mixed fortunes in their early Cup encounters. A 1–0 European Cup-Winners' Cup win in Belgium against the part-timers of La Gantoise, a very rigid side and the first Belgian team to compete in the competition, was followed, on the last day of September, by a 4–1 dismissal from the League Cup at Roker Park. Early in October Budgie opened his Cup-Winners' Cup account and sent West Ham through to the next round with the equaliser in the Upton Park leg of the encounter with the 'Buffaloes of Ghent'. The game ended 1–1. John recalled:

> Nobody rated the Belgians because no one had heard of them. But they were tough and gave us two hard games. They defended at home and attacked away. I'm not sure this was a conscious tactic, but it was an odd way of doing things. But we could have scored half-a-dozen goals that night.

Budgie's goal came 11 minutes after the Belgian opener and it was a good one. Sissons sped along the left wing and his long, diagonal centre was swept, first time, into the net by Byrne. This was one success, but it had to be set against an endless catalogue of near misses. Sissons hit the side-netting twice and was also denied by a post. Hurst forced Armand Seghers to make the save of the night and maybe his life.

The Hammers were into the last 16 of a major European tournament, at the time second only to the European Cup, but the team did not have to be reminded that their first match had been only the preliminary round of the competition.

In mid-November, in the Division One Highbury confrontation with Arsenal, Budgie got the second goal in West Ham's 3–0 win. It was one of his 29 goals that season that would keep him the Hammers' top scorer; Hurst was second highest with 19.

Just three days after the game at Highbury, Budgie won his 10th England cap in a 2–1 win over the Welsh at Wembley. Budgie had been brought into the England side to take the place of the former East Ham Boys' player Terry Venables (he'd played alongside Ronnie Boyce in that team). Venables had been expected to face the Welsh having been in Ramsey's side that had drawn 2–2 with Belgium on 21 October at Wembley, but as discussed earlier he had mentioned 'Sid'.

Date:	18 November 1964
Location:	Wembley
Competition:	Friendly
Fixture:	England v Wales
Result:	2–1 (HT 1–0)
England scorers:	Wignall (2)
Wales scorer:	C. Jones
Team:	Waiters, A.K. (Blackpool), Cohen, G.R. (Fulham), Thomson, R.A. (Wolverhampton Wanderers), Bailey, M.A. (Wolverhampton Wanderers), Flowers, R. (Wolverhampton Wanderers) captain, Young, G.M. (Sheffield Wednesday), Thompson, P. (Liverpool), Hunt, R. (Liverpool), Wignall, F. (Nottingham Forest), Byrne, J.J. (West Ham United), Hinton, A.T. (Nottingham Forest).

With three days respite John ran out onto his home pitch to face Leeds in Division One. After beating Welsh international 'keeper Gary Sprake to a Sissons pass, John walked a second goal into the Leeds net as the Hammers, in sixth spot in the League, beat the third-placed Peacocks 3–1.

Czech it out
The next European challenge was the visit of Sparta Prague to London's Docklands. West Ham were not seen as a very attack-minded side at the time, and the cushion of a couple of goals, traditionally expected for the away leg of a tie, was not a foregone conclusion. It was thought that Peters and Ronnie Boyce would hold the key in midfield. Ron Greenwood's plan was to let Sparta

do their defensive stuff (being the away team) and try to out-manoeuvre them. The idea was that this would give West Ham control of the game, allowing Hurst, Budgie and Johnny Sissons to devote their concentration to goal-getting. Simple! As is so often the case, it didn't work out.

West Ham opened the game with some intent. For nearly an hour the Irons flung themselves at Sparta's white-clad, hacking, solidly-drilled defence. The East Europeans never had less than seven men back and at times this went up to nine. It didn't make for exciting football, but for Prague it was effective, with the burly, uncompromising Gura closely marking Byrne, the equally daunting Steiningel holding on to Hurst and the towering Kos sweeping up behind the defence. The hopes of the East End seemed to lie with young Sissons. The left-winger did well against Dyba early on, but their outside-right was a hard-running defender and gave Sissons a difficult match. By half-time Dyba, alongside Voja and Mraz, who had focused on Boyce and Peters in midfield, had cut off the supply lines to Sissons. With Bobby Moore out injured, the side looked to Martin Peters for inspiration, but it was not forthcoming.

The plans had gone awry. It began to look like one of those nights that Irons fans know only too well; a cursed evening, when everything the Hammers tried just would not come off. A frustrating 0–0 was in prospect with the match degenerating into a form of trench warfare. Out on the right, Sparta conceded one of the string of free kicks. This time Alan Sealey tried to make something from a curling ball into the goalmouth. It was beaten out by a defender and landed at the feet of John Bond. If West Ham fans could have voted for a player to collect from about 25 yards out, Bond would have won the poll. Every pair of West Ham eyes turned to him. It was clear that the Czechs had no idea of the potential danger; they showed no sign of looking to cover the inevitable explosion. In what seemed like slow motion and awed silence, the mighty Muffin brought his left foot back. He struck the ball and the contact was audible from the back of the North Bank – 'TOMHP!' It was a belter; a scorcher, a rocket launcher, which tore into the Czech net despite coming from the 'wrong' foot. The men from Prague stood in shock and awe as Upton Park exploded.

With just over half an hour of the leg remaining the West Ham board and Greenwood must have been grateful that Bond had recently turned down the chance to sign for Queen's Park Rangers. John was something of a penalty and dead ball expert and although a defender, he played a number of games as centre-forward in the late 1950s, and throughout his career scored his share of goals (the first against Sparta was his 34th for the club – he was to score one more before he made his 428th and final appearance for West Ham). For all this, until Bond bashed the bomb that blasted Prague, he hadn't scored for over a year!

Then Budgie began to buzz like only he could, spraying passes around and opening up space. The Czechs were clearly thrown by all the movement and with under 10 minutes left Byrne sent a perfect ball to Ronnie Boyce, Sealey picked up Ticker's volley on the left-hand edge of the Czech penalty area and the former Orient man struck it firm and quick. The ball hit the far post. As it came out one of the Sparta defenders inadvertently chipped the ball back to Sammy. This time he relaxed and cracked in a shot that left Kramerius, the Prague 'keeper, who had played with distinction, with no chance. Sealey was euphoric after scoring his first goal since the start of April.

Abandoning defence (the Czechs had punted the ball out of the ground four times in an effort to waste time) Sparta charged the West Ham half with an almost kamikaze spirit. Even in the last minute they were still looking for blood when Mraz swept a shot across the unprotected mouth of Standen's goal, but it was to no avail; the Irons survived with focused belligerence and the West Ham players now understood that Sparta's defence was not impregnable.

5 December saw the Irons back to League business. Byrne was unlucky not to push his goal haul up a notch when he hit the bar during the 0–0 draw with Leicester at Upton Park, but he was compensated by winning a bet with Alan Sealey that at half-time Ron Greenwood would say, 'Go out there and win'. Four days later it was Sparta again. Moore, having missed the first leg with a rare injury, couldn't make the second leg either, so Boyce was assigned the role of sweeper. Every West Ham player understood that their side had a tenuous foothold in Europe, and that something really special was going to be required. In London the Czechs had proved to be a skilful team, but they were also a hard, disciplined outfit, with little conscience or reliance on an ethical sporting code. As the West Ham plane landed on Czech soil Sparta were comfortable leaders of their League. The Irons were facing dangerous and experienced opponents, as well as a huge, hostile horde of supporters. But these considerations were not the only influences working against the Hammers. West Ham had been told, as was the case in the first leg, that Spanish officials would control the game in Prague. However, on the night of the game the whistle belonged to a Bulgarian referee, Hlavni Dinov, whose preference for the Eastern Europeans over the East Enders gave the Hammers little in the way of protection.

The game was marked by the brilliance of Ronnie Boyce. He was always a quick and adaptable player but on that early December evening he was to be West Ham's epiphany, covering the entire stern section of claret and blue terrain while Byrne and Sissons were lone heroes in front, linking up with each other and holding possession until support arrived. The Czechs launched a continuous and ferocious attack on the East Londoners' defensive formation, but the West Ham rearguard were magnificent, as Byrne marshalled the whole side into a kind of dynamic protective system. In the 13th minute Budgie scuttled on to a long clearance from Bond. Liberating himself from the desperate arms of Tichy he squared the ball to Sissons and the young winghound made no mistake from 20 yards out. The move was an exemplary lesson in the art of 'constant football', often mistaken for simplistic counter-attack. This means understanding defensive play as the precursor of attack, but at the same time not seeing them as different things; there is no dichotomy. In recognition of this the Irons' posse of 120 flying supporters broke into exultant song.

For all this, Sparta resisted and they were helped outrageously as the partiality of the on-field adjudicators reached its peak in the 36th minute. Bond was blatantly pushed and as he tumbled to the earth his hand touched the ball. Like a waiting jackal Dinov pounced on the prone Hammer and awarded a penalty against him. Standen watched Mraz carefully as the Sparta forward placed the ball with purposeful intent on the mark in front of the waiting keeper. The West Ham custodian hunkered down and fixed his eyes on the penalty-taker. As the ball was hit, Standen flew to his distant left. Mraz, glaring, fists compressed as stone, watched as the West Ham goalie moved towards the Czech projectile. The crowd sighed as the Hammers man denied the Czechs a goal.

The Czechs scored in the 68th and 88th minutes. Both the goals followed mistakes of the type that past and present followers of West Ham are familiar with. Masek seized the first: while Boyce stood motionless, Standen pushed a Taborsky long shot onto the bar, then lost his footing to facilitate the Mraz equaliser. The second came at a point when no fewer than 18 players populated the penalty area. Mraz was allowed to flip a header by Kraus into the net. However, these were the only moments in the game when Boyce was still; during the rest of the match he was a Trojan, a bustling minesweeper in defence.

John Sissons and Johnny Byrne played a superlative game. They were loners up front, but when the ball came up to them they held it until things developed around them. Although West Ham lost the game 2–1, the cockney boys went through 3–2 over the two legs. But the desperate nature of the game was shown by the cuts and bruises that the West Ham players sustained. Sealey was taken to hospital immediately after the game to receive seven stitches to bind a hideous gash on his left shin. The injury put him out of action for the best part of a month. This apart, the result had been a real achievement for the East London side. West Ham had controlled affairs and they never lacked innovation. They had out-thought and out-played class opposition with style and courage, as a team.

League toil

Greenwood's team were fourth in Division One as Fulham set out on their journey to meet the Hammers. West Ham were seven points behind the leaders with a game in hand but it was to be their highest placing in the 1964–65 season. Fulham had two goals disallowed as Byrne scored a brace to take his term's tally to 19 and send Fulham home on the end of a 2–0 defeat. John was again on target at the City Ground but this time it was West Ham who went away pointless, Forest just getting the better of a five-goal game. Ten minutes of Birmingham's visit to Upton Park had ticked by when City's Brian Sharples hit home with a glancing header from a free kick by Alec Jackson. The Hammers seemed to be facing the prospect of three consecutive League defeats until Byrne put the Irons level with a penalty on the half-hour. Defender Joe Kirkup gave West Ham the points in the 71st minute.

With the New Year not two weeks old the Birmingham Blues made their second trip of the season to Upton Park for the start of the Hammers' defence of the FA Cup. It was the third time in two weeks that West Ham had faced the boys from St Andrews and the visitors were 2–0 up for most of the first half until, with 41 minutes gone, Sissons drew Schofield from his goal and made an elegant chipped pass for Byrne to strike with his special blend of velocity and power. Budgie's shots were not like those of John Bond; they were sharp weapons, wrought out of a combination of swiftness and subtlety of strike; force being directed and focused on a confined area. For the most part Bond hit through the ball, similar to a Joe Louis hook. Power was applied over a wide area at the end of a broad arc. In contrast the majority of Byrne's strikes were analogous to a Muhammad Ali jab; the seeming lightness of contact disguised a cobra-like impact. The definite nature of the goal seemed to inspire the home side and the outcome was a 4–2 win.

With just over two weeks of 1965 gone Sissons was again the Byrne provider when Budgie netted after 17 minutes at White Hart Lane. The goal cancelled out an earlier effort by Jimmy Greaves, but it was Spurs who were to be 3–2 victors, to the delight of most of the 50,000 supporters present. West Ham's next League encounter had looked like a 2–2 draw before Budgie pleased the Boleyn Ground supporters, capitalizing on Adam Blacklaw's mistake when the Burnley 'keeper failed to hold a cannonball shot from Sissons. But the joy was short-lived, as before the end of January West Ham had released their grip on the first major trophy the club had won, losing 1–0 to Chelsea in front of 37,000 unhappy claret and blue faithful.

The Hammers' fifth 3–2 loss of the season was enacted on 20 February in the side's fifth consecutive away defeat. Byrne's hook with 20 minutes to play seemed to allow West Ham to leave Roker Park with a 1–1 draw, but a 20-yard missile from Hurst just eight minutes later left the Hammers looking certain to take two points from the match. It was not to be. Two late goals from Nick Sharkey lifted Sunderland out of the relegation zone.

The Swiss roll

West Ham faced Lausanne in the next leg of their Continental pilgrimage as the first stirrings of spring were felt in the foothills of the Alps. As Lausanne was snowbound the game was postponed for a week so West Ham supporters had to revise their plans for the journey, which cost £13 10s, including refreshments on the plane from London and a trip around the Lake from Geneva to Lausanne. For 25s travelling Hammers could also have a dinner at a 'first-class hotel' in the host city.

The Swiss side's manager, Karl Rappan, was very much the father figure of his nation's football. He had 40 years experience as manager, coach and player. He believed in flexibility and skill in attack and clever strategy in defence. Rappan had coached the Swiss national side and had been named the 'master of Swiss soccer'. His Verrou 'bolt' system was unique. It was based on a highly mobile game, and required 10 men to theoretically do the work of 13.

West Ham had met Lausanne before. In 1936 the Swiss had won 1–0. They were the only team to beat the Hammers on a triumphant tour of Switzerland. In 1946 the Hammers more than avenged that defeat, thrashing the Alpine lads 7–1. But in the 1960s Lausanne were a different prospect. They were unlike the Czechs of Prague and a world away from the Ghent Belgians. They were much more supple and adaptable. They had seven Swiss internationals in their ranks, including right back Andre Grobéty, a dark, compact player with over 30 caps, and centre-back Heinz Schneiter, the tall, commanding pivot of the side, who had cost a five figure fee when transferred from Young Boys in 1962. Lausanne also boasted left back Eric Polencent, an Under-23 international at the time. He had won himself a place in the team only a short time before, at the expense of the more experienced Hunziker.

In fact Lausanne was more or less the Swiss national side, which had recently beaten Northern Ireland in a World Cup qualifying match in Belfast. This was part of their eventual group-winning performance that emulated their feat in the same competition in 1962 and would take them to England for the final stages in 1966.

Rappan's men were top of their League as they faced West Ham and would, by the end of the season, be Swiss champions for the sixth time, as their manager had predicted, a forecast that included his side taking the Cup-Winners' Cup. They had won the Swiss Cup against Chaux-de-Fonds 2–0 in front of 51,000 in the Wankdorf stadium and were experienced European warriors, having fought campaigns in the Cup-Winners' and Fairs Cups. So far in the tournament of 1964–65 they had accounted for Honved, the crack Hungarian side, 2–1 on aggregate and Slavia Sofia of Bucharest, 4–3 after a play-off in Rome.

West Ham came to the Olympic stadium, in the shadow of the Alps, with the intention of playing defensively to set up the second leg on level terms. Despite recent snow the pitch was in good condition. Brian Dear was playing his first senior game outside Britain following the injury to Eddie Bovington.

The Swiss had a number of chances in the tense first 20 minutes, as West Ham were struggling to find the form that had eluded them since they were knocked out of the FA Cup. The Swiss international wing-half, 30-year-old Kurt Armbruster, who had been among the squad named for the World Cup in Chile, thumped the ball against the bar from 18 yards out and had another long-range effort headed away by Kirkup. Standen failed to hold a shot from the Lausanne outside-left Charles Hertig (who made his debut for Switzerland in the last European Nations cup series against Holland), but Peters was there to clear things up. Dutch international Pierre Kerkhoffs, centre-forward and top goalscorer for PSV Eindhoven in 1963–64, who had been Switzerland's leading marksman that season, flashed a rising shot inches wide. He was potentially the most dangerous of the Lausanne forwards, but fluffed a couple more good chances during the game. Had West Ham allowed the Swiss to score early the home side might well have gone on to build up a commanding lead, but as it was the Hammers settled down to some solid defensive work and took a firm grip on the task that they had begun to realise was not nearly as difficult as they had at first thought. Soon they were confident enough to press forward when the opportunity arose, as it did when Dear cheekily flicked the ball into the net only to be told that the offside rule had denied him. Around the half-hour mark, as the Hammers made another of their few upfield sorties, Lausanne conceded an indirect free kick. Ronnie Boyce drove the ball over their wall at Rene Kunzi, a Swiss 'B' international. It was as good as in the net but the 'keeper instinctively blocked, although the resultant ricochet was picked up by Dear to score his first European goal.

The irony was that if Kunzi had allowed the ball to pass untouched into the net a goal couldn't have been given, as the kick was indirect. To that extent West Ham had the fates on their side. To their credit, following the Hammers' goal, Lausanne made even greater efforts to break through, but the claret and blue defence stood firm until half-time. Moore and Boyce, often playing behind their own full-backs, quietly and efficiently broke up many a Swiss move in its infancy. Brown, shadowing Kerkhoffs faithfully for much of the match, rarely put a foot wrong and Kirkup and Peters made sure that the Lausanne wingers were given the minimum of opportunities to break through.

Immediately after the interval, West Ham set out to improve their already healthy position with another goal. The Hammers' solid endeavour was rewarded in the 53rd minute. The Swiss wasted a free-kick by blasting it at Peters in the West Ham wall. Moore bounced the loose ball to Dear, who flicked it to Byrne on the edge of the Irons penalty area. Ignoring the heavy pitch, Budgie smartly swept round one defender after another 85-yard run, racing into his opponents' penalty box. He held off a final tackle to send in a well-placed clip shot. Kunzi touched the ball but could not prevent the Hammers' second goal. Reporter and Hammers fan Peter Lorenzo commented: 'Byrne tonight scored one of the most spectacular goals of his many splendoured career to highlight West Ham's superb first-leg victory.'

Ron Greenwood was to call this a 'brilliant goal' and it was every bit as good as anything seen in Brazil or Italy. John's analysis gave nothing away though: 'I just kept going and then hit it,' he said. Rappan, however, was more loquacious:

> Johnny Byrne's goal was a masterpiece. Our defenders did nothing wrong because he was unstoppable. When I was playing as a boy there was a coach who said to me, 'If you can keep moving and

thinking at the same time, and if you can turn and direct the ball with both feet, change your pace in split second and time your running perfectly and at the end of it all have made no mistakes, and be able to shoot with force and accuracy, you will be a player like no player who has lived'. Well, I have seen this player and his name is Johnny Byrne.

After Byrne's goal West Ham sensibly concentrated on defence and Lausanne's attempts to close the margin became more and more frantic. Just as their supporters were preparing to give up on them, they at last received the one chance West Ham allowed them in the whole second half. Peters misplaced a clearance in his own packed 18-yard box and Robert Hosp, the Swiss inside-left, an attacking player with a keen eye for a goalscoring opportunity who had made half a dozen international appearances, promptly slammed the ball into the net.

With the spectators now urging them on to even greater efforts, the home side forced three quick corners. However, when the final whistle sounded they had failed to close on the Irons, thanks to the headwork of Joe Kirkup, Moore's cool brain and the resilience of Ken Brown. West Ham had done well, but the game had turned into something of an intellectual battle for possession. The 500 travelling Irons sent chants of 'East Lon-don' echoing across the Alps as the 25,000 Lausanne supporters applauded the cockney boys off the park. West Ham had looked worthy of a place among four of the best cup-fighting clubs in Europe. The Swiss had played neat, thoughtful football, but the Hammers had dampened their thrust and in the process quelled their ability to break through the protective network laid down by the West Ham defence.

The supporter celebrations were not confined to within the Swiss borders. When the fans got back to the Docklands there was plenty of cheap booze flying about. While everyone was keeping track of the game, a lorry, parked in Silver Town, just down the Barking Road from the West Ham ground, had been relieved of its load of whisky. The 'chaps' had moved quickly. Some, allegedly, had even been used to toast the West Ham victory at a Mayor's Party following a Council meeting on the night of the match.

After the game Greenwood expressed his delight and commented,

> We did everything we came out here to do. We gave away a silly goal but the team played magnificently after the first 20 minutes... We were too defensive at this stage when we should have been going for more goals. We got a bit cocky and let Lausanne come back at us when we did not look in danger.

Ron had now seen the Swiss three times, once away from home. He said that they had played better than he had expected. In other Cup-Winners' Cup games the Germans, Munich 1860, had a 4–0 first leg advantage over Legia Warsaw, while Torino had beaten the Finns, Haka Valkeakoski, 5–0.

North and South Bank prices were 6s for the second leg match against the Swiss. Enclosures were 7s 6d, 15s and £1. The game itself was played with much more abandon than the tight first match. Shots and near misses made it an exciting night, appreciated by the 32,000 who turned out to cheer the Hammers on, yet again breaking the record in terms of club profits. Once more West Ham realised that the one-goal lead would not be enough in the way of insurance and that they would have to attack. It made for a good old-fashioned game of football. The Irons' non-stop offensive was met by Lausanne fighting to get back into the tie. This gave rise to some fine entertainment. From the kick-off both sides took risks and West Ham made a fantastic start when Hurst twice rattled the woodwork. Kunzi saved splendidly from a Dear effort but was lucky to deny Byrne. The Hammers blitzed them. The big Lausanne defenders kicked and volleyed shots clear. At one point the visitors gave away three corners in 30 seconds. But, with less than 10 minutes to half-time, the Swiss threw a counter-punch. The entire West Ham defence was caught napping for the first time in the leg by Lausanne wing-half Richard Durr. The lanky, long-striding linkman, who had played in the Chile World Cup and had appeared regularly in the national team, took the ball to the right corner-flag and crossed it quickly into the goalmouth. Kerkhoffs headed home. The game didn't really need lifting but this goal did just that. Within five minutes West Ham had scored twice. They were given the first by centre-back Ely Tacchella. The Swiss international swept Sealey's centre past his own goalkeeper. Alan also played a part in the second goal when he hit a hard drive at Kunzi, which the 'keeper could only palm away. The ball seemed to go over the byline, but Brian 'Stag' Dear, from an extremely acute angle, planted it high in the net.

That should have settled the issue, but the Swiss were unwilling to give in. Four minutes after the interval they forced the industrious Kirkup to make a mistake to allow Hertig to cut in from the left and hit the ball with his right foot into the far corner of the net. For a tempestuous 10 minutes the Hammers were under extreme pressure that included a Kerkhoffs effort that was somehow foiled by Standen's legs. West Ham then applied some extra pace, trying to outrun the Swiss, who were clearly seeking to slow the game down (which would not have suited the Irons). This began to alter the way the game was going. On the hour the home side forced a corner. Sealey sent a curler into the goalmouth and Peters, the outstanding player on a night of many heroes, calmly converted.

Though they now seemed to be fighting a lost cause, the Swiss soldiered on gallantly. Hosp smashed a shot against Standen's bar and 10 minutes from time outside-right Norbert Eschmann scored the game's most spectacular goal with an overhead kick that left Standen rooted to the ground in disbelief and earned rapturous applause from even the Hammers fans. Eschmann was a fine forward who had been signed from Stade Français two seasons before. He had won more than dozen Swiss caps and had broken a leg in Chile during his country's World Cup campaign. He was the Swiss youth team coach and had done much to guide the tactics that had taken Lausanne so far.

With barely a minute to go, Dear thumped the ball into the net to clinch victory. Taking this tie had been no mean achievement. West Ham had been the only side to beat the Swiss at home that season. Boyce, playing at right-half, had been immaculate, prising open the Lausanne defence. Just a few days later he became a father for the first time. Hurst had been a tower of strength and Byrne linked defence and attack with panache. Moore was his usual implacable self and Peters appeared to be the perfect full-back. They all looked England class, and with the World Cup just over a year away it seemed as if West Ham might have four or five players in Alf Ramsey's squad.

Za-Za-Zaragoza

In the semi-final of the Cup-Winners' Cup West Ham were first out of the draw to face the team Greenwood and most of his players wanted to avoid, the Spanish side, Real Zaragoza. Their ground was 200 miles from the nearest airport, in Barcelona. They were, by far, the best team the Hammers had come up against in the competition. The club included practically the whole Spanish national side. It was going to be a difficult tie.

Before that fearful encounter the Irons faced a tough First Division schedule: Arsenal at Upton Park, then Villa and Leeds away. Johnny scored a penalty and the winner with three minutes to go in the 2–1 defeat of the Gunners; at Villa Park he made the score 2–2 just before the hour and 13 minutes later supplied the cross for Dear to convert and give West Ham both points; and it was his cross, fumbled by double-chasing Leeds' 'keeper Gary Sprake, which led to Dear's equaliser, although Leeds took the points with a scrambled goal late on from the right foot of Billy Bremner.

The first leg of the 1965 European Cup-Winners' Cup semi-final was played out at the Boleyn Ground. The 'Words of Welcome' in the Hammers programme that night were headed, *Bienvenida a Nuestros Invitados*. Geoff Hurst and Ron Boyce had been to see the Spanish play in the previous round against Cardiff in Wales a month earlier. They sang the praises of 'Las Cinquos Magnificos'. Budgie recalled:

Zaragoza's 'Magnificent Five' front men were five internationals. Before they had knocked out Cardiff they'd seen Dundee off. Ron used to prepare for games and let you know exactly what to expect from who you would be playing against. He'd prepare special dossiers on each player. He was usually spot on but he got it wrong with Zaragoza as far as their centre-forward was concerned. Ken Brown did for him from the start. Ron didn't really want that. He was a purist.

The 'Magnificent Five' included Marcelino, Villa and Lapetra, who replaced the great Gento as Spain's outside-left. They had helped Zaragoza find European glory the previous season, winning the Inter Cities Fairs Cup, the trophy that would evolve into the UEFA Cup. They had beaten Barcelona and Atlético Madrid in the process of claiming the Franco National Cup that had qualified them to take part in the Cup-Winners' Cup. Zaragoza could score goals. Their victory over Valetta of Malta in the preliminary round of the tournament had proved this. The Spanish had won 8–1 over the two legs. Greenwood was destined to be vindicated when he predicted that they would be tough and uncompromising in defence and quicksilver, lethal destroyers in attack.

The big Wednesday night came and in the first couple of minutes Marcelino went close, but with just nine minutes gone a packed crowd saw local boy Dear get his eighth goal in as many games. The move began with Hurst, who sent a pass bouncing out to Sissons on the left, who cleverly drew Cortizo out of position, then crossed towards the far post where Dear was waiting to head it home. Less than a quarter of an hour later, Budgie got a cracker. Moore chipped a free-kick upfield, and this was collected by the alert Brown, who had forsaken the magnificent Marcelino to work on the right wing. Ken crossed to Sissons. For a second Sissons looked like losing control, but he flicked the ball into the middle for Byrne who took the pass on his chest, let it drop and volleyed home in one clear and flowing movement. The ball smashed into the roof of the net past the prancing Yarza. Budgie had made contact from almost 20 yards out!

Throughout the first half Dear and Sissons lashed wicked-looking shots inches over. Marcelino shot wide and D'Arcy dos Santos, better known to the Zaragoza fans as Canario, almost scored. West Ham had the potential to kill the tie in the second period, but were never going to score a hatful. Greenwood had opted for a cautious approach in the second half and his side came out after the break with a nine-man defence. The crowd hated it. The Hammers had just two front men and relied on the 'big boot' to find them. The home side lost momentum, and gave their opponents' shaky defence a rest. This allowed the fast, highly skilled Spanish attack of Marcelino, Lapetra and Canario to take advantage. The Spanish now looked quite capable of outsmarting Moore and his defence.

After hitting the post from the right in the 53rd minute, Canario halved West Ham's lead after 10 minutes of the second-half. The experienced Brazilian wandered out to the left, tapped the ball through Moore's legs, dribbled into the six-yard box and then shot at the Hammers 'keeper. The ball hit Standen on the arm and he effectively scooped the ball into the net.

Boyce had a great chance to make it 3–1, but slashed wide. Canario had a better opportunity to supply the equaliser, but his shot went high into the silent crowd. After that Zaragoza were happy to play out time, confident that they could take the tie in front of their own supporters. The Spanish defence, which had lumped the ball with all the thunder of a Fourth Division side in the first half, grew more confident as West Ham, desperately needing goals, faltered and slid back on the defensive. The giant Santamaria inspired some excellent defensive play which the two lonely striking Hammers and the occasional three-pronged attacks could not break in the second half. This said, as Byrne remembered:

> Ken Brown had a great game, the best I'd seen him play. He got the
> better of Marcelino in the air every time. You couldn't have asked
> for more of him.

The 35,000 Hammers fans rose as one person to applaud the Spaniards at the close. For the West Ham players there were only boos and hope. But the result gave the Irons some kind of chance for the second leg, although, by the next morning, most of the national newspapers had already written them off as finalists.

Greenwood was disappointed after getting two early goals. He noted that the Spanish had played better as the game went on and were as good as he thought they would be. He saw it as the toughest game West Ham had played since he had become manager. However, he claimed that the Irons had, 'out-Continentalled the Continentals'. The Zaragoza manager was very pleased with the result, but he said that he did not expect an easy game on his team's home turf. However, Budgie later said, 'Most of us, me and Bobby included, didn't think a one-goal lead would do. We expected the worst in Spain.'

Byrne burnt

As it turned out, the first leg of the European Cup-Winners' Cup semi-final was to be the last game Budgie would play for West Ham that season. At one stage in 1965 it was predicted that Byrne and Jimmy Greaves would be England's strike partners in the 1966 World Cup finals. His performances that season had certainly made him look like his country's number-one striker, in spite of fierce opposition from the likes of Greaves, Bobby Smith, Ray Crawford, Roger Hunt and Geoff Hurst. But a cartilage injury sustained when winning his 11th cap in a tough encounter with Scotland at Wembley, although no one realised it at the time, marked the conclusion of Byrne's international career and the start of his problems as a player. Byrne had again replaced Terry Venables in the England side. Injury had obliged the Chelsea midfielder to withdraw from Ramsey's squad for the second time in four games, having played in the 1–1 draw with Holland in Amsterdam.

John faced the Scots just three days after he had scored for West Ham against Real Zaragoza. Usually a side is not thought to have achieved a great deal by managing a home draw, but with just nine men for most of the second half England had accomplished much at Wembley as the spring of 1965 began to be felt. The game was level when left-back Ray Wilson was forced to limp from the Wembley pitch (he was later taken to hospital with badly torn rib muscles). With only 10 men England were obliged to move Byrne to left-back as part of a defiant defensive action. He came up against the tricky Willie Henderson. The Scottish winger played a quick one-two and if Byrne had been an ordinary forward he would have followed the ball when it went inside him. But at West Ham he had been taught about every job on the field and Budgie, instead of ball-watching, did what a good defender should do – he turned with his opponent. His studs caught in the thick Wembley turf and his knee went. After 20 minutes on the sideline, with England beset on every side, he returned to the fray, every step agonisingly painful, to help his country fight on against the odds.

Not for the first time the Wembley pitch had ruined the balance of a game that had promised a great deal, particularly for the English side. Scotland showed all their inherent qualities of talent and battling prowess, but were not able to quite harness the skills and experience of the side to full effect, to the extent that they found themselves dictated to by just 10 and then nine Englishmen for much of the match. Many nominated Nobby Stiles as the man of the match for his hard but skilful tackling of his teammates Crerand and Law. Jack Charlton had also been uncompromising and had handled his first full international well. Barry Bridges was perhaps the most notable player in the English attack. He made four clear chances, while ceaselessly on the run making space for others, and was pivotal in the work to put England 2–0 ahead after 35 minutes. Law reduced the lead with a shot which deceived Gordon Banks in its flight five minutes before half-time and the Scots drew level by way of Ian St John, after George Cohen had kneed a Wilson shot off the line.

Following his team's brave efforts Alf Ramsey said that his fighting side had been 'magnificent' but spoke of his regret that the team would not be kept together for the next four matches because of club commitments that included European games.

Date:	10 April 1965
Location:	Wembley
Competition:	Home Championship
Fixture:	England v Scotland
Result:	2–2 (HT 2–1)
England scorers:	R. Charlton, Greaves
Scotland scorers:	Law (40 mins), St John (59 mins)
Team:	Banks, G. (Leicester City), Cohen, G.R. (Fulham), Wilson, R. (Everton), Stiles, N.P. (Manchester United), Charlton, J. (Leeds United), Moore, R.F.C. (West Ham United) captain, Thompson, P. (Liverpool), Greaves, J.P. (Tottenham Hotspur), Bridges, B.J. (Chelsea), Byrne, J.J. (West Ham United), Charlton, R. (Manchester United).
Scotland:	Brown (Tottenham Hotspur), Hamilton (Dundee), McCreadie (Chelsea), Crerand (Manchester United), McNeill (Celtic), Greig (Rangers), Henderson (Rangers), Collins (Leeds United), St John (Liverpool), Law (Manchester United), Wilson (Rangers).
Attendance:	98,199
Referee:	Istvan Zsolt (Hungary)

West Ham's League term concluded just five days before the second leg of the semi-final of the Cup-Winners' Cup; they finished ninth in the First Division. The Hammers had only drawn four games all season, equal fewest ever with the 1934–35 campaign. A programme announcement listed season ticket prices for 1965–66 at £11 and £13.

Byrne, of course, missed the second match against Zaragoza. He had been West Ham's inspiration during their FA Cup achievements of the previous season, and had been the symbol of the Hammers' attitude throughout their historic European run. West Ham's 1–1 draw in Spain, with John Sissons scoring the vital goal for the Irons, a powerful right-foot shot, not the usual artillery piece favoured by the prodigious wideman, made the Hammers the second British team to reach the final of a major European tournament after Spurs, who had won the European Cup-Winners' Cup three years previously. But it was the Hammers who would become the first British team to win European glory in Britain. And, unlike the Tottenham side, these Irons were all English and West Ham went into the final with the best record of any British club in Europe.

The Wembley final against Munich 1860 saw both teams play the fast, open football that the 100,000 spectators had wanted to see. Munich tried to match West Ham by playing an attacking game, and this made for an entertaining match that swung back and forth, but in the end two goals from Budgie's good friend Alan Sealey made the Hammers comfortable winners.

It should really have been 'Byrne's Night', but, as was his way, Budgie, who watched his teammates' fantastic Wembley victory, later commented that it: '…was Sammy's finest hour and his night'.

CHAPTER 12

Searing Embers

B Y THE mid-sixties Johnny Byrne was a seasoned professional at West Ham. However, partly because of his injury, but also due to his lifestyle, it was likely that his best playing days had passed by the start of the 1965–66 season. That term it seemed that his body and soul would hardly allow him to string more than half-a-dozen matches together and he missed great chunks of the season. Yet Budgie never stopped learning and he perhaps learnt most from his manager at Upton Park. He recalled:

> Ron Greenwood was very dedicated to football and was a superb reader of the game. Many a time when we were in trouble Ron, in his own quiet way, came in at half-time and put things right.
>
> Most of us knew that Ron had tremendous knowledge of football and a fantastic understanding of the game. He studied football and was always looking to learn more about it. To me he often seemed to be having a different experience watching a match from most people. Ron saw things others missed. He was always concerned about the way soccer should be played. He was a practical man but at the same time, to him football, played well, was a kind of art. He set out to make his sides open and he wanted to see his players make the game attractive. Most of all he was a decent man and believed in playing the game honestly. For Ron, football was about using your head, your brain as much as your body.

Such an example would prove of great value to Byrne in the future.

Although injured Budgie went with the club to America in the summer of 1965. His wife, Margaret, had asked if he could go on tour, saying, 'Don't for God's sake leave him behind. He'll be terrible'. Greenwood decided to take him because of his value in terms of squad morale and in order that some therapeutic work could be carried out on his knee injury. So, three weeks after their European Cup-Winners' Cup triumph at Wembley, West Ham were again taking part in the New York International Tournament. Byrne was able to start the opening game that the Hammers lost to an All Star side called the New Yorkers 2–1 at Randalls Island. West Ham then met Munich 1860 in a repeat of the Cup-Winners' Cup Final. The Irons beat the Germans 2–1. Peters and Sealey scored against a half-strength Munich side. Budgie recalled:

> We'd gone to America before the Cup year. It had helped us build a
> team out of ourselves and Ron had said if we won the Cup-Winners'
> Cup we'd go again. After we beat Munich in the States they took us
> out to a German beer garden. After that neither side won a match.
>
> I nearly put a complete end to my career when we were over
> there. We'd had a few drinks and I jumped off a stagecoach! Bill
> Jenkins, the club physio, was so angry he nearly throttled me and
> told me I'd let everybody down. Bill worked hard on the injury, I'd
> broken a bone in my foot; he got me more or less fit for the last
> match of the tour. Bad really, but Bill's reaction still makes me laugh.

After the defeat of Munich the Irons met Portuguesa in the Shea Stadium, which had never before been used for soccer. It was a tremendous arena that hosted a legendary Beatles concert, but the venue outshone the game. West Ham lost 6–3. The scoreline flattered the Brazilians, as the Hammers squandered a string of chances, but it really was a case of South American football beating the British brand.

In the next game West Ham were beaten again by the New Yorkers; this time the score was 3–1. Games against the Italians, Varese, and another match against Portuguesa followed. The East Londoners could not qualify whatever they did so these games became no more than practice matches. All in all the tour was something of a flop as far as the Irons were concerned. West Ham looked a shadow of the team that had done so well in the US in the summer of 1963. The side were clearly exhausted: the energy, urgency and enthusiasm was simply not there. Greenwood called his team's performances 'disgraceful', but added:

> Still, the beatings we have taken over here should have cut us down
> to size. After this we will not start the new season with any pre-
> conceived notions of our own greatness, and that is a good thing.

The 'Greenwood School of Esteem Management' and 'You are not as good as you think you are' psychology took its inevitable toll and, exacerbated by a pre-season tour of Germany, where West Ham lost 1–0 to FVB Stuttgart, beat Eintracht Frankfurt 2–1 and drew 1–1 in yet another game with Munich 1860, was perhaps not the best way to start a new season. The Hammers returned to England physically battered with Byrne, Ken Brown, Alan Sealey and Brian Dear all on the long-term injured list, and mentally deflated.

Budgie missed the opening game of the 1965–66 season, a 3–0 pasting at the Hawthorns, and didn't get on the scoresheet until the start of September when West Ham lost 5–3 at Bramall Lane. The Blades had only scored three goals before that match but against West Ham they managed to get their biggest win since returning to the First Division in 1961. However, Budgie showed some of his former touch when in mid-September he claimed West Ham's third goal in the 3–3 League Cup draw at Twerton Park.

For all this, West Ham were in 18th place in the League when they faced the side just below them, Blackpool, at Upton Park. The Irons had only won two games in their first 10 in Division One. Hurst benefited from the remnants of a brilliant Tony Waiters save, following Byrne's efforts, in the final minute to give the Hammers a point.

Beware of Greeks bearing footballs

West Ham's last game in September saw Third Division Bristol Rovers at Upton Park for the replay of the second round of the League Cup. Budgie scored the opening goal of the game, just before the half-hour mark, and the winner, giving West Ham the better of a 3–2 scoreline with just 10 minutes of the match remaining. Not long after this Budgie was sidelined for two months, missing nine First Division and League Cup games. He returned for the Hammers' first match in defence of the European Cup-Winners' Cup against the Greek side Olympiakos, towards the end of September (as holders of

the Cup-Winners' Cup West Ham were given a bye in the first round). The first leg took place at the Boleyn Ground and was marked by the visitors' penchant for spitting, kicking and elbowing. Picking up on a pass from Moore, Hurst blasted West Ham into a 24th-minute lead. The big Hammers striker got a second with his head around 20 minutes later. Byrne made a contribution just over 10 minutes after half-time, jumping on a mistake by the Greek keeper Fronimidis to produce a 3–0 lead for the rampant Irons. Brabrook nodded in his club's fourth with 72 minutes gone.

Budgie returned to First Division action against Everton at the Boleyn Ground; his side had only three teams below them in the League at that point. Brian Labone, the massive England centre-half, gave Byrne a bad time, but this didn't prevent John from supplying the cross that gifted Sissons the first goal of the game, which West Ham won 3–0.

On the first day of December 126 Hammers fans and 40,000 others gave the Irons a warm welcome to Greece. Fireworks, that exploded and flamed as the West Ham players made a pre-match inspection of the pitch, brought the massive Olympiakos soccer bowl alive. The firework show was in full flow as the game started and continued after its conclusion. A flare pumped out flame and smoke in Jim Standen's goal as he made himself ready for the kick-off.

The visitors had a couple of shots early on. One, from Martin Peters, was particularly unlucky, being just inches wide, but West Ham's first goal was a bit fortunate. Stefanakos missed a chip forward by Sissons and Peters scored with an angled shot that was deflected past Fronimidis by a defender. Peters later claimed that he had meant it to go to Budgie.

West Ham's second goal came when a Byrne pass freed Johnny Sissons to weave his way around a couple of defenders and send a perfect cross to the head of Peters. Eddie Bovington scored a strange own-goal three minutes later, lofting the ball past the bewildered Standen.

In the last part of the match the Greek World Cup captain, Polychoniou, converted a penalty after a mysterious infringement by Ken Brown, the details of which were only known to the referee Mr Bachramov. Moore, Peters and especially Hurst would have cause to remember this official after he had run a line in the 1966 World Cup final.

After the game Greenwood identified Standen as man-of-the-match, pointing out the magnificence of two saves in the first part of the game. However, according to Polychoniou:

Byrne was magnificent in the first leg but in the second game it was he who drew the side together. He could read our game, but trying to predict what he was going to do, well, you might as well have tried to read the wind.

After Peters moved to centre-forward, he was injured when I tackled him not too long after the game started, Byrne became an attacking midfield player and was able to get West Ham started again and again. I think if he had not have been in the West Ham team that Olympiakos would have won that game and maybe the round.

However, Budgie remembered the nomadic West Ham fans:

They went crazy at the end, singing '*Bubbles*' and that and the police had to tell them to be quiet as they were winding up the Greek supporters who didn't like losing the tie one bit.

Byrne – bringer of hope

The following Saturday West Ham, in 17th position in Division One, were at Old Trafford where Manchester United, sitting at number eight in the League, were still unbeaten. Had either of Byrne's shots that struck the woodwork in the seventh and 77th minutes gone in the Reds might have lost their record, but they didn't and the game ended goalless.

Budgie's final goal of 1965 came in the first leg of the League Cup semi-final against Cardiff City at Upton Park. The Bluebirds had defeated Crewe Alexandra, Portsmouth, Reading and Ipswich Town on their way to the last four. For 85 minutes it was a one-sided match, despite the visitors' tough tactics, and the Hammers came through 5–2 winners.

John got his first goal of 1966 in the final minute of the Hammers' early January 2–1 First Division defeat at St James' Park. After this Byrne had to contend with another lengthy period of injury but he was back in Europe for the third round of the Cup-Winners' Cup in early March against Aufbau Magdeburg from East Germany.

For a team well experienced in this grade of football, West Ham were easily thrown out of their stride by Ernst Kümmel's FC Magdeburg at Upton Park, a sound but far from great German team that nevertheless seemed to be able to break the timing of Greenwood's side, whose efforts looked hurried. Strangely the Irons adopted a 'route one' tactic that resulted in giving the possession to the Germans. The Hammers snatched at shots and the ball flew high or wide again and again, even from close range. At the same time the Germans, through their close covering, intelligent marking and quick interception, forced West Ham to make errors. Busch swept up behind a four-man defensive line, while Segger and Seguin harried the Hammers in midfield. Magdeburg were able to launch continual counter-attacks, keeping the off-form Boyce and the diligent Peters busy for long periods. Byrne was tightly marshalled throughout; Hurst was given neither a second of time nor an inch of space. Brabrook hardly saw a chink of light on the right and Sissons was isolated upfront for great chunks of the match.

As such West Ham had to wait until a minute after the interval for any hope, and it was Budgie who gave it to them when he sent Peters a perfect cross into the net, after Hurst had just failed to meet the ball with his head. Thereafter, the Irons snapped out of their lethargy to launch successive raids on the German positions, but few were well constructed and none were concluded by a goal. In the end it was clear that the Hammers had unconsciously taken on 'hit-and-run' tactics. West Ham had thrown away most of their chances of building a tie-winning lead by trying smash their way through the defensive wall the Germans had erected. The semi-finals looked a long way off with the prospect of facing the effective, fit, fast and earnest Magdeburg on their own turf.

Final semi-final

At the beginning of March Budgie scored the second of two West Ham goals in the opening nine minutes of the Irons' 4–2 home win against Aston Villa, but this was to cut little ice with the West Ham fans, who, about 100 hours later, booed his name as it was announced at the start of the first leg of the League Cup Final at Upton Park. It was clear they expected Byrne to be as devastating as he was before his injury and that anything else was just not good enough. The 1966 League Cup final was to be staged over two legs. The following season and thereafter (until the demolition of the Twin Towers) the League Cup final would be one game, staged at Wembley. So the Hammers were not to grace the national stadium for the finals of three different cup competitions in three successive years.

Byrne silenced his detractors when he banged in the last of the tie's three goals in the final 20 seconds of the match to the protests of the West Bromwich players who insisted that he had fouled 'keeper Ray Potter in the process. The father of the well-known actor and West Ham supporter Glenn Murphy (of *London's Burning* fame) an East End pugilist of some renown, a contender in the highest echelons of British boxing during the mid/late 1950s, had attended the Upton Park leg of the League Cup Final. Terry Murphy was in the player's bar with Bobby and several other players. Tongue in cheek, particularly given Budgie's performance, Terry said that he was going to 'clobber' Budgie for a mistake he had made during the match. Terry later assured Byrne that the comment had been ironic, but immediately after the remark John Charles, one of the club's many comedians, ran to the dressing room to let John know what Terry had said. Byrne took the news seriously and headed home via one of the dark side exits of the Boleyn Ground. Greenwood got to hear of the situation and, taking it as seriously as Budgie, banned Murphy from the players' bar. The prohibition stood even after Terry's personal reassurance to John that he had not been serious. In the early years of the 21st century, after his years as landlord of the legendary rock venue the Bridge House in Canning Town, East London, Terry still found the reaction to his comment startling.

Budgie did not make the Hammers side that drew with Magdeburg in Germany to put the Hammers into the semi-final of the Cup-Winners' Cup, but he played in the second leg of the League Cup final at the Hawthorns. West Brom had learnt well from watching how West Ham combined a tight, disciplined defence with free-running play that motivated forward movement while drawing opposing defences out of position. On their home ground, in front of a crowd of 32,000, the Baggies demonstrated that they were able to mirror and counter the West Ham style.

The Albion players almost replicated the tactics that Preston had used against West Ham during the FA Cup final of 1964. They ran, chased and shot, peppering the claret and blue defence that had looked almost impenetrable in European competition over nearly two seasons. The pressure led to John Kaye levelling the aggregate scores after just 10 minutes, while injury to the Irons' centre-half Ken Brown left gaping holes in the Hammers defence. It was a rare mistake by Byrne that gave West Brom their second. Budgie returned the ball to Standen but the prolific Tony Brown took advantage of a poorly directed header with less than 20 minutes gone. Before the half-hour mark Clive Clark made it 3–0 and on 34 minutes the Albion captain Graham Williams shot from 30 yards and saw the ball ricochet in off of a post.

Two long-range efforts from Byrne flew over the bar and a Brabrook header hit a post to add to the seemingly never-ending list of West Ham 'ifs'. Martin Peters wore the number three shirt at left-back; Greenwood had hoped that he would provide an extra offensive weapon, overlapping and joining the attack by ghosting in from deep positions, but Peters was obliged to stay in defence to allow Bobby Moore to cover Albion's deep-lying centre-forward, John Kaye, who dragged Moore into midfield. After the break Greenwood told Moore and Peters to switch roles, and constant attacks throughout the second 45 minutes led to Peters heading a goal with 15 minutes to go, but the match had been killed off in the first half. West Ham had lost a Cup final for the first time in 43 years and it would be Albion who would contest the Inter Cities Fairs Cup the following season.

Now the whole of West Ham's season hung on 5 April, the day the Hammers would run out at Upton Park in the first leg of the European Cup-Winners' Cup semi-final to face Borussia Dortmund. Borussia boasted the services of the German international, Sigi Held, and the man with the kangaroo kick, Lothar Emmerich, the left-winger who would face Bobby Moore again in the 1966 World Cup final. As a team, Borussia had more class than any side left in the competition. They were one of the best clubs in Europe at the time, and were sitting at the top of West German football. They had smashed Floriana (Malta) 5–1 and 8–0, but had to work hard against CSKA, the Bulgarian Cup-holders. In the second leg a 3–0 lead was almost cancelled by a 4–2 defeat in Sofia. In the quarter-finals Dortmund managed to craft a 1–1 draw against Atlético Madrid and won 1–0 at home.

When they came to Upton Park Borussia had no intention of following the tradition of teams playing away in Europe. They set about attacking the West Ham defence at every opportunity. The night did not begin too promisingly for the Hammers. Byrne was captain in place of Moore, who was having difficulties with Greenwood over money. Bobby was the last but one man to take the field and was booed as he emerged from the tunnel. But Moore was not distracted and went about stamping his authority on the game. He was superb, as was Byrne, who darted about incisively, looking revitalised in the role of out-and-out striker. Brown stuck relentlessly to his job and Peters was at his omnipresent best, putting the Hammers in front just before half-time. Greenwood had brought the 32-year-old Jimmy Bloomfield into the side – he was an old pal from Ron's days at Brentford – and it was he who gave Peters the ball midway into Borussia's half. With Budgie running free on the left it looked as if the movement would continue that way, but Peters suddenly cut inside, drifted past two defenders and put the ball past Tilkowski with an aggressive, low drive. This would not be the last time the German 'keeper would be beaten by Peters; Tilkowski would collect a World Cup runners-up medal just a few months later.

West Ham pushed inexorably forward in search of a second goal, but it did not come. In the final stages of the game Borussia went on the offensive and provided a dramatic finish to a brilliant and combative encounter. They struck twice in the final four minutes through West Germany's top marksman, Lothar Emmerich. First Libuda, a ghost-like figure, gave Emmerich the opportunity to net from 12 yards, then a few dozen seconds elapsed and with only two minutes left to play Held crossed from the left and it was Emmerich, lurking by the far post, who slipped the ball slickly beyond Standen. The German had claimed both his goals by way of his right foot; his left had done all the damage in the competition until it came to the East End. Emmerich had given the Irons a mountain to climb in the second leg; the Germans were unbeaten at home that season.

Dortmund had shown themselves to be an efficient, skilled side that possessed a resolute spirit. The match had pulsated with the very soul of football and West Ham had done well to dominate for much of the game. In his post-match analysis, although he was later to confess that he thought West Ham had no chance in Germany, Ron Greenwood said:

> The way it ended was cruel but a game lasts 90 minutes. We have not yet given up hope. Dortmund are a good side, but they were not in it. I told my players how good this West German side was to buck them up. But we did not let them be good. I thought Bloomfield was the best player on the field and Byrne has been appointed captain for the rest of the season.

Things looked as if they were turning around when the Hammers beat Spurs at White Hart Lane. Byrne scored the first of West Ham's four and the Hammers defence limited Tottenham to the single reply. This was the start of a bright period for Budgie in the League, although he was out again for West Ham's 6–2 defeat at Stamford Bridge.

John's next appearance for the Hammers was in Germany. He recalled the hours before the crunch match against Dortmund:

> For two days before the match with Borussia we were talking about needing to get an early goal and the importance of holding the Germans off in the first part of the game. The away goals meant that we had to win 2–0 or 3–1. But it was our eighth European game in 18 months and we'd always scored in the away leg. At the Rote Erde stadium, Dortmund, who were on top of their league, scored with the first movement of the game. Such is life!

The Germans cut the West Ham defence in two when Sturm gave Sigi Held a chance to cross the ball to Lothar Emmerich. The tall, round-shouldered winger headed against the bar, but made sure of the rebound after just 27 seconds.

Emmerich had an awkward gait and moderate ability, but he had a feel for scoring goals and on 13 April 1966 he was not satisfied with the one. He scored again in the 29th minute with a fierce shot from a free-kick following a foul by Bobby Moore. West Ham built their defensive wall with meticulous care, but the lethal left foot, unleashed after a swift, seven pace run-up, found a gap that did not seem to exist. This brought his goal tally to 43 that winter.

Byrne described Emmerich as:

...a player that you might get the better of and forget about, but he was a bloke who could win a game, maybe a tournament, in a flash.

He hit a West Ham post so hard that the ball went for a throw in! West Ham persisted trying to play football and fought on long after the tie had been won and lost. Byrne managed to get on the scoresheet two minutes before half-time after Brabrook broke free on the right and Budgie headed his centre past Tilkowski. But with only three minutes left, Cyliax, the German right-back, came galloping up the field and his 25-yard shot hit Brown before spinning over Standen's head. West Ham were beaten 3–1.

During the period that included the two Cup-Winners' Cup games with Dortmund, Greenwood had been arguing with his skipper Bobby Moore about wages; the debate was about two pounds. Johnny Byrne did his best with the responsibility of captaincy, but his style was very different to Moore's approach to leadership. Unlike Bobby, Budgie was a talker on the park. At the same time John was not an experienced captain at top level, although Moore was no ordinary skipper, and even the most knowledgeable commander would have been unworthy to fill his boots. The debates that err toward the role of captain being irrelevant or merely symbolic cannot be applied to Moore or his professional context in the 1960s. Malcolm Allison and Noel Cantwell were the founder members of the legendary 'Academy'. When they left Upton Park Bobby took over as the informal leader of the club's professionals. It was he who interpreted and built on Greenwood's tactics on the field and he that made any strategy work; West Ham played around Bobby Moore. The cost of Greenwood's and the club's meanness and the bickering that resulted had huge financial repercussions for West Ham and long-lasting effects.

In the European Cup-Winners' Cup final at Glasgow's Hampden Park,

Borussia met Liverpool, a side conditioned to European football the previous season, but the Germans were stronger all round, with a particularly formidable defence and tactically more sound overall. Held put the Germans ahead after the interval only for Roger Hunt to equalise from a controversial centre. That might have upset less resilient teams than Dortmund, but they just kept going like a Tiger tank. With only seconds left Hunt failed with a simple chance and the match went into extra-time. In the 107th minute the Liverpool Scottish international goalkeeper, Tommy Lawrence, under pressure from Held, was forced to punch the ball from the edge of his area. Failure to 'hold the ball' was, in those days, seen as a nasty foreign weakness. Libuda pounced on the clearance and blasted from 40 yards out. As the ball flew, nasty and full, it took a deflection off the Liverpool centre-half Ron Yeats and rolled past the stranded Lawrence. West Ham had been knocked out of the tournament by the European Cup-Winners' Cup-winners.

West Ham had matched Liverpool in the Charity Shield at the start of the 1965–66 season and at Anfield in the League. Both Liverpool and Dortmund went on to become veterans of European competition and this allowed Liverpool to build the foundations on which they were to become one of the world's super clubs by the last part of the 20th century. Who knows what would have happened to the Hammers, including the England striker Johnny Byrne, if they had been led into those semi-final games by the only captain most of the West Ham side had known as professional footballers, the greatest-ever England skipper, the man who would inspire his country to win the World Cup just a few weeks later. And what would have been the effect on Byrne's chances of being selected for the England World Cup 22 if he had been part of a successful European trophy-winning side just weeks before the biggest sporting tournament ever to be held in Britain?

Marking time

The Hammers were in 12th place in Division One when John netted a penalty in the Irons' 2–1 win over Arsenal at Upton Park after Northern Ireland international Terry Neill had tripped Hurst. There were two more Byrne penalties against Tottenham at the Boleyn Ground, giving West Ham a convincing 2–0 win. The first was awarded after Phil Beal rugby-tackled Byrne and the second was given as the punishment for Joe Kinnear punching the ball from under the bar. Hammer of the Year Geoff Hurst hit the inside of a post, while England rival Jimmy Greaves missed an open goal from two yards.

Johnny's fourth penalty in three games and his fifth goal in four starts came in the home win against Manchester United. The Hammers were in a mid-table position; United were in fourth place. The gates of the Boleyn Ground were locked half-an-hour before kick-off on a season's-best crowd of 36,416. Thousands were shut out. This was West Ham's 64th match of the term and the last game in front of the Upton Park fans that season. Bobby Charlton celebrated his selection as Footballer of the Year with a stunning display of skill; he seemed to cut into the West Ham defence as and when he felt like it. However, surprisingly for an end-of-season, rather meaningless match, the game took on the feel of a cup-tie and it was the Hammers who led with 28 minutes on the clock; Hurst hit home after a scramble in front of the United goal following the blocking of a John Sissons shot.

The Irons experienced long moments where they were totally outplayed but they increased their lead when, after a shower of bottles from the terraces, Budgie hit his spot-kick in recompense for full-back Shay Brennan chopping down Martin Peters. Former West Ham skipper and Republic of Ireland international defender Noel Cantwell, who was constantly hissed at by the hardcore Hammers fans in the Chicken Run east stand (he had recently written an article criticising West Ham) pulled one back for the Red Devils, but Hurst headed in a Sissons corner to put West Ham back in front in the 73rd minute. Although United's John Aston made it 3–2 with a dozen minutes of the match left to play, the Hammers held on in front of England manager Alf Ramsey who had the upcoming game against Yugoslavia on his mind.

In the final match of the season Jackie Sinclair's left-foot gave him his 24th goal of the season for Leicester. His initial shot hit a stanchion at the back of the net with such force that it flew back out on to the pitch. This happened so fast that some players thought the ball had hit the bar. Byrne headed in off a post just before the quarter-hour, but Dougan replied with his 20th of the season with 20 minutes left on the clock.

What went wrong?
At the end of the season only five teams had won at Upton Park: Leicester City, Liverpool, Fulham, Nottingham Forest and Borussia Dortmund. West Ham had played 20 cup ties. In the League, five goals were conceded at Forest, Leeds and Sheffield United. Chelsea managed six at Stamford Bridge, prior to which Bobby Moore had been stripped of his captaincy. West Ham had won nothing. What had happened? That question was asked for a decade after 1965 and is

still being asked today by those who knew the club in the 1960s. The 'social culture' of West Ham was certainly a factor in the relative demise of the Hammers after 1965, but an aspect of West Ham's success was also probably part of the reason why the side was unable to sustain its achievement of the mid-sixties: consistency of selection. In the Cup-winning season Greenwood had called on 22 players. But five of those played no more than half a dozen matches. Another three turned out for the club less than 15 times each. For most of the games Greenwood relied on the 11 players who would win the FA Cup. It was typical of West Ham and Greenwood that a few days before the Cup Final of 1964 the eleven that would face Preston at Wembley were playing a London select side in John Lyall's testimonial. Being a 'London thing' the game was never going to be any less than demanding, and although West Ham won 5–0, with Hurst scoring four, it was not the best preparation for the biggest game in West Ham's history. It is true that the match had been arranged months earlier and that 18,000 turned up to pay tribute to one of the club's most loyal and unluckiest servants, but West Ham thought nothing of postponing League or Cup games at the drop of a hat and the match would probably have drawn an even bigger crowd after the FA Cup Final.

After one of the most demanding and financially rewarding seasons the club had ever known, not a single new player was brought to Upton Park for the 1964–65 season. This time a squad of 21 was used to defend the FA Cup, as well as contest the League Cup, the European Cup-Winners' Cup and cover the League programme, but again, in the main, it was the FA Cup Final side plus Martin Peters that bore the majority of the burden. Between 1963 and 1966 West Ham were playing a major game every three or four days. International players like Hurst, Moore, to a lesser extent Byrne and later Peters had an even heavier schedule. Even after the end of the domestic season there were still international games and Greenwood's tours of America, Europe and Africa. This being the case, it seems likely that the West Ham board and maybe the club manager were not ready to invest in their success or were willing to see players burn themselves out and hope that the youth policy on which the West Ham side of the sixties had been built would produce ready-made replacements. Unfortunately the plan failed, although sufficient talent did come through to maintain mediocre Cup and First Division performances for the better part of a decade.

West Ham's fall to mundane levels wasn't, contrary to football folklore, due to the fact that West Ham were 'soft'; there has always been a hard streak in

West Ham sides. Andy Malcolm, John Bond, Eddie Bovington, John Charles and Billy Bonds, who I once saw stare down Norman Hunter, Jack Charlton and Billy Bremner at the same time, are all fine examples of the Hammers' tougher qualities. The truth is that the Hammers, under Greenwood and later John Lyall, were constantly searching for or 'creating' space, but having found or made space, they were unable to adequately respond when well-theorised and rehearsed moves fell apart. Greenwood's complicated mission to produce dazzling soccer all too often simply faltered. The 'West Ham way', as this was known, was a gossamer construction, a shining idea, and it made West Ham, at times, a beautiful phenomenon, but with no more than a suggestion of durability that was quickly smashed when the aggression of English football, the charge, encroached on the dream. When former Hammers Malcolm Musgrove and Frank O'Farrell took the model to Old Trafford Denis Law called it '...fannying about' and suggested that it was in fact a form of 'over-coaching'. This being the case it seems that West Ham's decline was due to a number of factors:

1. Over playing a restricted squad.

2. Over coaching this limited group.

3. Over reliance on youth development/under investment in the first-team squad.

4. Over indulgence by the over-taxed players in pursuits involving alcohol.

After his injury Byrne had fought his way back into England reckoning. But he had been out of the international picture for months at a crucial time and by the early summer of 1966 England had a more austere plan of attack. Ramsey had a runner, Roger Hunt, alongside Geoff Hurst.

With the World Cup finals just weeks away four Hammers were in the England tournament squad of 28 at Lilleshall on 6 June. Hurst and Peters joined Moore and Byrne (who had been called up to replace the injured Fred Pickering of Everton) to prepare for the biggest challenge ever faced by English football. The players were given kit and smart, expensive Burberry raincoats to protect their England sports jackets and slacks from the trials of an English summer. However, after a friendly with Yugoslavia Ramsey had to reduce his squad to 22. Everton's Brian Labone, who had come into the 28 for Chelsea's injured Marvin Hinton, had himself been obliged to withdraw wounded. This meant five players had to be given the sad tidings. Ramsey called Bobby Tambling, Keith Newton, Gordon Milne, Peter Thompson and Budgie together and informed them, quite straightforwardly, that they hadn't made the final pool of 22 players for the tournament. Years later Sir Alf Ramsey related to Budgie how leaving him out of the World Cup squad had been one of the hardest decisions he'd ever had to make. The fact that John had also pulled a hamstring during training at Lilleshall would not have helped his cause. Budgie saw Alf as an honest man and a fair manager. Of course, England won the World Cup but Alf never forgot the players he left out and made sure that they all had tickets for England's games.

On that early June evening in 1966, as the disappointed rejects stood looking dejectedly at the floor, Alf asked them if they had any questions. Only Budgie raised his hand. Ramsey looked to him for his query. Johnny paused for a second and then asked, 'Can we keep the coats Alf?'

CHAPTER 13

Final Flickers

IN EARLY May, at Wembley Pool, before the 1966–67 season kicked off, Johnny Byrne, along with Moore, Hurst, Peters and Boyce, won the indoor London Five-a-Side Championship. However, it seemed that before the cheers following England's World Cup success in 1966 had melted away the first game of West Ham's 1966–67 season, against Chelsea, was underway. Byrne was in the West Ham team that was led out onto the pitch by the World Cup-winning trio, Martin Peters, Bobby Moore and Geoff Hurst, to be greeted by the proud 36,000 cockney fans at Upton Park. The Chelsea 'keeper, Peter 'The Cat' Bonetti, played like all of his nine lives depended on it to make the glory short-lived as the Hammers lost the match 2–1. This was beginning of a poor start for West Ham. Greenwood's side went five games without a win. It was clear that Budgie was not the player he had been. He scored in West Ham's 2–1 defeat at Highbury, but the crucial spark had dimmed. As the season developed, West Ham's form became increasingly erratic. The ability to score goals was still there, but seemingly in the wrong place, at the wrong time, as far as the Hammers were concerned.

The early September trip to Manchester City started out as the Hammers' sixth attempt to win a League game. The Irons had come close the previous week but a midweek draw with Liverpool at Upton Park had been the second time in seven days that a last-minute goal had denied them victory. West Ham made their way to Maine Road with just two points from five games, an embarrassing total for a side with three World Cup victors in its ranks. The Irons continued to spread the gospel of attractive, cultured football, but it was points that the team desperately needed.

City were smarting from a three-goal defeat at Villa Park and were up for a fight, looking to get back on track. As such it was not surprising that the home side had the better of the game in its early stages. The Hammers goalie, Standen, who had been criticised in the media after letting in a dozen goals in the opening games of the season, five of them at Leicester where Greenwood's boys lost 5–4, made three outstanding saves to keep the Manchester Blues at bay, allowing his club to weather the storm, although there were to be one or two more scares when gaps appeared in front of goal as centre-half Ken Brown, making his first appearance of the season in place of Eddie Bovington, was pulled out of position chasing the shadow of the elusive Mike Summerbee.

There were defensive lessons to heed – there were always some when the Hammers took the field – but in the pure art of football few could equal their flair and imagination. In the 22nd minute came a flash of tension and nerves. Hurst made a perfectly timed run to expose three City defenders, who were caught square. The big striker homed in to meet Boyce's superb diagonal pass and plant his shot clinically past keeper Harry Dowd. The impact was startling. Sissons and Brabrook took a grip on the midfield while Hurst constantly turned the City defence, switching play with raking crossfield passes while his charging forays through the middle posed more difficulties than the Manchester defence could handle. Byrne played with gazelle-like swiftness, dropping deep to pick up the ball, darting off on diversionary runs; the movement of the entire side was mesmerising. The parts seemed to have fallen into place as Peters, Boyce and Moore ran riot, changing roles and weaving patterns that bewildered their opponents. This was gorgeous, breath-taking play, full of quality, poise and style; an example of the 'beautiful game' at its most lovely. Boyce ran 20 yards to crack home Hurst's cross on the volley for West Ham's second. Sissons picked his spot through a crowd of players after Denis Burnett had set him up following a fine overlapping run down the right. Three goals between the 22nd and 42nd minutes destroyed Joe Mercer's team, who tried bravely to respond after the break although Standen kept them out. Hurst converted a solo effort to finish City, whose only reply came via Colin Bell.

Later that month Johnny netted a fine trawl of four goals and Geoff Hurst claimed two in the Football League's 12–0 win over the Irish League. This seemed to invigorate Budgie. In the same month he made it 2–0 to the cockney boys at Hillsborough with a diving header and on the first day of October West Ham, in 19th place in Division One, achieved their third win of the season (all their victories had taken place away from the Boleyn Ground). Sunderland were 1–0 ahead when the Rokermen's keeper Jim Montgomery flattened Hurst. John had to have two goes at the penalty that gave him the Hammers' first goal in a 4–2 victory at Roker Park. Two weeks later Budgie was on the mark again at Craven Cottage, but the Irons made their way home on the end of a 4–2 defeat.

West Ham picked up their first home League win at the end of October beating Nottingham Forest 3–1. This was achieved without either Byrne or Sissons in the side; both had been dropped for the game. John was back for the Guy Fawkes Day Upton Park confrontation with Fulham. Budgie didn't score but he was central to the 6–1 thrashing of the Cottagers. In one way or another he created Hurst's four hits and had a crucial hand in both the goals Martin Peters claimed.

Leeds larruped in League Cup

Having disposed of Spurs and Arsenal in the League Cup, the Hammers set up a meeting with Leeds United at the Boleyn Ground on 7 November. John, who all season had looked a shadow of the player that had graced the claret and blue in 1964–65, seemed to recapture something that night. He was to mastermind a historic demolition of the proud Peacocks with an irresistible performance.

Having won the Second Division title in 1963–64 Leeds had been Division One runners-up in the following two seasons and FA Cup finalists in 1965. The side was the foundation of the great Peacocks team of the seventies, founded on an intimidating defence. For a 10-year period from the mid-sixties few sides could match them, and during that time they would become League Champions and one of the most feared sides on the planet. Their ranks included England World Cup hero Jack Charlton and the fiery Scot Billy Bremner, as well as the uncompromising Norman 'bite your legs' Hunter, a fearsome and merciless tackler. Hunter might have played in Alf Ramsey's World Cup-winning team if anything had happened to Bobby Moore. Johnny Giles, Paul Madeley and Jimmy Greenhoff made up the midfield. Although missing regular 'keeper Gary Sprake, his deputy, David Harvey, did not disgrace himself. However, Budgie recalled:

> Big centre-backs never liked playing against me. To be fair I didn't
> like playing against them, but I had a habit of confusing them and
> playing around them. Leeds were one of the best teams in Europe in
> 1966 and although I didn't score I had a good game against Jack
> Charlton.

In fact Byrne destroyed Charlton that night and orchestrated one of the best-ever performances by a West Ham side.

Before the match the Leeds manager Don Revie, who, to the great cost of English football, succeeded Alf Ramsey as manager of the national side in 1974, told the press that his team would be playing for a draw, but in the event West Ham achieved their biggest-ever win in the League Cup, a feat that would become a fond tale in Hammers folklore.

In the opening minutes Bremner uncompromisingly challenged Moore, who was crunched against the Chicken Run fencing on the halfway line. Byrne and Ken Brown thundered in shots that Harvey somehow kept out in the opening minute but he could not prevent the Irons from opening the scoring just 60 seconds later when the mercurial Byrne, baffling the Leeds defence, slipped the ball out to Sissons on the left wing. Sissons, without a second thought, curled the ball into the net. After just 90 seconds Leeds were forced to abandon Revie's plan and push forward.

The referee's timepiece hadn't ticked to the 25th minute of the game when Byrne put Brabrook clear with a fantastic reverse pass and the winger went past Willie Bell before squaring the ball for Sissons to score his and the Hammers' second.

This was a turning point. Byrne had drawn the England centre-half to the edge of the penalty area, at which point Budgie froze on the ball. This confused Big Jack, who took root, unable to decide what to do. At that crucial moment Byrne flicked into life and sent the ball to Bovington, at which point Charlton looked a beaten man.

In a very similar move little more than 10 minutes later, Peters sent Brabrook away and the Irons' outside-right again picked out Sissons. A low shot beat Harvey and completed Johnny's hat-trick; before this game the young left-winger had only scored once in the 1966–67 season. The heat was not off. The Boleyn men were in some kind of feeding frenzy and four minutes before half-time Sissons, who now seemed to be everywhere, sent a long, penetrating cross into the Leeds area. The effort was half cleared and Brabrook picked up the ball; he sent it to the head of Martin Peters, who directed it straight to Byrne. Johnny's striker's instinct caused him to hit the ball first time and although Paul Reaney and Charlton made contact, Budgie's shot appeared to hit Geoff Hurst on the back of his legs and flew into the net; Hurst took the credit.

After the half-time entertainment treat of the British Legion band, Leeds changed shape for the second-half and the alteration seemed to have stopped the rot. But the sides were less than a quarter of an hour back on the park when Byrne lured Jack Charlton to the byline. John survived the centre-half's mad lunge and, displaying magnificent control, juggled the ball three times, then sent it to Hurst, who, after rounding a defender, drove the ball home low and hard. Leeds held out for another 20 minutes, but Revie's side were now in disarray and Peters was not slow to take advantage of their disorientation. He snaked round two defenders before smashing a powerful right-foot shot beyond the hapless, helpless Harvey. With nine minutes of the game remaining Jim Standen took a long goal kick that found the head of Brabrook. Byrne picked up the nod and turned the ball into the path of Hurst, who made no mistake, scoring West Ham's seventh goal.

Budgie had taken Jack Charlton, England's World Cup-winning centre-half, to pieces and to the cleaners. Johnny was to see this display by the Hammers as the '…finest exhibition of soccer by West Ham in London'. It was a virtuoso performance from Byrne. After the game he emerged from the players' entrance wearing a fashionable sheepskin coat and John Charles, the Canning Town-born West Ham defender, who had played well himself that night, shouted, 'Here he is – the wolf in sheep's clothing!' The smile on John's face was as magnificent as the skill he had shown that evening. The next morning's newspapers were unanimous in their praise of West Ham's emphatic rout of the Yorkshiremen and Byrne's display in particular. Not for the first time Budgie was described as 'The nearest thing we have in English football to a Di Stefano'. Billy Bremner was much more accurate in his appraisal of Byrne and the game:

> In those days, you didn't go to Upton Park and defend, that was not the way to play against Ron Greenwood's sides. You had to attack them. After a while people come to see that and that's why players liked to play against West Ham. When they beat us in the League Cup Johnny Byrne played great. He was a player that didn't seem to need room to turn or much time to pass or shoot. He was able to change direction or what he was going to do in an instant; he had a very agile footballing brain, so it was impossible to anticipate what he was going to do next. The way he could kill the ball with his chest and in the same movement volley it out to a winger was phenomenal. I mean other players could do that, but he done it so quick and in one continuous motion. Of course, the bigger the centre-half the better time he had playing them. He tortured Jack Charlton that day; murdered him. Jack didn't have a bad game; he was a real good defender. Not much went past Big Jack. It's just that

no one could have stopped Byrne that day. He seemed to relish battling one-to-one with big defenders. He'd back into them and then just twist away. It was not only the move but the way he moved. He was very much an individual, but whenever I played against him or saw him play he led his line and was always working to bring other West Ham or England players into the game. Budgie Byrne certainly was part of the difference between us and West Ham in that League Cup game, but he was always the player who made West Ham work; like when he had a good game, West Ham had a good game. But Leeds United played all wrong that night, right from the start, and that didn't help.

It had been Byrne's continual spray of accurate passes that had crippled Leeds, carving out openings that tore the Elland Road boys' normally solid defence to shreds. Billy Bremner had been given the job of marking Byrne, but when Budgie laid on the opening goal Bremner had been obliged to abandon his defensive duties to support the Leeds attack. It was then that Budgie began to carve up Jack Charlton. The humiliating defeat brought a vitriolic response from Revie. He told his shocked side: 'Don't ever lose to that team again!' And they didn't, until the League Cup replay at Elland Road in October 1971.

It was about this time that the West Ham board and management decided it would be a great idea to cram a friendly game in Egypt into their team's tight schedule. There were a more than a few 'dicky tummies' over the next few weeks.

Spurs splattered

Five days on from the triumph over Leeds the Hammers made their way to White Hart Lane for a League encounter. The Spurs team, managed by Bill Nicholson, included Pat Jennings, Cyril Knowles, Allan Mullery, Mike England, Dave Mackay, Jimmy Greaves, Alan Gilzean and Terry Venables and both teams provided a brilliant display of attacking football.

Jimmy Greaves hit the bar in the first minute, then scored from a penalty after being laid low and nailed by Eddie Bovington. Dagenham lad Greaves missed his second spot-kick of the game (the first time he had failed to put away a penalty as a Tottenham player) after Bobby Moore had handled the ball. Byrne seemed to be involved in everything except goalkeeping and covering the ball boys. He worked up and down the pitch, seemingly tireless, constantly animated and up for the fight.

In all Spurs struck post and bar three times. Budgie, Peter Brabrook, John

Sissons and Geoff Hurst scored for the Hammers, with Terry Venables and Alan Gilzean adding to the Greaves penalty. West Ham had inflicted defeat on the Spurs of North London in their own cockerel's roost, always a great event for East London, but the fact that this game was dubbed by the press the 'best game of the year', a term that included England's World Cup victory at Wembley, made it doubly pleasurable, even though one of West Ham's best defenders was the woodwork.

In a 3–0 Upton Park win against one-off-the-bottom Newcastle, Budgie scored West Ham's second with a penalty, making it four wins in a row for the Irons, who had netted 20 times in the course of those games. As such, it looked like things might be turning around, but in late November the Hammers, in 18th place in Division One, ran out onto the Elland Road pitch. In the final few seconds of the match Byrne came close to salvaging a point when he shaved Gary Sprake's bar, but in the end Leeds gained some revenge for the League Cup massacre at Upton Park, winning 2–1.

The League Cup win over Leeds had pushed West Ham into the quarter-finals of that competition and brought a visit to Bloomfield Road. Blackpool, propping up the First Division, destined to become Division Two by the sea, didn't really present West Ham with too many problems. Hurst got a couple in the first half, one from nearly 20 yards out, and Byrne grabbed a third early in the second period to finish a good 3–1 away win. West Ham were bound for their sixth Cup semi-final in four seasons.

Chelsea trauma

There were 47,805 Londoners at Stamford Bridge on 17 December 1966. Chelsea were in second place in the First Division table, just two points behind Manchester United, but they had only won three games at Stamford Bridge that term and West Ham, trailing the Pensioners by nine points, looked to be ahead early on when Byrne was called offside. However, the Hammers went ahead after 24 minutes. Ex-Chelsea man Brabrook knocked in a swinging corner from Sissons. The dexterous Byrne, who fought off two defenders after collecting a pass from Hurst, laid the ball in the path of Peters, who stabbed it home to make the score 2–0 to the Irons. Chelsea replied with a couple of chances but West Ham looked to be coasting, although in the dying minutes of the first half Tommy Baldwin scored for the Blues after a goalmouth ruck, picking up on a rebound off the post from a Bobby Tambling shot, set up by a Ron Harris free-kick.

Five minutes into the second half Tony Hateley scored from 25 yards out and on the hour Chelsea took the lead for the first and only time in the game with a Charlie Cooke goal, which, typical of the flamboyant Scot, was the best goal of the game; it was a terrific volley via Baldwin's delicate chip that had followed the hard work of Hateley. The Hammers drew level when, taking a pass from Brabrook, Sissons beat Bonetti with a curving drive sent in from the back of the penalty area. The 'Cat' sprang too early and the ball went through his paws.

With just over half an hour to go, Sissons got his second, a belter from 40 yards. Bonetti touched the ball but it was unstoppable. Two minutes later the Blues' skipper 'Chopper' Harris handled a Sissons cross in the area. Byrne took the penalty to see Bonetti make a marvellous save, turning it onto the post. But John coolly gathered the rebound, swerved past Eddie McCreadie and ex-Hammer Kirkup, to make it 5–3 to the Hammers.

Injury forced the tough-tackling John Charles to withdraw and West Ham brought on substitute Burnett. Charlo had controlled the dangerous Tambling for most of the afternoon, but now, freed from his shackles, Tambling began to cause havoc. With 10 minutes left Moore was judged to have fouled Hateley as Ken Brown failed to manage a John Hollins cross. Bobby Tambling scored from the spot but had shot before Standen had readied himself. Chelsea equalised in the last minute of injury time by way of Tambling's shin. It was really Charlie Cooke's cross shot that did the damage, following a characteristic raid down the left wing, dribbling a threatening path, passing through Moore as if he was a phantom. But the goal gave Tambling a Chelsea goalscoring record (129), beating Roy Bentley's mark. It was the last kick of the game.

During the 10-goal party at Stamford Bridge West Ham had been superior technically, but the all-out attacking strategy of the Hammers had left them open to counter-attacks. The fluidity of the passing and creative running had made the game an attractive spectacle. Chelsea were an exceptionally fit side and had relied on their front running, overlapping style with no orthodox wingers, while the Irons switched to a 3–3–4 formation with John Charles, Ken Brown and Bobby Moore at the back. Reporter John Steggles wrote that the match was, 'The greatest display of attacking football I have ever seen.' But maybe Chelsea manager Tommy Docherty summed up the match from a pragmatic point of view: 'It was great entertainment, but entertainment doesn't bring results.' Maybe he should have explained that one to Ron Greenwood.

West Brom... again

West Ham travelled to Blackpool again on Boxing Day. Budgie struck his side's third in the 80th minute and the Hammers went back to London 4–1 winners. The teams met again at Upton Park 24 hours later. John's 14th-minute strike separated the sides until there were just 10 minutes of the game left to play, at which point Bobby Moore made a rare strike from over 30 yards out. It was a glorious goal, but Mooro just turned his back and walked back into defence; he always saw goal celebrations as a waste of energy. Goals from Hurst and Peters followed.

West Ham had scored 32 times in just nine League games in November and December, but the League Cup seemed to become the focus for West Ham's season at this point. The Hammers won just one of their next eight games in the First Division. In retrospect the concentration on the possibility of a European Fairs Cup place looked ill-advised in mid-January. The first leg of the semi-final was something of a nightmare that began 60 seconds after the kick-off with a long ball into the Hammers area that met the head of Jeff Astle and it was 1–0 to West Bromwich Albion. Clive Clark doubled the lead and Astle went on to complete a hat-trick before half-time. West Ham, although the leading scorers in the First Division, did not have a reply.

Before the second leg of the League Cup final West Ham were taken to a replay by Third Division Swindon in the FA Cup. At the County Ground the Hammers were relieved to draw level in the 78th minute when Byrne's well-taken corner was converted by Sissons. But two late goals from the Robins disgraced West Ham. After the game Greenwood commented that 'This was the blackest month we have known.'

Things were destined to become even grimmer. At Upton Park West Ham looked to turn a 4–0 deficit into a passport for the inaugural Wembley League Cup final, making that event an all-London affair against Queen's Park Rangers. It was also a chance to force a fourth successive Cup Final appearance for Moore and Hurst and a hat-trick of Wembley finals for Martin Peters. These dreams looked a little more corporeal when the news came through that Ken Foggo would replace Astle in the Albion side and even more so when Budgie scored in the 13th minute, but despite passionate support and a true battling spirit, Hurst was surrounded by three defenders for most of the match and although he broke lose 10 minutes before half-time, Albion forced a 2–2 draw. For the second year running West Bromwich Albion had beaten West Ham over two legs in the League Cup.

Goodbye Johnny, goodbye

The let down of the League Cup semi-final was followed by a home draw against Sunderland. It was Budgie's 205th and final match in his familiar number nine Hammers shirt. The four goals the two teams shared included Johnny Byrne's 107th and last for West Ham. Byrne had a good game and John's career at Upton Park might have concluded with a win if Hurst had succeeded in netting the penalty given after Byrne was tripped in the box, but Geoff redeemed himself by heading home Budgie's last-minute cross that had, typically, been achieved from what seemed like an impossibly tight angle.

Budgie had only missed five games during his last months with West Ham. The side were in a respectable mid-table position, with no real fear of relegation, but also with no chance of winning anything. As such the club's decision to sell Byrne was partly based on his relatively erratic form, but his departure had much more to do with timing.

John was always to claim that if it hadn't have been for his weight and the problems with his knee he might well have stayed on at West Ham and eventually taken up management in the English context. However, reflecting on his career he confessed: 'I was probably not as dedicated as I should have been'. There was certainly something of the George Best about Budgie. However, he also made the point:

> I was targeted by some of the hardest men the game had seen; the big galoots, the likes of Jackie Charlton and Ian Ure. I shall remember Ure as long as I live. We were playing Arsenal at Upton Park. I had come out wide, very wide to the wing and knocked the ball back to Geoff Hurst, who whacked it into the net.
>
> It could have been 10 or 15 seconds later when Ure came storming into me. There was a wall around the Upton Park pitch and I was sent flying over the top of it and landed in the terraces. Four or five years after this, every time Ure returned to Upton Park he received a terrible roasting from the West Ham supporters.
>
> People like him didn't help me. Neither did the likes of Jackie Charlton.

From West Ham's point of view the late winter/early spring of 1967 was the best time to negotiate Byrne's transfer. During the season he had shown he was still able to play to a high standard, which had allowed the cost of his contract to appreciate relative to the previous season, when Byrne was seen by some not so much as an investment whose returns would gradually diminish from then on, but as a near hopelessly crocked striker with a propensity to party and put on weight. The potential fee he could command would not grow after the spring of 1967. At the same time West Ham were at a stage in the season and a position in the First Division to allow Greenwood to blood a replacement in the heat of competition.

There were rumours that Budgie would go to First Division Stoke City and link up with his former England colleague George Eastman, but Johnny Byrne was destined to return to his former club, Crystal Palace, who were, in 1967, plying their trade in the old Division Two.

For the record

Budgie's career at West Ham had been fast and furious. He had burnt like an inferno, hot and fast, but in the end he had quite literally burnt out. But it had been a glorious conflagration; a rollercoaster ride, a firework show of a time, full of colour, incident, drama, adventure and thrills. Just a glace at his West Ham career details betrays the hectic nature of his time at the top table of English football:

First game: 17 March 1962
Last game: 11 February 1967
Played 205 out of a possible 269 (76.58 percent)
Scored: 107 (better than one goal every two games)

If one needs a concrete example of the difference Johnny Byrne made to West Ham it helps to compare the club's statistical record with and without him:

West Ham with Johnny Byrne

	P	W	L	D	F	A	
1961–62	11	3	5	3	14	20	–6
1962–63	36	12	13	11	84	73	+11
1963–64	46	21	15	10	108	93	+15
1964–65	44	21	18	5	103	110	–7
1965–66	38	15	14	6	116	118	–4
1966–67	32	11	12	9	90	69	+21
Total	209	83	77	44	515	483	+32

Won: 39.23 percent of games

Lost: 36.84

Drew: 23.93

Scored: 2.36 goals per game

Conceded: 2.31 goals per game

210 points out of 418 = success rate of 50.02 percent

West Ham without Johnny Byrne

	P	W	L	D	F	A	
1962–63	13	6	5	2	27	18	+9
1963–64	10	3	3	4	19	19	
1964–65	10	5	4	1	20	18	+2
1965–66	24	10	8	6	45	48	–3
1966–67	5	4	1	0	11	4	+7
Total	73	28	21	13	122	107	+15

Won: 38.3 percent of games

Lost: 28.76

Drew: 32.94

Scored: 1.67 goals per game

Conceded: 1.46 goals per game

69 points out of a possible 146 = 47.26 percent success rate

Total

1961–62	11	3	5	3	14	20	–6
	49	18	18	13	111	91	+20
1963–64	56	24	18	14	127	112	+15
1964–65	54	26	22	6	123	128	–5
1965–66	62	25	22	15	161	166	–5
1966–67	37	15	13	9	101	73	+28
Total	269	111	98	60	637	590	+47

Won: 41.26 percent of games

Lost: 36.53

Drew: 32.21

Scored: 2.36 goals per game

Conceded: 2.18 goals per game

282 points out of 548 = 51.04 percent success

At first sight these figures seem to reveal little. However, if one compares the goal and win averages and the success rate of the Hammers when Byrne was present in the West Ham side to the same statistics for the matches he missed, an indication of the effect of his presence in is suggested. With John in the first team West Ham were more successful (based on two points for a win, one for a draw and none for a loss, consistent with Football League rules of the time, although the above figures include Cup matches) there being a 50.02 percent success rate with John and a 47.26 percent rating without him in the side. Goal average and difference figures demonstrate that, in the main and overall, the Hammers scored more goals when Byrne played; the team's victories were more emphatic, draws were higher scoring and there was more of a reply in defeat. This suggests a certain type of spirit was stirred when Johnny Byrne was in West Ham's ranks.

John's years with West Ham were a golden era for the club, and his career with the Hammers, although short, had been action-packed and successful:

March 1962	Johnny Byrne is transferred from Crystal Palace as part of a £65,000 deal, a record fee between English clubs.
February 1964	West Ham reach the semi-final of the League Cup (v Leicester, West Ham lose 3–6 on aggregate).
July 1963	West Ham become the International Soccer League Champions in the USA.
May 1964	West Ham win the FA Cup (v Preston North End, 3–2).
September 1964	First West Ham match in a European Competition (v La Gantoise in the Cup-Winners' Cup).
May 1965	West Ham win the European Cup-Winners' Cup (v TSV Munchen, 2–0).
March 1966	West Ham reach the final of the League Cup (v WBA, West Ham lose 5–3 on aggregate).
April 1966	West Ham reach the semi-final of the European Cup-Winners' Cup (v Borussia Dortmund, West Ham lose 2–5 on aggregate).
May 1966	Johnny included in England's World Cup Squad of 28. West Ham win the London five-a-side Championships with Johnny in the side.
July 1966	England win the World Cup. Bobby Moore, Martin Peters and Geoff Hurst, all West Ham players, take part. Hurst scores three and Peters one in the 4–2 win for England.

Budgie's swan song with West Ham had been the three-game, 17-goal celebration that started on Bonfire Night 1966 with the 6–1 rout of Fulham, then went on to crush Leeds, humble Spurs on their own turf and generate a bizarre 5–5 draw at Stamford Bridge a month later. This typified the spirit of West Ham with Budgie Byrne.

Like the first British European Cup-winning team, Glasgow Celtic, all of whom were born within 20 miles of Celtic Park, this West Ham side had grown up together; they understood each other, sang the same songs and laughed at the same jokes. In fact John played, during his entire first-team career at West Ham, with only 41 other professionals. The names of those he lined up alongside read like a who's who of West Ham United and English football in the mid to late sixties:

George Andrew	Trevor Dawkins	Bobby Moore
Dave Bickles	Brian Dear	Malcolm Musgrove
Peter Bennett	John Dick	Martin Peters
Jimmy Bloomfield	Alan Dickie	Eddie Presland
John Bond	Bobby Ferguson	Harry Redknapp
Ronnie Boyce	Bobby Howe	Brian Rhodes
Eddie Bovington	Roger Hugo	Alan Sealey
Peter Brabrook	Geoff Hurst	Tony Scott
Martin Britt	Joe Kirkup	John Sissons
Ken Brown	Bill Kitchener	Jim Standen
Jack Burkett	Lawrie Leslie	Ron Tindall
Denis Burnett	Bill Lansdowne	Derek Woodley
John Charles	John Lyall	Phil Woosnam
Ian Crawford	Colin Mackleworth	

The above assembly is no mean bunch. It includes all the members of the FA Cup and European Cup-Winners' Cup teams, several players who had or would win full caps and many more that had represented their nation at youth and Under-23 levels, as well as others who had gained selection for international squads.

Twenty percent of them became first-class managers or top coaches… and John was the best of them all.

Of course, as an England player he turned out with 31 of the very best, including most of the 1966 World Cup-winning side:

Armfield, J.C. (Blackpool)

Banks, G. (Leicester City)

Bailey, M.A. (Wolverhampton Wanderers)

Bridges, B.J. (Chelsea),

Charlton, J. (Leeds United)

Charlton, R. (Manchester United)

Cohen, G.R. (Fulham)

Crawford, R. (Ipswich Town)

Douglas, B. (Blackburn Rovers)

Eastham, G.E. (Arsenal)

Flowers, R. (Wolverhampton Wanderers)

Greaves, J.P. (Tottenham Hotspur)

Haynes, J.N. (Fulham)

Hinton, A.T. (Nottingham Forest)

Hunt, R. (Liverpool)

Kay, A.H. (Everton)

Melia, J.J. (Liverpool)

Milne, G. (Liverpool)

Moore, R.F.C. (West Ham United)

Norman, M. (Tottenham Hotspur)

Paine, T.L. (Southampton)

Robson, R.W. (West Bromwich Albion)

Springett, R.D.G. (Sheffield Wednesday)

Stiles, N.P. (Manchester United)

Swan, P. (Sheffield Wednesday)

Thompson, P. (Liverpool)

Thomson, R.A. (Wolverhampton Wanderers)

Waiters, A.K. (Blackpool)

Wignall, F. (Nottingham Forest)

Wilson, R. (Everton)

Young, G.M. (Sheffield Wednesday)

Byrne not only played with the best. His international appearances against Portugal, the Scottish sides of the sixties and Brazil, together with his European adventures with West Ham, ensured that he also encountered the some of best players to kick a ball in the history of the beautiful game.

Back to Palace

Greenwood had announced after the Cup defeats that changes were necessary. To that end Budgie Byrne returned to his former club after five years at Upton Park. Although it was clear that Byrne was past his best, the Crystal Palace board were keen to have him back at Selhurst Park. He was, for Palace, something of the past that could give them hope for the future. It was thought that he might bring modernisation with him, and there were some unexpressed hopes that he would eventually manage the side. Ron Greenwood was also keeping a promise. Unlike many players John did not make any money 'on the side' when he moved to Upton Park; that wasn't 'the West Ham way' and it certainly went against all of Greenwood's highly cherished principles. However, Greenwood had assured John that when the right time came for him to leave the Boleyn Ground he would make sure John would be looked after financially and Byrne's return to Crystal Palace offered more than would have been on offer at Stoke.

West Ham finished the season on a low note with seven defeats and a draw against Manchester City in the final game. The Hammers ended up in 16th place in the First Division table, although they were scoring goals all season. In fact only the Champions, Manchester United, scored more than West Ham in the League. The Irons got 80, and the Reds netted 84. However, the United defence let in just 45, while West Ham conceded 84. West Ham scored a hundred goals in all competitions. Geoff Hurst, who was voted Hammer of the Year, got 41 of these. Billy Bonds, the first of Greenwood's new intake, arrived on the last Saturday of the 1966–67 term. Bonds had been in the Charlton team that West Ham had defeated on their way to winning the London Five-a-Side Championships before the start of the season.

CHAPTER 14

Blistering Palace

J OHNNY Byrne returned to Crystal Palace for a fee of £45,000 in February 1967, just a few months after his fantastic display for West Ham against Leeds in the League Cup. It was a relatively high fee and, as Greenwood had promised, Budgie's departure from West Ham had been lucrative for him. But it also meant that the Hammers had paid £13,000 for half a decade of high-quality football from one of the best players of the era. Good business, but with stronger leadership West Ham could have got so much more from Johnny and he might have become one of the greatest players ever to emerge from English football.

John's return to Selhurst Park had much to do with Arthur Wait. He had been chairman of Crystal Palace when John first joined the club and was still in charge when Budgie returned to the site of his youthful glories. Wait and his board saw Byrne as having the qualities to push Palace into the modern era and at the same time as a 'name' that they hoped would pull supporters into the ground. However, as John admitted: 'I was thicker round the middle and the quick bursts had gone'.

Bert Head, who had taken over as manager of Crystal Palace in 1966, had no desire to have the flamboyant, opinionated and in his view 'over the hill' Byrne at Selhurst Park. Head remembered how Byrne had cockily torn his Swindon Town side apart in the League Cup and FA Cup in 1963–64. At the same time, although Head was to take Palace into Division One in 1969, for the first time in the club's history, he was a manager of the old school and as such was something of an anathema to a player like Johnny Byrne, who had worked with some of the finest managers in the English game; managers like Alf Ramsey and Ron Greenwood had consulted with John when he had played for them and looked to him for advice. As such the Head/Byrne combination was a partnership doomed from the outset. Some years later the former Hammers defender and Manchester City manager Malcolm Allison would replace Head at Sehurst Park. Allison and Byrne might well have been a perfect combination, both having astute footballing minds and sharing a love of soccer panache. However, John had to deal with Bert, who for Byrne did not provide the best example of managerial competence. According to Budgie: 'His knowledge of the game didn't tally with mine'. And satirising Head's rural origins he commented, 'I felt he would have been more suited to selling cattle'. John saw his new manager as something of a joke and Palace's position did, at times, seem tragi-comic.

BERT HEAD

Journeyman winger Mark Lazarus joined the club in the December after Byrne returned to Palace. He had done the rounds with London sides and was a widely travelled and experienced player. He had started with Leyton Orient, moved to Queen's Park Rangers and then was involved in a big transfer to Wolves. He returned to Rangers, then went to Brentford and back to Rangers before joining Palace. This was not the end of his roving, as in 1969 he completed the circle by going back to Brisbane Road. He was a big man for a wide player, quite roly-poly towards the end of his career, but his goals were always followed by his traditional celebration – a lap of honour. On one occasion Lazarus extended his festivities to a full three minutes and, as he ran round the field shaking hands with supporters, Budgie was left wondering whether Lazarus had done this for his benefit.

John understood that his best days were behind him but he had returned to Palace because he felt he had a lot of football left in him and that his experience could help the club where he had started out. However, good performances were few and far between and the crowd were cruel to their former hero. Thus the inevitable clash between Byrne and Head was not long in coming. Following a particularly poor game for Budgie, Bert called John to his office. Head, a big man physically, told Byrne, 'You're not playing too well, boy.' John, not really appreciating Head's tone, nevertheless thought it best not to be too confrontational and said to his manager, 'Well boss, I'm trying.' John used the term 'boss' because that was how Head required his players to refer to him, but Budgie resented Head's insistence on this. Byrne had been on first-name terms with Greenwood, Ramsey and Winterbottom and really couldn't place Head above these towering examples of managerial intellect, excellence and civility.

Head continued to complain but John interrupted the flow by saying, 'Boss, if we played to our strengths and weaknesses, then we'd have a bit of a chance'. The Palace side had responded to Byrne's presence by pumping balls all around the former England man and this was not something that Budgie saw as effective, given his style of play. Head looked his star striker straight in the eye and, in Budgie's words, '...with a nasty, savage look told me, "I don't need you. I don't need football".'

John had too much Irish in him and had spent too long in the East End to take that kind of goading. He leant over Head's big desk and responded: 'Well, if that's how you feel, why don't you do us all a favour and fuck off? Football would be better without you.'

From open-mouthed astonishment Bert went into something of a 'wobbly', to the extent that John was expecting to be physically assaulted. However, the confrontation ended with Budgie leaving the room. Head never learnt the skill of tolerating genius. It is perhaps a pity he was not able to do what Geoff Hurst had done. For Hurst: 'There was never a dull moment with Budgie around, but without his help it would have been a lot more difficult for me to have succeeded in my role.'

And it is true that Budgie could have done an awful lot for Crystal Palace.

Late bloom

John had something of an Indian summer in terms of his international career when in 1967 he was called into an English Football Association side as a late replacement. His weight problems were becoming more serious, to the extent that Alf Ramsey christened him 'the Toby Jug'. The team were classed as an FA eleven and were bound for Montreal, Canada, to play in a tournament against teams from Brazil, Russia, Mexico and Germany. Ramsey hadn't forgotten Budgie. He knew John would be good for team morale and an asset socially, but due to his difficulties in keeping his weight down Ramsey had not seen Byrne as a first-choice player in the party. However, the first game of the tournament was something of a shambles and Alf turned to Byrne. In response Budgie punished himself in training and helped England win the tournament.

This was to be a source of great pride to Budgie for the rest of his days.

It was during 1967 that the African Football Confederation argued at a FIFA congress that the FASA and the apartheid South African government conspired to:

1. Keep 'non-racial' soccer teams and leagues out of municipal sports grounds.
2. Finance 'establishment' black teams with the help of big business.
3. Persecute anti-apartheid sporting officials.

It was becoming clear to everyone, inside and outside of South Africa, that the world was not going to accept the notion of racially segregated sport and that the vast majority of South Africans, black and white, knew that this congress would be a powerful signal that archaic and inhumane regimes like the one that ruled South Africa had no future. Even apartheid's most vociferous supporters could see the time was coming for some strategy of damage limitation.

Flight to Fulham

Byrne lasted just over a year at Selhurst Park. He managed to score only five goals in 36 Second Division matches before March 1968 when his opportunity

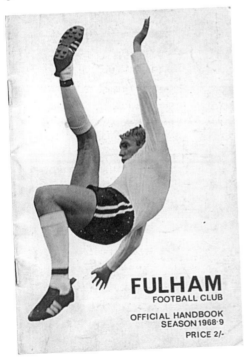

FULHAM
FOOTBALL CLUB
OFFICIAL HANDBOOK
SEASON 1968-9
PRICE 2/-

to escape Head's domination came. During the last part of the 1967–68 season the Palace team were returning to London from Blackburn. Having changed trains at Manchester, they met up with the Fulham side in the refreshment car of a Euston-bound express. After a short discussion, Bobby Robson, then manager of Fulham (who would go on to manage a string of clubs in England and Europe as well as the English national side, before his tenure at Newcastle) signed Byrne on the train for £25,000 just 15 minutes before the transfer deadline, in a last-minute bid to stave off relegation from the First Division. John recalled: 'I only took five minutes to say yes'. It was hoped that John would revive his goal-scoring touch by linking up with his great friend and schoolboy hero Johnny Haynes, the man who gave Byrne his 'Budgie' nickname.

John made his debut for the Cottagers on 23 March 1968 in the home game against Arsenal. The Gunners came away with an easy 3–1 victory. For John:

> Fulham had been the laughing stock of English soccer for a number of years; this might have had something to do with the comedian Tommy Trinder being the chairman of the club. Like West Ham it was a friendly club but without the professional organisation and discipline I had got used to at West Ham. Robson had been a player at the club but as a young manager he had a hard time with players like John Dempsey, who would later join Dave Sexton at Chelsea. Dempsey was a manager's nightmare. Whatever was arranged for training he would mess up. If you had hurdles to go over he'd smash them up. If there were balls in the middle of the field he'd kick them out of the park into the river. He was never on time for training and Robson used to fine him £1 for every minute he was late, but it didn't do much good.

Around the time of Byrne's move to Craven Cottage the FASA, in an attempt to have the FIFA suspension lifted, organised a match between (white) Highlands Park and (black) Orlando Pirates in Swaziland. However, the South African Minister of the Interior threatened to deny passports to all participants and fans and this caused the match to be cancelled. The effect of this was the further erosion of FASA's relationship with FIFA, the latter having granted permission for the match to be played.

As hard as Robson tried it seemed that Fulham's fate was sealed. Haynes, like Byrne, was coming to the end of his long and distinguished career and Fulham crashed from the First to the Third Division in two years. John spent 12 months at Craven Cottage, scoring two goals in 19 appearances (three as substitute), mostly playing as a central defender. His final game in Britain was, perhaps fittingly, played at Selhurst Park in April 1969. The result allowed Palace to win a place in Division One for the first time in their history, but under the dubious leadership of Bert Head they lasted just four seasons. By 1976 they were again a Third Division side.

After their relegation Fulham started looking for new blood and it seemed that John was not in the club's long-term plans. Byrne had been putting on even more weight and there was a lot more of the 5ft 8in Byrne than the 11st 7lb Budgie of 1964 vintage. There was also concern about his knee and doubt that it would withstand another long English season. John remembered the conclusion of his playing career in England:

> Fulham finally gave me a free transfer. Basically it was because they were economizing and, although they wanted to renew my contract, I would have to take a cut in my wages. I couldn't accept this, as I was a family man with four children. It was alright for Johnny Haynes. He accepted the cut, as he was still single. So by my not resigning, the club were obliged to give me a free transfer.

Looking to other shores

In May 1969 John was playing snooker in a London cricket club, where he spent much of his free time during periods of injury and between the conclusion and start of the English football seasons. As he played he was conscious of the very limited options he had in the English game. He knew the injury to his knee had finished his chances of playing football at the top level in England, and would perhaps deny him any part in the professional game. In the middle of this contemplation of his future he was given a message that his wife, Margaret, had telephoned asking him to contact her urgently. He got to the telephone and while he was still puzzling about how she had tracked him down, Margaret said 'Johnny, (she never referred to him as Budgie) Bobby Keetch wants you to phone him at this number in Durban'. At first John thought she had said 'Durham', having no idea where Durban was. Budgie knew Keetch well; he had played for Fulham, Queen's Park Rangers and as an amateur at Upton Park. John got Keetch's number from Margaret and booked a call to Durban (as had to be done in those days).

The call arrived an hour later and the familiar cockney tones of Keetch heralded what was to be the beginning of Budgie's South African soccer odyssey. The former Fulham man invited John to Durban that weekend with a view to turning out for Durban City on the Sunday. When Bobby told him of the sun, wine and women it struck Budgie that Keetch hadn't changed much since his days in English football, but the description immediately appealed to Byrne.

Keetch told John that the game in South Africa was of a fair standard, but as a former English international Budgie would be an instant draw and association football in Africa desperately needed players of Byrne's calibre. Any complications seemed to be overcome when Keetch let John know that there was a return ticket waiting for him at Heathrow, that he would meet Byrne at Johannesburg airport and from there they would fly down to Durban together. All Budgie had to do was pack a bag and his boots and get on the plane in London. The plan was to spend a day or two in Durban, play for City, and John would be back home by Tuesday. Everything would be paid for.

Byrne knew of players who, having come to the end of their best years, had taken up the game in Hong Kong and Australia. His former England and Fulham teammate Johnny Haynes had himself visited South Africa. Budgie had also been to Africa with West Ham, and his former West Ham teammate and the then manager of Norwich, John Bond, had also journeyed to that part of the world. When Budgie got back to the snooker table he asked if anyone knew anything about South Africa. No one did.

John obtained clearance to play in South Africa from Fulham and the English FA He then told Margaret that he was going to South Africa on business, packed his bag and made for the airport to board a Boeing 707. Within a few hours he had opened the gateway to a new life and was standing in Jan Smuts Airport, Johannesburg. True to his word Keetch was waiting for him. During the hour's flight to Durban Keetch told John that the Sunday match against Highland Park was a big game and as such there would be around 30,000 spectators.

Budgie had no way of knowing that the weekend visit to Durban would be the start of a new era for him, one that would bring success in more arenas than just on the field of play. He would never have guessed that as the 1970s began he would lead Durban City to South African Cup and League triumphs. He would certainly have laughed if he had been told that what started as a weekend jaunt would be extended to a 31-year stay in South Africa, that it would become his home and he would spend the rest of his days under African skies.

Johnny Byrne successfully takes a penalty for the Hammers at Upton Park.

John Charles, West Ham's first black player.

Hammers players ready to board the team bus, c.1965. Budgie is in the driving seat of course.

Another mid-1960s Hammers photo call. Back Row: Brown, Bond, Peters, Standen, Burkett, Moore. Front Row: Brabrook, Boyce, Byrne, Hurst, Sissons.

Martin Peters, the maestro.

Bobby Moore, captain of all the Hammers.

Geoff Hurst pictured after the 1966 success the Hammers trio enjoyed with England.

Martin Peters, at the same time.

Bobby Moore.

Budgie on 23 August 1966, a day when he scored at Highbury but West Ham lost 2-1.

Johnny Byrne in October 1966 during pre-match warm-up, with Ronnie Boyce also pictured.

West Ham 1966–67.

Jim Standen clears the ball over his bar in a 3–2 home defeat by Everton on 8 October 1966.

Budgie limbering up before a match in October 1966.

Martin Peters tangles with Liverpool's Roger Hunt at Anfield. Both were players in England's winning World Cup team of 1966.

Moore leads the travelling Hammers out, with Johnny Byrne behind (as usual).

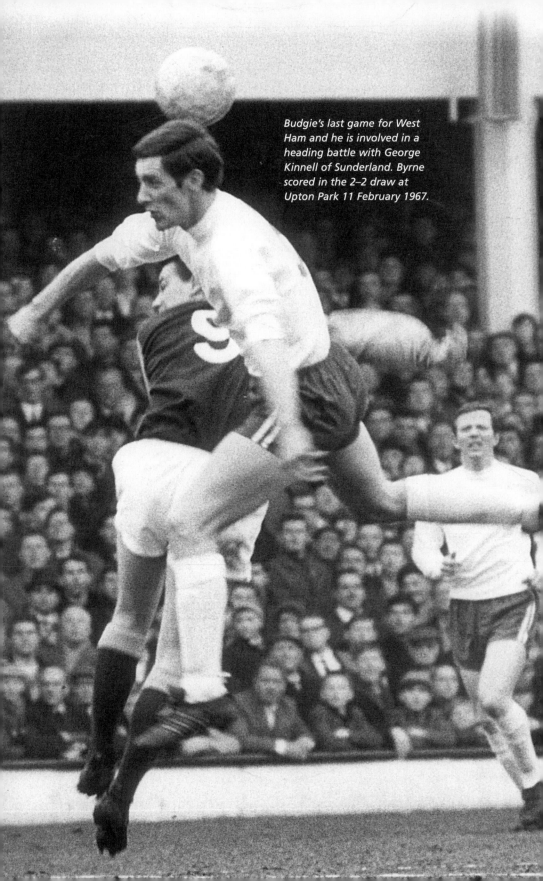

Budgie's last game for West Ham and he is involved in a heading battle with George Kinnell of Sunderland. Byrne scored in the 2–2 draw at Upton Park 11 February 1967.

Geoff Hurst.

Mark Lazarus of Crystal Palace in early 1969.

John Bond (extreme left) and Ken Brown (second right) moved on to the less salubrious stage of Torquay United in the late 1960s.

Johnny Haynes, who had coined the name 'Budgie', was still at Fulham when Byrne moved there in 1968.

Willie Morgan in mid-1970s action with Fulham's Alan Mullery.

A Fulham team group that includes Johnny Byrne on the front row, between Johnny Haynes and Frank Large.

CHAPTER 15

A Phoenix Rising

A S THE 1970s began, perhaps, if John had known about all the difficulties of playing football in South Africa that would come in the next quarter of a century, he might have thought twice about taking up the challenge of working in football in that country. Bobby Keetch recalled:

When Budgie came to South Africa I had not been playing in the country very long myself. It was nothing like playing in England. Things happened almost from day to day. A lot of it was about having a good time, although a professional player will nearly always do his best on the field, the conditions at times and the life around the game made it all a bit disorganised. But it suited a lot of us at the time. There were players who fitted in there that just wouldn't have fitted in anywhere else and we pleased a lot of people.

When John finally arrived in Durban he was confronted by an environment and culture very different from the East End of London or his Surrey roots. It was very much an African city, with strong elements of its colonial past still quite tangible.

Probably the first European to see the bay around which Durban was to develop was Vasco da Gama on his pioneering sea voyage to India in 1497. The Zulu called the area, in the Province of KwaZulu-Natal, the ancestral home of the Nguni people, Tekweni. The region is famed for its mild, sunny winter climate and abundance of vegetation encouraged by a subtropical climate that provides sunshine for at least 320 days a year. Temperatures range from 16°C to 25°C during the winter months of June, July and August. Summer temperatures can reach a humid 32°C as the equatorial current of the Indian Ocean, which the city overlooks and is the source of a vast stream of warm, blue water flowing south-west through the Mozambique Channel, makes itself felt. Seawater temperatures along the coast are Mediterranean in summer at 24°C, but even in the winter they seldom fall below 19°C – 10°C above the Mediterranean in the same season. The warm coast, decked in radiant golden sands, together with the lush sub-tropical greenery surrounding the city, immediately seduced Budgie.

The city of Durban derives its name from Sir Benjamin D'Urban who was governor of the Cape Colony at the time of the first successful colonial settlement in 1835. Over the years the city was colonised by Dutch and then English traders and Indian labourers who were brought to Durban in the 19th century to work in the emerging sugar industry. With them came traders, whose descendants form a large percentage of Durban's modern population. One can still see the Sugar Terminal, the crowning achievement of an industry that indelibly changed the face of the former Zulu realm. From the time 'sweet sand' was offered to King Shaka by early British adventurers in exchange for hunting rights, to the arrival of indentured plantation labour from India and the re-moulding of the coastal vegetation, sugar has remained an omnipresent force that took Durban into the modern world.

Durban was and is a major gateway to Africa and is the largest and busiest port city on the continent. Due to this, the South African road network seems to lead to Durban. The city itself has wide, clean streets that emanate from the Beachfront and run to the heart of Durban's Central Business District. When Johnny arrived in the city segregation had established separate business districts, of which 'Indian Town' was perhaps the most notable. This area was filled with curry houses and jewellers, and was a place where the purveyors of exquisite silk-and-gold attire rubbed shoulders with mendicants, holy men and street-hawkers.

Durban's first and longest-running sports venue is Greyville Racecourse, which has been part of the city's social life since the mid-19th century. It hosts the Gold Cup and Durban July Handicap, two of the country's biggest horse-racing events. In 1935, the centre of Greyville's circular track was sculpted into the Royal Durban Golf Club's championship course. This 6,000m, 71-rated venue offers the rare experience of pausing on fairway or green as the field thunders by on race-days. When Budgie got to Durban Greyville was a favourite training venue for Durban City Football Club.

By the late 1960s South Africa had a long tradition of attracting British players of the highest calibre – the likes of Stanley Matthews and Danny Blanchflower – and from the development of the NFL a steady stream of professionals had come from the English and Scottish Leagues, including a number of former West Ham players, like Keetch, Eddie Lewis, Dave Sexton and Andy Malcolm. Others Hammers would follow Budgie: Geoff Hurst, Joe Kirkup, Bobby Moore, Eddie Presland, John Sissons, Alan Stephenson, Trevor Dawkins, Perry Suckling, Johnny Ayris, Ted MacDougall and Tony Smith would all spend time playing or coaching and managing in South Africa.

Bobby Keetch, who had arrived in South Africa to join Durban City at the start of the 1969 season, wanted Budgie to come to Durban because of his exemplary record in England that by itself made an impressive CV:

Club	Season	League		Internationals	
		Matches	*Goals*	*Matches*	*Goals*
Crystal Palace	1956–57	14	1		
	1957–58	28	7		
	1958–59	45	17		
	1959–60	41	16		
	1960–61	42	30		
	1961–62	32	14	1	
West Ham	1961–62	11	1		
	1962–63	37	9	1	2
	1963–64	33	24	7	6
	1964–65	34	25	2	
	1965–66	23	9		
Crystal Palace	1966–67	14	1		
	1967–68	22	4		
Fulham	1967–68	5			
	1968–69	14	2		
Total		395	160	11	8

Team	Appearances	Goals
England Under-23	7	6
Football League	3	0
Total	10	6

On arrival in Durban, Keetch and Byrne were met by Durban City officials including Norman Elliott, known as 'The Silver Fox' within South African football. Elliott had founded the club in May 1959 on a budget of £500, half of which he had borrowed from his brother. Over time City had become one of the best sides in South Africa and had brought a number of fine players to the country to wear the blue and white hoops of City. The 'Banana Boys' had a brief but glittering history, regularly winning honours in the 'non-coloured' sphere of South African football from the very start. Durban City had won the first NFL Championship in 1959 and only lost the title in a play-off with Highland Park having finished the league schedule level on points with Highland. City's record in knock-out competitions, like the Castle Cup and the National Bowl, was also impressive:

Durban City honours up to the arrival of Johnny Byrne 1959–69

Year	Honours
1959	NFL Champions
1960	NFL Runners-up; Castle Cup
1961	NFL Champions; National Bowl
1962	Castle Cup
1964	NFL Runners-up; Castle Cup; National Bowl
1968	Castle Cup; National Bowl

The club also shared the Champion of Champions competition, which brought together the major trophy-winning sides, three times and won it outright once in the early sixties. Durban had a record of good results in other competitions like the Benson and Hedges Cup, the Coca-Cola Shield and the BP Cup.

Although a 'white' club, competing in segregated competitions, much of Durban City's support came from the local Indian community and Byrne was introduced to the non-white supporters' club committee, who presented him with traditional garlands. Seven hours of negotiations followed and at the end of it John had no idea what fee he was to be paid for his services, Keetch having acted as his broker.

There was no time for acclimatisation to the sultry, mid-season conditions of Sunday soccer in South Africa. John's expectations of the South African sun were soon dampened. His first visit to the country was during a period when, in his words, 'it rained fit enough to drown a duck' and it had been like that for three days. For all this, Budgie enjoyed the game at the packed New Kingsmead ground, but he was exhausted at its conclusion. His side lost 2–3 to Highland, but Budgie was impressed by the standard of the game and he decided to extend his stay for a further week. City's next match was against local and traditional rivals Durban United, a game that provoked a deal of passion in the city.

The following Sunday brought Budgie's first taste of a South African local derby. The love/hate feelings between the camps that made up the 30,000 crowd were palpable. United destroyed Byrne and his side 5–1. But even that score flattered City. Budgie could not remember being part of a side so comprehensively beaten. However, having come to the end of the 'temporary agreement' cobbled together between Elliott and Keetch, John entered personal negotiations with 'The Silver Fox' and eventually, after 10 days in Durban, signed a two-year contact with City. His signing on fee was £5,000 but the contract virtually committed him to his new club for the rest of his life. This would turn out to allow Elliott to cause John grief in the future.

John telephoned Margaret and told her that they were going to live in South Africa and asked her to organise their property and arrange for their four children, Kevin, David, Mark and Karen, to be taken out of school. Before flying back to Britain to finalise arrangements, John made one more appearance in South Africa, but as far as he was concerned, this one almost cost him his life. He was asked to referee a game between two black sides at the Merebank Stadium. Budgie blew the whistle, calling the team captains together for the spin and to ask them to produce their team sheets. At this point one skipper refused to show Byrne his sheet, as he did not want Budgie to manage the game. Suddenly the crowd started to jeer at Byrne and there were cries of 'OFF! OFF! OFF!'

Within seconds a group of a dozen tough-looking policemen were on the field to escort John out of the ground and he left Merebank with something more than due haste. A friend, used to the foibles of the South African game, witnessed the events and later told John that it was fortunate that Budgie had not chosen to start the game. He told Byrne, 'The crowd would have swarmed onto the field and you could have been killed'. John had seen the nature of South African soccer, red in tooth and claw. The following morning he flew back to London, but unperturbed he was back in Durban three weeks later. In John's first season City finished sixth in the league and reached the semi-final of the National Bowl. John was to spend four years with Durban City.

Good-day sunshine

The modern soccer season in South Africa is played out between August and May but in the 1960s the season started in January and concluded during

October, although sometimes the playing term would stretch to November. However, such was the lack of competition that two teams could find themselves playing each other half-a-dozen times in a season. When John arrived in South Africa the crowds had begun to drift away from soccer and were picking their games rather than giving consistent support. At one time there were four clubs fighting for survival in the Durban area within a 50-mile radius: the three Durbans, City, United and Spurs, and Maritzburg. As such support was hard won.

The more one looks at football in the late 1960s and early 1970s in South Africa the picture that emerges is a sort of 'Dodge City' of soccer. It seemed to be dominated by characters that operated in, at times, outrageous fashion, driven by a cross between entrepreneurial spontaneity and backs-to-the-wall adventurism. The Maritzburg general manager, Barry Mills, who was at the helm of that club when they won the Castle Cup in 1968, was a fine example of this spirit. As a player he had been transferred from Durban City to Municipals, the side that would later became Maritzburg, for a 'fee' of... an

DURBAN CITY
vs
HIGHLANDS PARK
Kick-off 3.00 p.m. at New Kingsmead
Sunday, 13th August, 1967

CURTAIN RAISER D.&.C.F.A. League (Under 14)
Durban City vs Addington
Kick-off 1.45 p.m.

electric fan. In his managerial role Mills used a local African magic man 'Doctor Sunshine' in his game preparations, who seemed quite effective. The good doctor had been in attendance at Budgie's second South African game and claimed a deal of credit for the trouncing of City. However, before a subsequent match between the two clubs Elliott had found a former Sumo wrestler knocking around Durban and introduced him as 'Professor Chu' when he rolled onto the pitch to throw 'sacred salt' at the Sunshine man, to 'rid the arena of evil spirits'. It seemed to work as City won the match, and United hit their opponents' bar and had a goal disallowed. However, when the obese Chu moved on and took his powers elsewhere, Doctor Sunshine claimed that he had caused the 'foreign devil' to disappear, and restored faith in himself. It was later rumoured that the Sumo was really a former Tongan rugby player who was a working for an old Springbok pal selling sporting goods all over South Africa and, following employment by Elliott, had made a fair secondary income doing his Sumo bit on his travels around the country. However, this profitable enterprise came to a sudden and chaotic end when he was chased, fearing for his life, from a grudge croquet encounter between two Indian sides in Timbuktu.

Apparently Prof. Chu's saline antics had temporarily blinded a Hindu fakir who had been brought in by one of the rival teams to lay a curse on their opponents. The holy man, one Chandu McKrinnon, seemingly propelled by his 'brave heart' blood and straightforward agony, had grabbed a croquet hammer to sightlessly lash out at the lumbering South-Seaer. Chu, dodging furiously, responded with the plea, 'Keep yer fucking hair on Gandhi', delivered with a strong Antipodean accent. At this point, having offended both sets of players (unlike Elliott the team he was working for had really thought he was some kind of Shinto shaman) the sham Sumo took flight. In his rush to flee the scene the Tongan trampled a Buddhist monk and the ensuing mêlée escalated into a minor riot, but also created enough of a diversion to cover his escape.

As the 1970s began professional teams in South Africa didn't play on the same days. The vastness of the country meant that there were differences from day to day in conditions and the state of pitches depending on where one was in the country. A team might have found itself playing on a cool and rainy evening in Cape Town in midweek, and on the weekend sweltering in a packed stadium on a hot and humid Johannesburg day, then, a few days later, being required to deal with the altitude in the Transvaal. Not having the luxury of acclimatisation, some teams with more knowledgeable staff, like Byrne, went to altitude as late as possible to minimise effects. But these considerations made results and form unpredictable; a side could be well beaten in conditions that were alien to them, but they would reverse the form on their own turf. Often when John's side played away he would advise his colleagues to keep the ball on the ground, to slow the game down, so allowing themselves time to get some understanding the pitch and how the ball was reacting. This was an example of his knowledge of the game picked up from touring with England and West Ham and during the 1970 season Byrne's presence brought a level of professionalism to the Durban City set-up that had been missing before his arrival. This was supplemented when the former Fulham and England skipper,

Johnny Haynes .

Johnny Haynes, joined forces with his former England pupil. However, for Haynes it was a new lease of life. He remembered:

Budgie was instrumental in my coming out to South Africa after I had been given a free from Fulham and I have never regretted the move... I flew into Durban on a Tuesday morning and Elliott, immediately wanting his 'pound of flesh' from me, decided that I was to be in his line-up against Arcadia that night. Despite the long flight and the Durban heat I managed to last about an hour. That was my introduction to football in South Africa.

But Haynes could see that Byrne's playing days were numbered: 'At the time of my arrival Budgie was playing for Durban City but I realised that he couldn't carry on much longer due to his weight problem.'

Byrne described Johnny Haynes as having 'a built-in radar screen'. Haynes was Byrne's schoolboy hero and it was always his dream to become a professional and play alongside the England skipper. For Byrne:

Johnny Haynes was a great player. He was better player than Matthews, Greaves or Pelé. He led England in my first international game. He was difficult to play with, his reading and passing and know-how were so advanced that he did the unexpected and expected other players to know what he was going to do or what he wanted them to do. He could split a defence open with perfect passing that was the best I've ever seen.

Haynes was a professional, a purist and a perfectionist. John pointed out that:

He gave nothing less than 100 percent but maybe his greatest weakness was that he expected the same from others. He would get the hump with a player if a pass was inaccurate or if the bloke was not where he wanted him to be when he sent the ball in their direction.

On many occasions, in English football and in South Africa, Haynes let his temper get the better of him. For all that, although he liked a good time as much as any player, Haynes at the age of 40 was still a great credit to the game and a model professional. Byrne was always of the opinion that young players should model their technique on Haynes's style.

Johnny Haynes was born in Edmonton, London, on 17 October 1934. He played for England as a schoolboy and at youth level before gaining eight Under-23 caps. He turned out for his country on 56 occasions and also played for England 'B' and Football League sides. He might be thought of as English football's first real icon. He was the first British player to earn £100 a week and as England captain he had a celebrity girlfriend and marketing deals. But nowadays talking to Johnny does not involve fighting your way through a barrage of lawyers and agents.

Today he lives in a smart maisonette and finishes work at 11am. Haynes was in the vanguard of the Jimmy Hill-led emancipation from the maximum wage for footballers in 1961, but although now a pensioner he is still working for his third wife Avril. They run a dry cleaning firm and a contract cleaners together, rising at 4am each day and going to bed at 9pm.

> I was supposed to have been retired since I was 40, but that's all
> changed since I came to Edinburgh, and I quite enjoy driving around
> town when there are no cars around.

Haynes was a midfield visionary who could direct the ball with either foot from all points of the compass on to the head or boot of a colleague; he had the ability to drop his shoulder and drift past players on either side and he could score goals. He signed for Fulham as a junior and became professional with the club in May 1952. For most of the 17 years after that he was regarded as the club's best-ever player and thought of as a genius.

Budgie recalled seeing Haynes as a boy and being mesmerised by his skills. But these were hard-won treasures. Long after everyone else had finished training Haynes was still kicking balls from the half-way line on to a towel in the far corner. For Byrne, Haynes was: '...an inspiration, a perfectionist. One of the greatest footballers ever. He had it all.'

At 69 Haynes looked years younger than his age. Thirty years on from his playing days he was only 14lbs heavier than when he turned out for Durban

City. As he approached his seventieth year he still worked out regularly, but as in his playing days he remained a modest man.

In his long career with Fulham, his only league club, Haynes ran his midfield patch with a brand of autocracy that might have been compared to the Foreign Legion. At Craven Cottage he was unquestioned, even by the volatile Jimmy Hill or the dynamic Bobby Robson. It was the same with England: as captain, Haynes was indisputably in charge. On one occasion, three of his Fulham colleagues, Jim Langley, George Cohen and Alan Mullery, turned up just 10 minutes before a league match against Leeds United, having got lost after deciding to walk to the ground after their pre-match meal. Haynes tore into Langley in the dressing-room, but Fulham won 4–0, although the then teenagers Cohen and Mullery almost attacked their skipper because of the verbal abuse he gave them during the game.

Off the field Johnny Haynes was a different person. He was modest but very much a woman's man. One of his girlfriends was film actress Janet Scott and like Budgie he was partial to 'a suck of the sauce bottle', although unlike Byrne, Haynes was always mindful of the possible consequences of his behaviour, certainly after he became captain of England. He confessed:

> Sure, I lived the life. We had our fun but I wasn't a mug. I had a drink with the boys and went out now and again, nothing serious. There was never any scandal. When I became England captain from 1960–62, I knew I had to behave myself. I still went out but you had to be careful of what you did and who you did it with. It was part of the job. I never dodged training. Jimmy Hill and I were the best trainers in the business at Fulham. He'd run all day and all night if you let him.

> We'd all sorts of people at Fulham. One of my big mates was Bobby Keetch. Now he was a real man about town. After games, we'd go to a local in the King's Road, but Bob would be off with his briefcase to spend the weekend in Paris. He wasn't a big earner, he wasn't a star performer, he was a good pro who only played for Fulham and QPR, but he knew people outside the game. He was interested in art galleries and things like that.

> I never got married until I was 35, but did all right in that department. I pulled a few when I was younger. In all, I had a fabulous life, but I realised that it wouldn't go on forever and was all right as a consequence. Of course, it was probably easier in those

days to get away with anything like that. Now things are so covered by the press that if you put a foot out of place, somebody finds out about it.

A good night out, usually on Wednesdays, consisted of a couple of drinks in the Twenty-One Club in Curzon Street, followed by a visit to the Astor Club, which was populated by the most celebrated villains in London. Haynes recalled that he was on nodding terms with the Kray twins and a doorman called Sulky.

Haynes lived with his parents until he married for the first time. He bought a beautiful house in Epsom in his £20-a-week days and asked his mum and dad to leave their council flat in North London to live with him.

> It was a good influence having them there and they had a lovely life. They were a great mother and father 'cos they gave me everything they could afford. They always had football gear for me when things were expensive. You must remember that I started playing as a schoolboy just after World War Two. They always found the money. I never forgot that. They never inhibited me when they lived at my house. I had my S-type Jaguar and I got home when I got home. Sometimes I took girls back – not to stay, mind – but my parents were fine about it.

In the early to mid-1960s Johnny Haynes was the most recognisable face in football. He advertised Brylcreem and was the focal point of a Milk Marketing Board campaign. This brought him another £5,000 a year.

> I was the Beckham of my day, and was probably bigger than any of my managers, but it never occurred to me that I was. I never abused it. If you start thinking that way, you're setting off on a slippery slope. I was certainly the highest-paid footballer in the UK. I think it did other footballers a favour as well. Instead of going in for 30 or 40 quid a week, they'd go in a lot stronger. They had something to barter with.
>
> When I got my money, there was outrage in some quarters. There were a lot of people in the Football League who were absolutely mortified that the maximum wage was finished. They fought tooth-and-nail not to let it go, but Jimmy Hill simply wouldn't take 'no' for an answer, and in the end we won quite comfortably. People never said anything to me, but you could tell by their manner. The Football League secretary, Alan Hardaker, was very bitter.

Funnily enough, I didn't get a lot of letters on the subject. The only letters you usually get as a footballer are for autographs. In fact, I still get them. At least two a day come through that letterbox. I don't know whether it's the internet or not, but they know my address. It's a surprising amount of mail for someone of 69 who hasn't kicked a ball for 30-odd years. It makes me very proud.

Over nearly two decades Haynes turned out 658 times in Fulham's first team in both League and Cup matches, scoring 158 goals. His England career ended in September 1962 when the car in which he was being driven by a woman friend skidded on the Blackpool tramlines and collided with a vehicle. Ironically, he was making his way back to the team hotel to keep a 10.15pm curfew.

I was in hospital for three weeks and the main damage was to the cruciate ligament in my knee. I spent the next year getting myself as right as I could. I was 27 and it was a very sad end to my England career, but at least I had another seven years playing for Fulham... although I wasn't really fit.

Just before his international career finished Haynes led his country to a 9–3 win over Scotland at Wembley. The memory of that match still brings a smile to his face, but he is a man generous in victory:

I should have said something to Frank Haffey [the Scottish goalkeeper] that day because there were a few others to blame, don't worry about that. But you're so over the moon with what you've done, you don't think of other people's problems.

At that time Fulham were having more than their share of problems and managers were coming and going at Craven Cottage at an alarming rate. Haynes looked back on Bobby Robson's reign at the club:

He struggled for a long time, couldn't get a job anywhere. Then, fortunately, the Ipswich job came along and he went from strength to strength. He's had a terrific career since and I'm delighted for him. He's finished up a knight. He didn't get a knighthood for what he done on the playing field.

When Bobby Robson was sacked, the chairman Sir Eric Miller asked Haynes to take over as player-manager. From the start it was not a role he relished:

I still wanted to play and I didn't think you could do the two. I said I'd do it until they found somebody else, yet I jacked it in after a month. I'll never forget my first game which we won 5–1 against Blackpool. It was a tremendous feeling but it didn't last.

We had a game at Fulham and were struggling for goalkeepers. We put in a young guy and we got beaten 6–1. He had a nightmare but it wasn't his fault, he just wasn't ready. I sat on the touchline and thought to myself: 'You can't do this job 'cos these things are going to happen and there's nothing you can do about it'.

Haynes has lived in Edinburgh since his return to Britain from South Africa and has had time to contemplate his career:

I must be one of the few England captains who has finished up with nothing, I must be honest. A distinguished playing career, yeah, but you've probably got to do a bit more than that. Tom Finney and Stan Matthews were two of the few who just got a knighthood for football. How does it leave me? It does worry me a bit that some people have MBEs and OBEs. It gets to me. Yeah. I can look at some of the lists in football and find it very hard to work out. But that's the way it goes, I suppose.

The Kingsmead Kings – Durban double days

In 1970 Budgie played a midfield role for Durban with consummate genius and steered the side, which had been nicknamed the 'Kingsmead Kings', to the NFL Championship and victory in the Bowl, defeating Southern Suburbs 4–2 after two replays of the final (in the decade of the Bowl's history the final had never gone to a replay). It was the first time that this double had been achieved in the South African game.

For all this, Byrne's achievement had taken place in a country that was isolated as a sporting nation. He had started his first full South African season as it was announced that South Africa had been expelled from the Olympic movement.

At the beginning of 1971 Byrne, while maintaining a playing role, became City's coach following the forced resignation of the manager Marty Deetlifs and his coaches Danny le Roux and Ken Denysschen.

Managing a football club in the early 1970s was a demanding job, but in the South African context it was almost impossible. For example, John was now in charge of his former idol and mentor Johnny Haynes. The former Fulham and England captain hated to be chastised by a manager or a coach, even if he was wrong. John remembered an incident with Durban City in 1971:

Team spirit was low and there was constant bickering between players. Johnny had had a go at one or two players and this didn't help matters. I decided the only solution would be to call the squad together and thrash out the difference of opinions.

Before the meeting I had a chat with Johnny and told him that I was going to have a real go at him at the meeting. This way the rest of the players would think that I was not favouring him and it might solve the problem. I could then have a go at a few others as well. Haynsie wasn't very keen on the idea but he agreed to go along with it. So, after training that particular evening I assembled the lads in the clubhouse and proceeded to lay down the law.

"As you are the captain," I said to Haynes, "I'm going to have a go at you first."

I then threw a few verbal punches and I could see that a number of players present were sitting up, wide-eyed and listening in amazement. When I had ended my lecture to Haynes and was about to move on to someone else, Haynes leaned back in his chair and replied: "If you don't like it you can go and get stuffed."

I was completely thunderstruck and for once in my life was left completely speechless. If looks could have killed, then Haynsie was as good as dead. But this was typical of him.

Many of the players Byrne had to deal with during his first years of management in South Africa had seen better days, and quite a few had all but been transported as soccer miscreants. One shining example of such imports to City was Alec Munro, formerly of Bristol Rovers. He carried his nickname, 'Muffy', with him to Durban City in 1971. The moniker was bestowed on him because of his habit of wearing a wig. The football saying of the 1960s 'win or lose, go on the booze' might have been penned specifically with Munro in mind. On one occasion his 'celebrations' concluded with his admittance to hospital where, 'syrup' still precariously balanced on his head, he informed Elliott and Budgie that 'It was a hit and run job' and that he had 'just managed to roll out of the way'. In response Byrne made for the police station to find out the facts and if necessary press charges. However, the fact of the matter was that Munro had, alone and unaided, wrapped his car round a lamp-post. This said, Munro, who took up boxing for a while (his record was nine fights and eight losses) would give his all on the field of play, but his belligerence was always something of a threat.

City were on their way to play Germiston Callies and Elliott, who had had a few drinks during the flight, decided to give the team a reminder of his authority on the bus from the airport to the game. During this lecture The Silver Fox remarked that Munro was 'not worth two bob as a footballer'. No sooner had Elliott spat the words out than the huffy Muffy was on him. Munro hoisted Elliott into the air and throttled him. Everyone on the bus froze in a kind of disbelieving surprise and if it hadn't have been for another player pulling the toupée-topped Glaswegian away there is little doubt that angry Alec would have strangled The Silver Fox. Another 'Munro incident' occurred after Alec had been excused from training after informing the club that he was suffering from a virulent, near terminal bout of flu. However, on the evening of his reporting his diseased state the apparently ailing Muffy and a teammate, Tony Coleman, went out on a therapeutic tour of Durban bars.

Outside-left 'TC' had been on the books of Stoke City, Tranmere Rovers, Preston North End, Doncaster Rovers, Bangor City, Manchester City, Sheffield Wednesday, Blackpool and Southport, and would return to England to turn out for Stockport County in 1974. Eventually patient and nurse arrived at the pub where Johnny Haynes, Budgie and a couple of other players were contesting a dominoes match. Seeing Munro, Byrne queried the novel medical regime Alec was pioneering. It seems that Alec did not appreciate this concern about his treatment strategy and, showing admirable consistency, he went for Budgie's throat. To his credit the much-travelled Coleman intercepted the raging invalid and wrestled his charge to the floor, shouting 'Ignore him. It's the fever!' As the pair crashed about, the dominoes, although disturbed by the tremors from below, continued, John being keen to play off the double six he had in his hand.

Haynes, in his quiet, casual manner, looked over the top of the table at the two comrades floundering around on the floor and said 'Alec, if you want to fight piss off outside. If you want to have a drink, get up and sit down.' Munro staggered to a chair, apologised and ordered a drink. As this incident demonstrates, Haynes was a born leader and John was quick to make him the captain of Durban City when he took over at New Kingsmead.

Like the indomitable Munro, Tony Coleman was also a mixed blessing at New Kingsmead. His style was typified when he dropped his shorts to an opposing goalkeeper after smashing home a goal from the penalty spot. TC also had a run in with The Silver Fox. Coleman and Elliott had argued following a training session, with Coleman telling Elliott in no uncertain words where to stick the football club. During a Durban City Supporters Club dance Budgie found himself sitting next to Elliott as TC staggered up to the club founder to invite the top man at City outside in order to have his head smashed in. The conversation extended to include Byrne, Coleman calling him a 'rubbing rag'. Budgie stayed calm, mostly because he didn't have a clue what the expression meant. However, TC was also a battler on the field and had the ability to score goals of sheer quality, having a cultivated left foot.

Another troublesome player was Joe Fascione. He shaped up to Byrne following a game in Johannesburg. The side were ensconced in the airport bar when Fascione, who in common with many of his teammates liked a drink or seven, started to threaten Budgie, who had to be restrained from retaliation by other members of his side. But Munro was able to achieve what Byrne was prevented from doing when he gave Fascione a notably fine battering.

At the end of 1971 City finished third in the League and reached the Castle Cup final where they met Cape Town City. The Castle Cup was then the South African equivalent to the English FA Cup and was regarded as the showpiece of the South African soccer calendar. The two sides were deadly rivals when they met in the final in Johannesburg's Rand Stadium (South Africa's Wembley). According to Byrne the finalists 'hated the sight of each other'. The game went into extra-time but still the two teams were deadlocked. It was the first-ever final to result in a replay. Ronnie Mann, formerly of Aldershot, was Durban's hero, producing a superb hat-trick, only the second threesome scored in the final of this competition. Mann had scored over 30 goals that season and had been tipped for the title of 'Footballer of the Year'. Johnny Haynes recalled: 'Ronnie Mann, although he wasn't very big, used to score lots of goals'. But politics was a powerful consideration in South African football at that time. Footballer of the Year had never been won by a player born outside of South Africa.

Durban had not planned for the replay that would take place three days after the final and Elliott had arranged for his side to travel back in the supporters train, '*The Banana Express*'. '*BE*' trips involved all-night festivities and as such were not the best preparation for Cup final replays. However the Durban City supporters were, even more than usual, in party mood, so much so that Munro, who boarded the train with the rest of the team at midnight on Saturday, was not seen until the train pulled into Pietermaritzburg at midday on Sunday. Nobody, including Munro, knew where he'd been.

An early goal in the replay, played in Durban, killed the hopes of the New Kingsmead revellers. Byrne had persisted with the 4–2–4 formation against Cape Town's 4–3–3 but it seemed that the celebrations had cost the Durban side glory; they lost 2–1. For all this, the sides had provided some great entertainment and that year's contest would be remembered as one of the great encounters of the Castle Cup. Johnny Haynes told how he: '...thoroughly enjoyed playing in the Cup Final at the Rand Stadium. The atmosphere was fantastic but it was a pity that we lost in the replay'.

Cape Town proved to be that season's bogey side for City. They also put Byrne's side out of the Bowl at the semi-final stage.

As Byrne began to stamp his authority on the club, Durban City began to change. John negotiated the acquisition of a training ground, putting an end to a decade of using a hotchpotch of training venues, including Greyville racetrack, and the building of a club house, another first for Durban City.

Byrne's Boys were to contest the Castle Cup Final again in 1972, this time against local rivals Durban United. It was the first ever all-Natal final played in the Transvaal. More than 40,000 spectators saw the clubs equal each other's efforts after extra-time. Alan Skirton, who had played 144 games for Arsenal during the first six years of the 1960s, had pulled City level, obliging the clubs to do it all over again. Skirton remembered his friend's management style: 'I thought the world of Budgie. He was a most sincere fellow and a lovely man to play for. You just couldn't help to go out there and give your all for him.'

In the replay a controversial offside goal by United's Alec Morrison seemed to be a turning point and when Munro showed his consistency by punching Jim Scott inside the area, so giving away a penalty, it looked all over. City lost 5–2. But the season still ended in triumph for City as they won the Champion of Champions trophy, John's first success as a manager. This was followed by victory in the Coca-Cola Shield for the very first time and maybe the sweetest victory of all was City's fourth NFL championship. It was a glorious treble.

By the start of the next season Johnny Haynes and Bobby Keetch had left City (Haynes played his last South African season for Maritzburg). Haynes remembered his time at City with more than a degree of affection:

> The first couple of years that I was there City went great guns... I had a great time over there and played into my forties and only returned to England for good in 1985.

Looking beyond colour

The departure of Haynes in particular seemed to mark the start of a decline at City. The club were to finish in ninth place in the League, but Byrne would leave halfway through the season. The final straw seemed to be Durban's exit from the Castle Cup in the first round. The increasing cost of attracting players and their families from overseas proved difficult for City, which was effectively a one-man operation in the shape of Elliott. Byrne had introduced the likes of Haynes and Ray Crawford, the former England striker (who never really acclimatised to South Africa) but the flow of talent seemed to be drying up. Apart from this, at City Byrne knew that there was only one boss and that was Elliott; Budgie had to approve his every move with The Silver Fox. Elliott had done much to bring glory to Durban, but in the early 1970s his presence became more of a hindrance than a help in terms of the development of modern football in one of the biggest cities in the entire continent. At the same time Byrne had a bigger picture of the problems facing football in South Africa. John

had long believed that football had no future in that country if the game failed to develop local talent and that meant not just white kids. He saw the reliance on British and latterly European exports as souring the roots of the game in the country, which everybody knew were deeply set in the townships.

John, along with many other white South Africans, could not see how sport could prosper in the apartheid environment, cut off from the world and its own people. While he understood himself to be 'transient' in terms of South African soccer, John just did his job, but there came a moment when he perceived that he and his family were becoming African and it was then that he began to build his own philosophy of developing football in his adopted country.

To the south of Durban, across the Umbilo and Umhlatuzana Rivers, is the large Umlazi township. It has a population of almost two million. In a spirit of frustration with the system in general and Durban City in particular, John, working more quietly than covertly, with a shadowy group of unofficial black coaches and one or two trusted white players, including, at times, Arsenal's George Armstrong and Bobby Moore, helped to organise a number of coaching sessions around Umlazi. This was not a revolution but it was a chancy occupation and the start of what Budgie saw as a common-sense strategy for the future. It would be wrong to see Byrne as an anti-apartheid campaigner, he clearly was not, but change, in any society, is reliant on normal people: in South Africa this meant people who understood, at one level or another, that apartheid, segregation, and racism, are, at an everyday level, just plain stupid.

According to Tottenham-born Bobby Keetch:

> When you first went out there (South Africa) you didn't really notice it. You just take things for granted, but the longer you were there the more you said to yourself 'this can't last'. Rugby was the white game in South Africa, that and cricket. All the schools for white kids did rugby. It was only round the townships that you saw loads of football being played. There were black clubs of course, but they never got the backing or facilities that the white clubs had. Anyway, you'd often see a player who you thought, 'He could play alongside so and so' or 'if they had such and such' the whole side would do better. But 'so and so' and 'such and such' were often the wrong colour... the whole thing, looking back on it, was just daft.

For George Armstrong:

> The kids out in the townships showed fantastic ability, but then most of them spent all their spare time with a ball at their feet. They worked so hard and thought about what they were doing. They had masses of individual skill and you thought that if only they could work a bit on the tactical side, a bit more discipline, they would make wonderful players. More than anything else it struck you what a waste it was; all that enthusiasm.

According to Budgie the situation was idiotic but the response simple:

> If you were born into that situation it seemed like a natural thing. But being born and brought up in a different country and being out of South Africa every now and then helped you see how senseless the system was. As it turned out it could have been much nastier than it was and it's a credit to the country that it wasn't. But it was obvious that for South Africa to do what it could do in football everyone had to work together and the last 10 years have shown that to be right. Some time, not too far off, South Africa will win the World Cup and that will be because the whole country will have worked together. It's just teamwork... no team can be successful when its members are working against each other.

Durban disenchantment

Durban's seeming lack of ambition caused Byrne to feel that the time had come for him to leave City. So when George Eastman, the Hellenic skipper, suggested that John fly to Cape Town for a weekend to talk about the possibility of managing the Hellenic club, Byrne was ready to listen. Eastman might have taken the job himself but was not keen on a player-manager role. Byrne didn't quite know what to expect as he made a secret visit to Cape Town but he had always been a gambler and as he said, 'One is who one is' and he was prepared to take a chance.

With Hellenic offering more money and more scope for development along with the promise of a full-time management role (while with City John had worked for a tyre company, his football had been essentially a part-time occupation) it would have been hard for Byrne to turn down the move to Cape Town. However, things were not going to be easy. Byrne's contract with City was such that he was always going to have problems moving away from Durban. He had signed a two-year contract with Elliott as a player, but he had been with the club four seasons, and although Joe Kirkup, Byrne's former teammate at West Ham, was to take over as manager at New Kingsmead, City Tsar Elliott was reluctant to let his coach go.

Big Mal's All Stars

In the period between Byrne joining Hellenic and leaving Durban City the former West Ham player and Manchester City manager Malcolm Allison came to South Africa with his All Star British side. Included in his squad were Don Rogers, Frank McLintock, Rodney Marsh and George Armstrong, while Geoff Hurst and Derek Dougan were guesting for two other clubs. For Byrne:

> Rodney Marsh had more skill than any player I'd seen, including any of the Brazilians. He loved 'nutmegging' [sending the ball through his opponent's legs] nearly as much as scoring a goal! A Marsh party trick was to flip a jam tart on his foot, toss it into the air and catch it in his mouth. Rodney said his mum had helped him practice this as a boy, tossing him jam tarts as a reward.

> Rodney carried out an interesting tailoring job when he was in South Africa with Malcolm Allison. He wouldn't wear a long sleeved shirt so he tore the sleeves off and went out to play. Malcolm had done much the same thing at West Ham in the 1950s.

Allison assembled his team in Durban and various clubs drew on these players. City used the former Leeds and Wales goalkeeper Gary Sprake and former Everton player Alan Whittle (Sprake was not to do well during his time in South Africa). Allison, always a master of publicity, made sure he was seen with champagne, cigars and beautiful women, and his All Stars side was quickly dubbed 'Malcolm's Travelling Circus' by the press, as, like their leader, the squad preferred the nightlife and parties to playing soccer. Byrne took part in much of the 'socialising'. The players treated the tour like a holiday. Predictably the tourists were beaten by a South African based eleven at the Rand Stadium in a drama-packed match marred by the sending off of Tony Coleman following a fracas with goalkeeper Sprake. It also saw Rodney Marsh throw his shirt at Allison (the one with the sleeve job) in front of the 40,000 crowd. The game included the most blatant offside goal anyone in South Africa had ever seen. For all this, in the final match, in Cape Town, Allison's gang really turned it on. They buzzed, with Don Rogers and Marsh playing some incredible football.

CHAPTER 16

The Truth of Fire is that it

Never Dies

WITH a metropolitan population of around one million Cape Town is not as big as Durban, but it is one of the few great cities of the world where the periphery is cosmopolitan and developed while the centre of the city is something of a natural wilderness. Cape Town nestles up against a wildlife reserve directly in the middle of town, the massive 1,086 metre sandstone bulk of one of the world's best-known landmarks, Table Mountain, which is flanked by Devil's Peak, Lions Head and Signal Hill. This area has approximately 1,470 species of plants. Many of these appear nowhere else on earth, like the rare Silver Tree and the wild orchid Disa Uniflora. It is also home to baboons, dassies (a kind of antelope), porcupines, and a kind of mountain goat called a Himalayan Tahr, which was introduced by British colonialist Cecil Rhodes.

From atop Table Mountain, the flat summit of which measures nearly 3km from end to end, one can look out over the city and its beaches. The panorama stretches from Table Bay to False Bay and around the mountain to the Hout Bay Valley and Kommetjie. On a clear day one has a magnificent view across the Cape Flats to the Hottentots Holland Mountains. Table Mountain was named by Jan van Riebeeck on 6 April 1652 as he sailed towards what was to become Cape Town. His fort was Cape Town's first building. It was constructed because of the threat of war between Holland and Britain. The cornerstone of the castle was laid in 1666 and it was first occupied in 1674 by the forces attached to the Dutch East India Company, demonstrating Cape Town's long connection with Holland, the first European occupiers of the area.

A diversity of building styles reflect the various colonial powers that have called the Cape home. Dutch Cape architecture rubs elbows with minarets brought by Muslim slaves from East India. The invading English brought Georgian and Victorian styles. The Botanical Gardens, right by the Town Hall, reflect the English habit of putting beautiful parks in the middle of their cities. The old Supreme Court Building was designed by a Frenchman, and its style flaunts that fact. Thus the city's colonial past can be traced through its architecture, which is a testament of history from the 17th century on. As such, Cape Town has a structural design and lifestyle which are broadly cosmopolitan yet uniquely 'Capetonian', with many historical buildings still standing among the new skyscrapers, including the Castle of Good Hope, Cape Point – the place of the Meeting of Two Oceans and Robben Island, which houses the old maximum-security prison for political prisoners convicted during the apartheid era that included Nelson Mandela for 25 years.

Cape Town is home to a diversity of people and is a mixture of landscapes, from the mountains to lush indigenous gardens and many beautiful beaches. The wine country of Constantia, which was first planted in 1685, is almost part of the city. 'The Mother City', as Cape Town is sometimes called, has always had a bustling nightlife that includes a range of restaurants catering for the city's many varied cultures (there are 11 official languages in South Africa, including Afrikaans and English) and many clubs and pubs spread around the city.

The region has a near Mediterranean climate. In summer it is usually pleasantly warm. From September to March the high temperatures range from 19°C in September to 27°C in February. In the spring and summer period there is little rain and the hottest days are often cooled by pleasant breezes or strong winds. Bracing south-easterly winds occur in November and early December. Cape Town's winters are cool and wet, the daily highs are usually between 17°C and 19°C. Highest winter rainfall usually occurs in July and August, when icy north-westerly winds bring heavy showers to the Cape Peninsula. Light snow-fall can also occur in the mountains during this period. By Northern Hemisphere standards the conditions are mild, and rainfall is often followed by warm, sunny days. However, there are abrupt weather changes year-round. Fog is one cause; it spills down into the city from the mountains.

The N2 highway, connecting Cape Town international airport with the city, is lined with townships made up of densely-packed shacks and buildings. During the turbulent days of the apartheid government, these were no-go areas for whites. The maze of Khayelitsha was one of these. Like most townships it has a shebeen on almost every street block.

Hellenic

When Budgie arrived in Cape Town, Hellenic was one of its leading soccer clubs and a power in South African football. The club was founded in 1958 and fought its way up the regional divisions, winning promotion to the top flight of white South African football in 1963. However, it was under the influence of George Eastham that the 'Greek Club' really began to make its mark, playing in their white and blue, at Greenpoint Stadium, close to the cold Atlantic Ocean. After an indifferent start to 1971, in February Hellenic were beaten by Johnny Byrne's Durban City, a 6–0 walloping at Greenpoint, Hellenic's biggest-ever defeat, but the Cape Town side won the R12,500 Coca-Cola Shield, the BP League Cup and their first NFL Championship that year, while George Eastham had been awarded the *Sunday Express* Footballer of the Year prize. It would have been a near clean sweep for the Greeks but they were beaten, by a single goal, in the Bowl in October by Cape Town City, their bitter rivals from the other side of Table Mountain. It would have been hard to replicate such success and the next season the 'Glory Boys' of 1971 were limited to runners-up spot in the NFL, the Bowl and the Champion of Champions trophy.

At the end of 1972 Eastham returned to Stoke City in England but came back to South Africa in 1973 for secret talks with Johnny Byrne at Cape Town Airport. This led to Budgie taking up the managerial reigns at Hellenic. He couldn't have had a tougher start to his new job; Hellenic faced local rivals Cape Town City in the first round of the Castle Cup. Hellenic were beaten 1–0 after extra-time, but following the match Byrne found out that he was still on Durban City's books. Elliott had refused to release him and, resenting the fact that John had walked out mid-season, had suspended him for working with Hellenic. This was followed by the National Football League informing Byrne that he could take no further part in any football activities. Negotiations dragged on for three months, during which time Byrne was not allowed to sit on the Hellenic bench, or have any contact with the team. He was forced to organise covert meetings with his players and work through his assistant Wally Gould (who was to become manager of East London). In exasperation Hellenic officials and Byrne made three trips to Johannesburg to appeal to the NFL but lost the case as Budgie was still officially a City player, despite having no contract, and Elliott was digging in.

During his early discussions with Hellenic Byrne had been led to believe that the club were looking to become a totally professional side, but it was only after he had arrived from Durban that he found out that his new club were in no position to become a full-time concern. If he had known this when talking to Eastman Byrne might well have caught the first flight back to Durban and patched up his differences with The Silver Fox. Even though Hellenic won the Champion of Champions trophy in 1973, Byrne realised that the team lacked leadership and that this was holding the side back. After the conclusion of the season Byrne sorted out his problems with Elliott, by paying him compensation, and made a start rebuilding for the new term.

Budgie noticed a huge difference between working with Durban City and Hellenic. He was given a lot more responsibility in the day-to-day affairs of the club, but was also allowed to set a path for Hellenic's overall development. The Cape Town side had a tradition of bringing players of quality to South African football, exemplified in 1971 when George Eastham fielded a star-studded Hellenic side, which included Ian St John, Calvin Palmer, Gordon Banks and Willie Hunter. This had permanently raised the expectations of the 'Greeks' supporters; they had become used to a rich diet.

Soon after the end of the South African season Budgie returned to England and sought out Ron Greenwood, Malcolm Allison and his former teammate John Bond for help in finding players who would bring Hellenic success. When the new season got underway it didn't take long for the newly-formed side to impress. The leadership John saw as necessary was supplied by Bobby Moore (who came to the Hellenic on a short-term, eight-week contract from Fulham in May). With the monumental influence of the former West Ham and England captain the side Hellenic took the Coca-Cola Shield by beating Maritzburg in the two-leg final. At Greenpoint the teams fought out a 0–0 draw. Although Moore had visited South Africa before, and coached in Durban and Johannesburg, he had not played in the country, but with him and West Bromwich Albion legend Jeff Astle playing in the Hellenic ranks, the Greeks made their way to the Jan Smuts Stadium in Pietermaritzburg in confident mood. At one point Byrne's boys were 2–0 down, but the Cape Towners pulled their way back into the game and the equalising goal from Kenyan-born Andrew McBride, who had been an apprentice at Selhurst Park, gave Hellenic the Shield on the away goals rule.

Bobby Moore played well for Hellenic. For Byrne, Moore was a great example to the younger generation. In the two years he guested for Hellenic in the early 1970s Moore played in 17 games and was never on the losing side. The last game of these matches was on a Wednesday evening in June against Jewish Guild in a Castle Cup tie. Byrne had a number of injury problems but

Bobby was supremely confident and before the kick-off told his manager, 'There's no way we can get beaten'. Hellenic won 5–1. The Guild had George Best in their eleven as well as the former Hammer and Bournemouth goal machine, Ted Macdougall. The Scot didn't get a sniff of the ball as Bobby marked him out of the game. The next day the media hailed Moore's performance as the best ever by a sweeper since the beginning of semi-professional football in South Africa. Moore had a lot of time for South Africa. He loved the country and Byrne was confident that he would return to turn out for Hellenic when his English playing days were over. Sadly Mooro's time was short after he hung up his boots. When he left Hellenic they were knocked out of the Cup and then suffered defeat by East London. The club were seemingly anchored to the foot of the NFL that season, being plagued by injuries. It had been so bad that Byrne himself, now more than a little rotund, had been obliged to turn out for the reserves in April, but for all his extra bulk he still managed to grab a hat-trick.

Building foundations – a family affair

John had tremendous ambitions for his new club, saying that, 'Hellenic's image must be pushed to all corners of South Africa'. He believed that, 'To reach a goal you must set yourself an image' and he did just that. He began to build a side that would make a mark in South African football, but also helped to give the game in Cape Town a solid foundation for the future. During the period Byrne had been in South Africa the schools concentrated on rugby while football took a poor second place. He often argued that it was this that obliged clubs to turn to foreign players. However, he noticed that in high-school kids of the Cape, Natal and Transvaal would spend a great deal of their free time kicking tennis balls or footballs around during school breaks and that it was as rare to see a rugby ball at such times as it was after school hours in the townships. For all this, it was a difficult job to get coaches into schools and by the time white boys had completed their matriculation and army training they would not be available to clubs until they were 20. John's sons, David and Kevin, went to Sea Point High School, which was very much an institution devoted to rugby. When his boys started at the school it had no soccer teams playing in the school leagues but John's lads managed to win the prestigious Pro Nutro National Schools Tournament that started with well over 100 sides, which, as far as John was concerned, demonstrated what could be done. But Byrne knew that over the next 20 years few of the great players of South

African football would come from the whites-only high schools, and he hadn't been in Cape Town long when he began the same type of coaching efforts he had instigated around Durban.

Kevin was the first of John and Margaret's sons to follow in his dad's footsteps. While he was still at school the full-back skippered and coached his school team. As a teenager he showed his not inconsiderable skills for Hellenic, but a horrific car accident early in 1978 finished his playing career.

David scored his first professional goal for Hellenic early in 1978. He was just 18. He went to the US and spent 13 years playing in America before returning to South Africa in the mid-1990s where he played for a number of Cape clubs. In 2000 the veteran defender was in line to make South African football history, but a late season slip by his First Division team Avendale Athletico meant that this was not to be. David had turned out in the NFL, FPI, NPSL and NSL, and if Avendale had been promoted into the PSL the 40-year-old would have played at the highest level in four separate decades.

John's younger son Mark, like David, was also encouraged by his father to make an early entry into the professional game. He was only six when Budgie started to instruct him in the football arts and the youngster was able to trap a ball, play it with the inside and outside of his foot and even bring it down with his thigh before he was seven. Mark made his debut in 1979 at the age of 16 against Arcadia at Green Point Stadium. The strong defender was seen regularly playing for Hellenic over many seasons and also coached the side in the late 1990s. He once reflected on his family's footballing dynasty:

> At one stage David was with Santos, I was contracted to Hellenic,
> my dad was at Cape Town Spurs and Gavin Hunt, my brother-in-
> law, Karen's husband, was at Seven Stars.

Budgie 1 Apartheid 0

Because of apartheid South Africa was expelled from the United Nations in 1974 and it seems that the reverberations were felt by the nation's soccer administrators. From the start of the mid-seventies the tight control over soccer segregation was beginning to erode, more from a lack of enforcement than broad ranging changes in legislation, and teams of whites were turning out against teams made up of black players on an increasing number of occasions. A few multi-racial games took place – some made the newspapers but most didn't – but Johnny Byrne led Hellenic to their first nationally recognised trophy won in a competition that included clubs made up of the whole diversity of South African culture. In 1975 Hellenic retained the Champion of Champions trophy and in February were one of the eight sides to contest the first the multinational Champion of Champions title. The other sides were:

Kaizer Chiefs (Black)

Orlando Pirates (Black)

Arcadia Shepherds (White)

Bluff Rangers (Asian)

Aces United (Asian)

Blackpool (Coloured)

Claremont United (Coloured)

Hellenic and Kaizer Chiefs reached the two-legged final. This was the first time that white and black sides had the opportunity to play each other in a nationally recognised competition. The experienced English referee, Jack Taylor, who had officiated in the 1974 World Cup finals in Germany, would take charge of the match.

The first leg in Hartlevale passed without any controversy as Hellenic strolled to a 4–1 victory over the strangely subdued Chiefs. This said, Hellenic played exceptionally well with players like Dave Hudson and Des Backos excelling, but the overall the atmosphere stayed convivial. According to Byrne:

> The Kaizer lads seem a bit intimidated by the whole thing. It was like they had an entire country on their backs. We stayed at the same hotel in Cape Town and had a drink and a few laughs together. But the Chiefs weren't allowed in the night club in case they danced with white women, which was against the law. So we didn't go to the night club either.

It has to be said that Byrne was never for black versus white football, seeing it as divisive. The year before the historic encounter between Hellenic and Kaizer Chiefs a select white side had met a black select side in the final of a multinational tournament. The blacks had a goal disallowed and the Rand stadium nearly boiled over. In fact the black team refused to come out for the second half and it took a deal of persuasion to get them to finish the game. At this point John had argued that:

> The teams must be integrated in the future. Only then will things work out... I can't wait for the bridge to be crossed. It would only be a turn for the good and I hope I'm still in the game when multiracial soccer comes into being... It might seem one small step but, in actual fact, it will be a giant leap into a more fruitful and

happier soccer existence. Doors closed to us now will suddenly open and we can only go from strength to strength.

This was a brave statement for the time. It is quite amazing that he was allowed to stay in the game thereafter. It was one thing to play to the weaknesses of the system; playing but saying nothing, but an open attack on apartheid was unprecedented. For all this Byrne was vindicated in his opinion in the second leg Champion of Champions final. He recalled:

The second game was played at the Rand Stadium. Their supporters went wild when we scored early on. Their 'keeper, 'Baks' Setholodi, thought the goal was offside. Dave Hilley had made it for Jeff Cook. Hilley had come from behind the Chiefs' defence and was clearly on-side. But Baks sat in the back of the goal with the ball and wouldn't let the game go on. Then the beer cans started to come onto the pitch. So I called my players off. It was about 20 minutes later when we were asked to go back out, more or less to avoid a riot. The Hellenic chairman, Chris Christodolides, and myself, after talking with Kaizer Chiefs officials, asked Taylor to restart the game and once Eddie Lewis (formerly of Manchester United and West Ham) the Chiefs' coach, and their managing director, Ewert Nene, 'The Lip', as he was known, had given assurances that they would sort their supporters out, the game was restarted.

Some of our lads had already showered! We restarted, but Jack told us not to expect too many decisions to go our way. The Chiefs came out with more energy and seemed more determined and more physical than previously. Tackles ranged from bad to awful. I thought one challenge on Hudson was the worst I had ever seen anywhere. Don Reich also took some punishment, particularly from the Chiefs' captain Kaizer Motaung. The Chiefs were physically stronger than us and they knew that retaliation would have sent the crowd wild. There wasn't much Taylor could do and he knew it. He kept on asking the Hellenic players to 'bear with me and let's get the game over'. Had he sent someone off it might have sparked a riot. Kaizer won the game 2–1, to become the first black team to beat a white side, which seemed to keep their supporters happy, but we had won the final overall.

This showed that the 'inter-racial' concept was fraught with problems, in that it pitted one group against another. The effect was to create an even greater demand for multiracial football to be legitimised. History was made in 1976 when South Africa fielded their first multinational side against an Argentine Stars XI; the Rainbow XI won 5–1. This was the beginning of the end of segregated football. They also won a second game 2–0 and the final match concluded in a 1–1 draw.

As outlined above Johnny Byrne never doubted that football in South Africa should be multiracial, but it was not just the players he was thinking about. The fact that when he had been in charge of Durban City black people were not allowed to attend NFL games at New Kingsmead, except on rare occasions when they might be able to get hold of special permits which entitled them to buy tickets, left a bad taste in his mouth. In the *South African Soccer Weekly* John commented:

> If we are to get anywhere in the soccer world we have got to have conformity and we need help from everybody; sponsors, provincial administrators and even the government. Multiracial soccer would of course clear up everything for then obviously people of all colours would be allowed to watch their teams. Certainly we can never hope to get back into FIFA if the present rules on spectators, players and teams continue to exist.

This wasn't a new stance for Byrne: he'd been saying much the same thing since the early seventies in the context of what was a very definite apartheid regime, where sport was a central part of cultural and nationalist identity. John consistently took a position that was nothing less than dissident. Indeed, he argued that blacks and whites playing together was South African football's 'only hope', which clearly implied that the apartheid system was hopeless. Pragmatically John saw that the tremendous interest that the black population had in soccer reflected the game's potential and future in South Africa and argued that the desegregation of football would not only improve the sport but would also provide what he called a 'different insight into football'. He saw the raw talent the townships had produced and that black and white South Africans had been playing successfully in multiracial soccer for years. For example, Albert Johanneson had played for Leeds United in England from 1960 to 1970, scoring 48 goals in 170 League games, while the young Witts University goalkeeper, Gary Bailey, was attracting a deal of interest from English clubs (he would play nearly 300 games for Manchester United from 1978 to 1986). So there was certainly some commercial potential in developing talent on a multiracial basis. It was in the unity of blacks and whites that John saw the true strength of South African potential. In his view:

It is silly to talk about 'natural ability'. A young player, in a high school or a township, will become a good player only if they have the enthusiasm needed to work at the game and develop a personal discipline. Yeah, one kid might have good balance, another tremendous intelligence, but without the character and will all that will come to not very much. Look at Mooro... he couldn't run and wasn't that fond of heading the ball, but he worked and worked at making himself a player. Geoff Hurst was a great player, but not before he worked his arse off; practice, practice, rehearse, rehearse. To be honest the most talented players I've seen have come to nothing, but the workers, the ones who made the most of their strengths and worked on their weaknesses, they were the ones who would make it. Most of all, everyone has to learn to work together. Black and white, fast and slow, tough and clever. Then you got the best of all worlds and not stuck with just what you got.

Hellenic had been a pioneering club in terms of multiracial involvement. The Champion of Champions tournament was an example of this and it was after that game that John predicted that before the end of the century South African football would be a force. He was, of course, yet again, to be proved right.

In 1976 in Soweto, a small town that alongside others made up a township located just outside of Johannesburg, students and school children took part in a massive demonstration against apartheid and the attempt to enforce the use of the Afrikaans language for teaching in the township. Nearly seven hundred people died, most shot by the police. What occurred in Soweto during 1976 shocked the world and was an important step in the eventual change in South Africa's governmental policies. Not long after South Africa was expelled from FIFA the Football Council of South Africa was formed, led by George Thabe. The SASF almost immediately rejected the authority of the Football Council, but when one of the leaders of the Soweto protests, writer Steve Biko, was killed in police custody, the whole country shook. Biko had been the voice of black dissidence but also a symbol of general freedom. When the facts were digested it seemed all the more necessary for those involved in moving South Africa into the modern world to concentrate their efforts.

Around the same time one of England's 1966 World Cup heroes became the new chair of Hellenic. Alan Ball recalled: 'I played a season for Budgie and thoroughly enjoyed playing out there.'

Ball had seen the beginnings of John's family growing into football and remarked: 'David, Mark and Kevin were only youngsters then, but I could see that they had the potential to take after their famous father.'

These boys would grow to carry on their father's work and be among those that would prepare South Africa for football greatness and build on the foundations that were set in the 1970s, the culmination of which was the moment in 1978 when South Africa's soccer administrators lost the last shred of patience with the government and took the initiative by launching a new, multiracial, 24-club League, in two zones. The first games took place on 4 March 1978. Two weeks later Orlando Pirates made their first white signings, Phil Venter from Germiston Callies and Pedro Sculli from Lusitano. Venter recalled:

> I came from a right-wing, nationalist background. Both my grandfather and father belonged to the party and for a whole year after I'd joined the 'Buccaneers' my father never spoke to me. It was only when his black co-workers started talking to him about me that things began to change. After that he wholeheartedly accepted the fact that I had become a Pirate and his relationship with blacks improved remarkably.

Venter went on to play for the other two of Soweto's 'Big Three', Moroka Swallows and Kaizer Chiefs. He remembered:

> It was scary going into the townships to play but the atmosphere in the stadiums was something I shall always cherish. And I still get goose-bumps talking about it today. I participated in the 'muti' ceremonies. At Orlando it was big, but unlike Swallows we didn't have our skins cut. There was a guy somewhere in the township who used to hit us with sticks and do all sorts of funny things to us.
>
> Someone told me that once I pulled my black and white jersey on I would always be a Pirate no matter where I went. And I still support my former club today.

Soon managers and chairmen were making statements in the press about the new feeling of unity: '...we don't have white or black players... just soccer players', and '...we had to make sure the player was good and the type who had no race hang ups' '...our blokes are all race colour-blind... they are a team and that's about the end of the story'.

In terms of segregation this was not the end, but it certainly was part of the beginning of the end.

Push and run

In October 1982 Johnny Byrne resigned as manager of Hellenic. During the 1980s the club he had built had more than held its own in the top flight, and unlike many of its contemporaries it survived the volcanic changes in the South African game. In fact Hellenic had thrived. Budgie had pushed them to third place in the League, the Greeks fans had seen their club finish in the top four on three occasions and they would qualify for the Top 8 Cup in all but 1985, 1986 and 1988. However, one of the greatest achievements of the 1980s for Johnny Byrne and all those involved in South African football during that period occurred in 1985 when the unity talks between the SASF and the Football Council broke down and as a consequence, although amateur soccer remained racially segregated, 'non-racial' football in the National Soccer League (NSL) was ratified.

In the late 1980s Budgie entered into a protracted love/hate relationship with Hellenic. After returning to manage the club in 1988, he was dismissed in 1989 only to be reinstated in June 1990, the same year Nelson Mandela was released from prison and President de Klerk lifted the ban outlawing the African National Congress (ANC) and other Liberation organisations. At the time John Charles, West Ham's first-ever black player, heard from his old friend, teammate and drinking colleague:

> Budgie was a good bloke, game for anything. I went to the pub and the landlord said 'I met a mate of yours in South Africa, Budgie, he's given me a present for you' it was a scroll and it read 'Dear Charlo, now they've released Nelson Mandela, you can come out here and visit me'.

In 1991 Mandela became President of the African National Congress and in the same year the International Olympic Committee lifted the 21-year ban on South Africa. Within a year unity had been achieved between 'establishment' and 'non-racial' soccer federations. Local, provincial, and national amateur soccer leagues were reorganised along non-racial, democratic principles and South Africa was readmitted to international soccer. As if in celebration Johnny Byrne took Hellenic to runners-up spot in the League in 1992 and the following year was voted the nation's Coach of the Year, winning a free trip back to the UK for the FA Cup Final.

The development of South African political life continued to be mirrored in soccer when the country's Football Association was formed on non-racial, democratic principles in 1993 and in 1994 Nelson Mandela was inaugurated as

President of South Africa in the first democratic elections in the country's history. Not too long after his inauguration 'Madiba', as Mandela was affectionately known, along with 80,000 black and white fans, attended a match between South Africa and Zambia at Ellis Park, Johannesburg. As life grew in South Africa one was taken in England. In March of that year Budgie was back at the Boleyn Ground to pay tribute to his great friend Bobby Moore. He was present at the memorial match against an FA Premier League side in honour of the man that John knew as 'Mooro' – his skipper and captain of all the Hammers from the time he first took the field as West Ham's leader. Moore and Byrne, along with Johnny Haynes, were known as 'the terrible trio' in England during the 1960s. Bobby and Budgie were very close on and off the field and John always saw himself as owing a tremendous amount to Moore. For Budgie, 'Mooro was the greatest Hammer of them all'.

John took the Greeks to the final of the Coca-Cola Cup in 1994, but after an 18-year association with the club he was sacked for a second and last time in October 1995, just a few months after the Orlando Pirates won the African (club) Champions' Cup. It seemed that Byrne's job in soccer had been completed in more ways than one. John's son, David, took over as the Hellenic manager in 1998 for a short time before Gavin Hunt, Budgie's son-in-law, who like David had been a professional with 14 years service to the club under the eye of Budgie, moved into the manager's seat. David also managed First Division Avendale Athletico and became the assistant coach for Black Leopards (under Lidoda Duvha) when the Limpopo-based team were looking to build for the future after narrowly preserving their Premier Soccer League status. Hunt spent time as manager of Seven Stars. An uncompromising competitor on the field, he gave Seven Stars the war cry of 'Never Give Up', a rallying call that drove the club through the 1996–97 season undefeated, after they had narrowly missed out on promotion on three successive occasions.

The South African Premier League was created in 1996 at the same time President Mandela created a commission of inquiry to investigate and resolve the serious conflicts between the NSL and the SAFA over the control of soccer (and its growing revenues). And South African soccer came of age when that year the African Cup of Nations was won in Soccer City, Johannesburg. John had worked hard on this achievement with the national coaches and many of the players who were involved recognise his contribution to this day. But the joy of that day had come from the root of suffering; it had been a long road, the memory of which was renewed on 18 March 1997, when First Lady Hillary

Clinton and her daughter Chelsea visited Soweto to remember the uprisings that occurred there in 1976. Mrs Clinton bowed her head to remember one of the many that were killed during those riots, Hector Peterson, who was the first student killed among many young blacks that died that day.

Although football might do well to spend more time learning from its past, the game, on and off the field, should always look to move forward. It was the way of Johnny Byrne and his family seem to have followed his example. Mark, the youngest of the Byrne brothers and the 'baby' in professional soccer management, had been an outstanding defender for Hellenic in his prime and was always a keen student of the game. After a successful stint as player-manager with the amateur club Camps Bay, Mark took over from Colin Gie at Hellenic. David was to return to take over again in 2001 but was sacked as the side struggled against relegation. The former Liverpool goalkeeper, Bruce Grobbelaar, took over and managed to maintain the team's top-flight status, which meant that Hellenic were the only surviving team from the old NFL in the Premier Soccer League. Indeed the club have played in four incarnations of the elite of South African football; the Federation Professional League, the National Professional Soccer League, the National Soccer League and the Premier Soccer League. For all that, in the early years of the 21st century they were lucky to draw 500 spectators to watch home games.

South Africa qualified for the 1998 World Cup by beating Congo 1–0 at Soccer City in 1997. John took over the role as manager of Santos for the 1997–98 season after becoming owner of the club. With David's move to Santos (following a short stay at Michau Warriors, Port Elizabeth, as player manager) John took on the manager's job at Cape Town Spurs for a brief period. At the time of his death Budgie had recently rejoined Hellenic, under the management of his son Mark, as head of the club's Youth Academy. As such Budgie was still making history in the 1990s; Cape Town's four Premier Soccer League clubs, Spurs, Santos, Hellenic and Seven Stars, provided something of a first in world soccer in that they were coached by a father, two sons and a son-in-law. But this was nothing new. John constantly made history during his time in football, but, unusually for a man who relished being the centre of attention, most of his later achievements happened quietly and behind the scenes.

For example, Budgie had made his share of comments about referees, but unlike most managers he did something about refereeing standards, organising referee training facilities at Hellenic. Everyone knew John was a good talker, but his words were always very honest and he was a sincere man; he took these, his best qualities, into his career. Quick to speak his mind, when an official of a prominent club allegedly offered him R5,000 to throw a game in 1994 he let the world know: 'I said no, and told him where he could shove that R5,000'. He also said, 'I met some really good managers in the English soccer but there were also some who were a joke.'

Unlike many, John could tell the difference.

E p i l o g u e

Drums

JOHNNY 'Budgie' Byrne died at the age of 60. He was taken from this world and those who loved him, by a sudden heart attack. He was survived by his wife Margaret, sons Kevin, Mark and David, and daughter Karen. At the time, 27 October 1999, he was regarded as an institution in South African soccer, being the country's longest-serving football manager. His booming voice and a vocabulary that included many a colourful word from his London lexicon had dominated the game for nearly three decades, but underneath this he was a kind man who lived for football. He was never too busy to talk, and when you got him started, like his former colleague and lifelong friend John Bond, he had a fantastic memory of the games he played in, a quality rarely found in footballers at any level, but particularly in the professional ranks, where, for the most part, the men who made the game experience a kind of merging of memories, with just a few outstanding moments to mark their achievements.

John never really got the recognition he deserved in South Africa or England, but although an outgoing man, he was modest and preferred personal recognition to mass adulation. According to Ron Greenwood, Byrne was the catalyst for West Ham's 'golden era'. When the 1960s were still new Greenwood brought Johnny to Upton Park. Game for game, Byrne was comparable to Geoff Hurst as a goalscorer for England and West Ham and better than Vic Watson, West Ham's highest-ever goalscorer. He was the star of the West Ham team in those heady days of claret and blue glory. The side was built around Budgie and his great friend, Bobby Moore. For Greenwood, Johnny was a world-class and even a great player, having everything – all the talent, all the skills needed to perform at the highest level, conducting the Hammers attack, drawing on his repertoire of genius. In him were gathered all the attributes that typified what West Ham were about in those days.

Greenwood saw Byrne as an intelligent player, and cited one particular example of this footballing acumen operating in a game against the Spurs double-winning side. It was not a Cup or a League match, but matches between West Ham and Tottenham were always competitive. When the Hammers won a free-kick on the edge of the Spurs penalty area Danny Blanchflower knew the Irons well enough to spend a long time organising the defensive wall, pushing, pulling and giving orders. The Spurs 'keeper, Bill Brown, crouched while Maurice Norman, Dave Mackay and the rest prepared themselves. Byrne stepped up to take the kick. He could have chosen any number of well rehearsed moves, but did the simple thing and smacked the ball into the net. After the game he told his manager: 'They were all so worried about what we might do they missed the obvious – the big hole.'

The goal, for Greenwood, was 'all Byrne'; only Budgie had seen the chance or had the instinct to do what he had done. It exemplified John's opportunism and intelligence.

Byrne was small but solidly built, he had personality and other players took to him straight away, because of his attitude to the game, and how he took this into everyday life. Ken Brown, often Byrne's roommate during their time together at West Ham, recalled:

> For his size Budgie used to get whacked all over the park, but what a player! He could hold a ball, score goals and he loved his football. He always came up smiling and he loved life. I knew him ever since he came to West Ham when Ron asked me to room with him on away trips and 'look after him a bit'. I was proud Ron had asked me to do something like that but, bloody hell, he was a handful; lovely fella, but he was up to everything and always wanted to be doing something mischievous.

In many ways the Budgie you saw playing on the pitch was the man. Although he was born in leafy Surrey, Greenwood saw that the young Byrne had much in common with his cockney teammates. But first and foremost Ron recognised John's phenomenal balance, which with his short stride and practiced skill made him a fantastic ball player and a central figure in West Ham's success.

But the first season after the Cups – FA, Cup-Winners' and World – the Hammers fans found nothing to congratulate themselves about. Somewhere along the way the magic had died. Perhaps the 'Allison effect', the man who had founded West Ham's 'Academy', had finally worn off. Maybe Budgie's injury had robbed the side of too much. Bobby Moore had been the soul of West Ham, but his wrangles with the club about pay and West Ham's refusal to entertain approaches concerning him from other clubs, most notably Spurs, had turned his head away from Upton Park; from then on Bobby's team was England. Geoff Hurst, the pumping heart of the Hammers, and Martin Peters, who represented the football intellect that made West Ham, were often able to beat anyone, almost single-handedly, but looking to them week in and week out was indeed a big ask. However, to us romantics, the dreamers of the game, the key to fortune fading and dying at the Boleyn Ground was the demise of the miraculous 'Budgie' Byrne. He symbolised West Ham and their success in the sixties and as his spark dulled so the very soul and spirit of the Hammers was eclipsed. His skill, impudence, confidence, tenacity and optimism had personified the claret and blue Irons and what they would aspire to over the next 40 years. He stayed with us till the end. He was better than the rest, those that would follow and seek to fill his boots, English, Scottish and Italian.

In South Africa John established himself as one of the best coaches in the soccer history of that country. While managing was always second best to playing for Byrne, he derived a great deal of job satisfaction from his work in management. He was never with an unsuccessful club and loved seeing something that had started out as an idea come to fruition in the real world after he, his coaches and his players had spent weeks or months organising a move or a set of tactics. John was a master of the game plan. For example, he remembered a Hellenic match against Arcadia:

> After seeing Arcadia in action in Durban a week previously, I used
> a sweeper behind my centre-halves and although it might have not
> looked a pretty formation, especially at home, the move worked like
> a charm and Arcadia's front line never had a kick at the ball.

But Byrne was also able to moderate and change his strategy. This was perhaps his greatest quality as a manager; his gambling instinct together with his knowledge often paid off:

> Durban City were at home to Germiston Callies. I had to move
> Bobby Keetch into the midfield as an experiment but after 10
> minutes City were a goal down and I knew the plan wasn't working
> so I took off Brummie de Leur, who was coming into the side as a
> regular, put Keetch back at centre-half, brought Joe Fascione into
> the midfield and sent on another forward. We came away winning
> 2–1.

But Budgie had also experienced most sides of soccer. He said:

> ...my career... stands me in good stead as a coach or manager. I
> know all the little tricks... because I went through it all myself... It
> makes me appreciate where I went wrong, and I try to help players
> overcome these problems. It isn't easy, but when we work, we work,
> and when we play, we play.
>
> I think I've gained respect from my players because with this sort
> of attitude I'm close to them, sometimes I think I'm too close... you
> get the best out of everybody. You've got to live with them, eat with
> them, and drink with them and this is how we operate.

Hurst and Byrne

Former English international cricketer Mickey Stewart and good friend of
Budgie's once made the light-hearted comment that Byrne '...was the worst
cricket umpire I ever saw.' This was a good-humoured remark, but to a certain
extent it said something about the type of man John was. He had a mind for
the bigger picture, for him details followed from getting the general atmosphere
right – not the best attitude in terms of a cricketing official maybe, but in the
management of others it was a technique Byrne acquired well in advance of the
modern organisational gurus. But for John this was an instinctive response.
Geoff Hurst, remembering Budgie's arrival at West Ham, saw it as a seminal
moment in his career. According to Hurst, Budgie was a tremendous character
to have around the club. It was perhaps this that, in part, made West Ham a
team that players wanted to play for in the 1960s. It was a place where, under
the tutelage of Ron Greenwood, players like Hurst, Martin Peters and Bobby
Moore could develop, but with personalities like Budgie around it was also a
fun place for young men to be. His good humour extended to the pitch; in his
entire career he was never sent off.

Within this atmosphere Hurst and Byrne developed a creative partnership,
in which Geoff was happy to be the piston to John's spark. Looking back on
his career Sir Geoff rated Budgie as the best player he ever worked with; a great
player, in a different class to his peers. The pair played together for over five
years during West Ham's most successful era and for Hurst, together they were
the classic case of the big target man feeding off the sharp, quick and extremely
skilful smaller partner. Sir Geoff saw himself as learning a lot from Byrne after
Greenwood had converted Hurst from a work-horse wing-half to a
powerhouse striker in September 1962 and without Johnny's help it would

have been a lot more difficult for him to have made the transition successfully.

Ron Greenwood confirmed Geoff Hurst's view of Byrne when he stated that Budgie had helped Hurst become a world-class striker, but also said that he helped other teammates to prosper, being able to make a unique contribution to the West Ham side. Like Sir Geoff, Greenwood remembered Byrne as a great personality and an asset in the dressing room and said that Budgie was a pleasure to work with.

The partnership between Hurst and Byrne was very special. To begin with, Hurst just took the weight off Byrne. Their worth to each other was a bit hit-and-miss. Budgie was the star, once he found his real form, and Hurst the straight man. But, gradually, a real relationship grew. They were opposites in appearance and style: Hurst was the powerhouse, the strong running forward, Budgie the elegant artist. But it was this contrast that made them so effective. Between Hurst and Byrne they had everything to undermine opposing defences. Hurst, with his late, angled runs, his controlled power and aggression, his persistence and selflessness, posed one sort of problem, while Byrne, with his deft touches, instant control, ability to beat his man, quickness over the first vital yards and cheekiness, presented another, and both men knew exactly where the net was. They got more than 40 goals between them in each of their first two full seasons together. Byrne helped make Hurst, but in the end they were an equal and complementary partnership.

For another of Budgie's former strike partners, Brian Dear, Byrne was the most talented target man England produced in the last third of the 20th century. He commented:

> He played football like he played life. He gave everything he did 100 percent. Whether it was playing football or having a drink or a bet. He was totally committed! He did all the sweet things on the field; the rest of us just did the bits and pieces. Ron Greenwood used to call Budgie and Hurst Salmon and Chips. Johnny helped Geoff enormously. We were all lucky to have played with him.

Epitome of life
When John got to South Africa as a player and later as a manager he brought the same qualities he had displayed in the English game to the clubs he served. He had an ability to make groups of players feel good and within that work with them on their development. This mentality was the more effective in that

it was not contrived; it was as natural to Budgie as his laughter, his broad smile and wicked sense of humour. Johnny could be no other way and that was his most notable quality, even if it restricted his playing career. This being the case, it is perhaps very suitable that Crystal Palace chose to honour one of their favourite sons by naming a bar under the Arthur Wait Stand at Selhurst Park after him. A less well-known epitaph was that a football team was actually named after him, the 'Byrne Nitonians' who played in the Croydon Sunday League. In their first season the Nitonians won promotion, the next they were relegated. That might have made John smile. Perhaps a longer lasting memorial is the fact that Budgie remains a member of that small group of professionals to have played in five separate divisions of English professional football.

The minute's silence in memory of Budgie and his former teammate Dave Bickles before the UEFA Cup tie with Steaua Bucharest at Upton Park in 1999 was a perfectly observed tribute and this respect echoed the response of the South African press to the news of Byrne's untimely death. Hellenic coach Gavin Hunt described his father-in-law's passing in the *Cape Times* as a great loss to soccer. He said:

> The man was the epitome of life, always enthusiastic and never short of a joke or two, especially at social events. His presence at the annual awards ceremony for Cape soccer writers will be sorely missed.
>
> In his role as chief scout for Hellenic he has done wonders in a short time at the academy. Some of his protégés are already on the verge of breaking into the PSL side.
>
> His passing leaves a huge gap in our development set-up.

Kaizer Motaung, boss of the powerful Kaizer Chiefs club, and Jomo Sono, of Jomo Cosmos, both paid tribute to Byrne's soccer expertise and said the game would be a lot poorer without him. In the *Argus* newspaper, under the heading 'Football Mourns The Passing Of Budgie Byrne', Professor Ronnie Schloss, the Wits University FC president, said he had the highest regard for Byrne's football brain and went on: 'Many times I tried to get Byrne to come to Wits, but his love for Cape Town kept him away.'

Ron Greenwood commented that Byrne:

> ...was a delightful character as well as an immensely gifted player. He was all chat and humour. I visited him in hospital once, a Catholic hospital down Lambeth way, and he had the nuns there

running in circles for him – even putting his bets on. It was a great loss to English football when Johnny Byrne decided to emigrate to South Africa, but our loss was South Africa's gain.

For Johnny Haynes Byrne '...achieved considerable success for Durban City in the three years as a manager and then went on to do equally well for Hellenic.' And he was: '...one of the game's greatest characters, on and off the field.'

Harry Redknapp, whose first days at Upton Park were influenced by Byrne's performances, made the point that Johnny was the player Bobby Moore looked up to and that this was enough for anyone who had played for the Hammers to hold Byrne in the highest esteem. The manager of West Ham at the time of Budgie's death went on to tell of how John would always have a story to tell and was one of the game's great characters, an outgoing man. Even though he lived in South Africa Budgie phoned Chadwell Heath to talk about games on a weekly basis, being particularly interested in European ties. Redknapp identified Johnny Byrne as one of the greatest players to wear the West Ham colours, but said he was also an infectious personality who would be sadly missed by all at West Ham United.

Frank Lampard senior, Redknapp's assistant at Upton Park, was more succinct, saying that Byrne '...was the governor. Bobby was in awe of him. He was like the Pied Piper.'

Ken Dyer of the *London Evening Standard* wrote the following homage:

As someone who watched Budgie in his heyday I can't help thinking how much he would be worth these days – he would be priceless. Moore was always my boyhood hero, but Johnny Byrne wasn't far behind.

Well, although I rated Moore as the ultimate defender and a leader without peer, for what it's worth John was my hero, right from the moment he nearly knocked my head off during that reserve game at Upton Park. His price? No. I don't think of that at all. John was a man who purchased clubs, with money, as with Santos, but more often he bought the sides he played for and managed with something more than this; no chairman ever owned Budgie Byrne. If you ever really understood his motivation you'd realise, Byrne owned you!

He had a number of greatest moments. His debut for Crystal Palace and his first England game against Northern Ireland of course loomed large, but his most lasting memory in football was the FA Cup win with West Ham. John saw his two magnificent goals, which gave West Ham a 3–2 win in the quarter-final against Burnley, as being among his best, but the Wembley occasion and 'doing the lap of honour' was, 'the greatest feeling on earth' for Budgie. John also remembered the hundreds of thousands who turned out to watch West Ham bring the Cup back to the East End with great affection.

There were also some sad moments. John derived immense satisfaction from breaking the British transfer record when he moved to Upton Park, but he was sad to leave Crystal Palace and Arthur Rowe who had become a good friend and mentor.

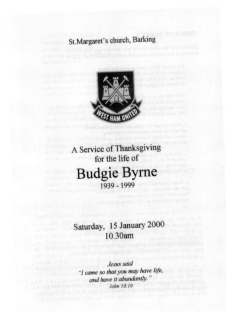

St.Margaret's church, Barking

A Service of Thanksgiving
for the life of
Budgie Byrne
1939 - 1999

Saturday, 15 January 2000
10.30am

*Jesus said
"I came so that you may have life,
and have it abundantly."
John 10:10*

Another bitter moment came when he injured his leg playing against Scotland at Wembley, which resulted in him missing the final of the European Cup-Winners' Cup against Munich 1860. John had to watch the Hammers win 2–0 from the stands.

However, Budgie was never a man to mourn the past. He always looked to the future, the next bet, game, goal, club or country. He would have approved of his long-time strike partner and friend Sir Geoff Hurst's contention that football is a game of tomorrows – that is where he would want us to look to. Days before his death John was looking ahead to the new season with an excitement that had been missing for a while. He had regretted leaving Santos two seasons before, after saving the club from relegation and, on the day he died, he was wearing a Santos shirt. However, typically of John, he had put the past behind him and was looking forward to the future. I attended the memorial service for John held at a pretty little church on the Essex/East London border, a place where many of my family have been christened, married and mourned. Margaret was there, of course, and it was our first meeting, which was strange as I had been writing this book for so many years and had had more than my share of conversations with John. Sir Geoff Hurst spoke well. In August 2002 I attended the funeral of John Charles, West Ham's first black player, who had played alongside both Bobby Moore and Johnny Byrne. The three were firm friends.

As I entered the little chapel just inside the East London cemetery, packed with people, I heard one of the tunes that Charlo had asked to be played:

We will fight for the right to be free
We will build our own society
And we will sing, we will sing
We will sing our own song

When the ancient drum rhythms ring
The voice of our forefathers sings
Forward Africa run
Our day of freedom has come
For me and for you
Amandla Awethu*

This made me think of Charlo, but also Budgie and Mooro, and picture the three young Hammers, all smart dressers and attractive young men in the early 1960s standing, smiling in the Black Lion pub, which, like my family home, was just a few minutes away from where we were. Johnny Byrne's life had been a song of freedom. As a young man he had used his skill and personality, along with his comrades at West Ham, to build a kind of affable community based around the club, but when he got to South Africa he had been part of the whole historical movement that had built a new society, building the game that the country loves best, preparing for the future by just working with the unifying factors of soccer to bring the 'day of freedom...Forward Africa run...'

In accordance with Budgie's request his ashes were returned to England and scattered on the Boleyn Ground pitch before the UEFA Cup game at Upton Park on Thursday 4 November 1999. Two years later Margaret donated some of Budgie's West Ham memorabilia to the club; five England caps, three England shirts, a League Cup final medal, Charity Shield mementoes, European souvenirs, his 'Hammer of the Year' (1964) Rose Bowl, a mounted boot last worn by John as well as presentation salvers, tankards, photographs, books and programmes. It was a wonderful gesture that will allow John to be appreciated and remembered by generations of supporters who were not even born at the time he graced Upton Park. However, his presence is in the breeze that blows across the Docklands of the East End and the wind that rushes across the vast South African veldt. As the sun breaks over Table Mountain and lights up London's river, which flows like an artery into the home of the

* Power to the People.

Hammers, Johnny Byrne's heart pounds like a thousand Zulu drums with the ever-beating pulse of cockney pride. Like captain Bobby, Budgie will never really die: along with Charlo and all the other Boleyn Boys who have gone before, he now inhabits the land of the hearts of all those who have loved and suffered with and for the claret and blue and we will hold him there forever.

A few years ago I wrote to John in South Africa asking him to add to a written memorial for Alan Sealey following the death of his good friend, gambling colleague and teammate. I have adapted part of that response to conclude this book.

> I would like to pay my respects to John's wife Margaret who is a fine lady. Unfortunately, the saddest part about life is that in time we all move on and invariably lose touch with one another. This was the case with John. It was probably due to the fact that he lived in South Africa for the last 30 years.

> I could write no end of stories about him. I do believe that I could tell a million tales about the man. John was a great character. Yes, John, you came, you conquered and you went, but you will be remembered in the football records at West Ham forever.

Appendix

Top League Football in South Africa in the last decade of the 'Byrne Years'

1992

		P	W	D	L	F	A	Pts
1.	Kaizer Chiefs (Johannesburg)	42	24	12	6	70	22	60
2.	Hellenic (Cape Town)	42	23	11	8	82	39	57
3.	Wits University (Johannesburg)	42	20	11	11	53	29	51
4.	Orlando Pirates (Johannesburg)	42	21	8	13	47	41	50
5.	Jomo Cosmos (Johannesburg)	42	18	11	13	64	49	47
6.	Mamelodi Sundowns (Pretoria)	42	16	15	11	62	49	47
7.	Witbank Aces (KwaMhlanga)	42	17	13	12	47	38	47
8.	Lightbody's Santos (Cape Town)	42	15	17	10	46	41	47
9.	Moroka Swallows (Johannesburg)	42	17	11	14	53	46	45
10.	Cape Town Spurs	42	13	17	12	47	43	43
11.	Fairway Stars (Witsieshoek)	42	15	13	14	40	40	43
12.	Ratanang	42	14	15	13	40	40	43
13.	Halls Dynamos (Johannesburg)	42	14	15	13	53	56	43
14.	Bloemfontein Celtic (B'fontein)	42	12	17	13	54	49	41
15.	Amazulu (Durban)	42	13	15	14	47	48	41
16.	Pretoria City	42	16	7	19	47	53	39
17.	Umtata Bush Bucks (Umtata)	42	12	14	16	33	42	38
18.	Highlands Park	42	13	11	18	36	38	37
19.	Crusaders United (Stanger)	42	11	13	18	34	58	35
20.	Vaal Reef Stars (Orkney)	42	12	10	20	32	53	34
21.	Manning Rangers (Durban)	42	9	11	22	40	58	29
22.	Dangerous Darkies (Nelspruit)	42	1	5	36	27	122	7

Top scorers: George Deamaley (Amazulu)   20 goals
Mark Williams (Hellenic)   20 goals
Player's Player of the Year: Stephan Khompela (Fairway Stars)

Changes after the season:
Ratanang Mahlosians of QwaQwa were bought by the owners of relegated Manning Rangers of Durban. Ratanang now play in Durban as Rangers, in all but name.
Highlands Park have become the second NSL club to change ownership and location this season. This Johannesburg club are now based in Welkom, Orange Free State.

1993

		P	W	D	L	F	A	Pts	
1.	Mamelodi Sundowns	38	24	7	7	69	31	55	
2.	Moroka Swallows	38	21	10	7	44	24	52	
3.	Amazulu	38	17	14	7	43	34	48	
4.	Orlando Pirates	38	15	13	10	52	42	43	
5.	Umtata Bucks	38	15	12	11	51	43	42	
6.	Kaizer Chiefs	38	15	12	11	42	35	42	
7.	Hellenic	38	14	13	11	58	50	41	
8.	Chatsworth Rangers	38	10	20	8	46	37	40	[*3]
9.	Pretoria City	38	11	17	10	39	40	39	[*4]
10.	Cape Town Spurs	38	13	11	14	43	37	37	
11.	Bloemfontein Celtic	38	13	11	14	36	45	37	
12.	Vaal Professionals	38	10	16	12	49	44	36	
13.	Qwa Qwa Stars	38	10	16	12	40	38	36	[*2]
14.	Witbank Aces	38	13	10	13	48	49	36	[*1]
15.	D'Alberton Callies	38	14	8	16	44	48	36	
16.	Wits University	38	14	8	16	37	42	36	
17.	Dynamos	38	8	17	13	41	41	33	
18.	Jomo Cosmos	38	10	12	16	39	48	32	
19.	Lightbody's Santos	38	7	15	16	29	45	29	
20.	Welkom Eagles	38	1	6	31	23	97	8	[*5]

[*1] Total Aces were renamed Witbank Aces.
[*2] Score Stars were renamed Qwa Qwa Stars.
[*3] Ratanang Mahlosians (Qwa Qwa) were bought by the owners of relegated side (1992) Manning Rangers (Durban), played as Rangers in Durban and were subsequently renamed Chatsworth Rangers.
[*4] Albany City were renamed Pretoria City.
[*5] Highland Park (Johannesburg) changed owners and were relocated to Welkom, playing as Welkom Eagles.

Relegated: Dynamos, Jomo Cosmos, Lightbody's Santos, Welkom Eagles.
Promoted: Royal Tigers, Real Rovers.

1994

		P	W	D	L	F	A	Pts	
1.	Orlando Pirates	34	18	13	3	45	14	50	[*]
2.	Cape Town Spurs	34	17	15	2	59	21	49	
3.	Umtata Bucks	34	18	5	11	51	32	41	
4.	Mamelodi Sundowns	34	18	5	11	64	47	41	
5.	Kaizer Chiefs	34	16	8	10	37	29	40	
6.	Hellenic	34	17	5	12	53	49	39	

7.	Wits University	34	14	10	10	38	24	38	
8.	Qwa Qwa Stars	34	11	15	8	41	33	37	
9.	Vaal Professionals	34	10	17	7	36	38	36	[*]
10.	Moroka Swallows	34	11	11	12	38	42	33	
11.	Witbank Aces	34	11	10	13	50	46	32	
12.	Real Rovers	34	12	8	14	57	62	32	
13.	Amazulu	34	10	10	14	32	41	30	
14.	Manning Rangers	34	8	13	13	31	36	29	
15.	Bloemfontein Celtic	34	12	4	18	51	58	28	
16.	D'Alberton Callies	34	6	13	15	32	49	25	
17.	Pretoria City	34	9	7	18	35	54	25	
18.	Royal Tigers	34	1	5	28	16	91	7	

[*] Pirates awarded one point, Vaal deducted one point: Vaal failed to produce ID cards.

Promoted: Jomo Cosmos, African Wanderers, Rabali Blackpool.

1995

		P	W	D	L	F	A	Pts	
1.	Cape Town Spurs	34	21	8	5	52	20	71	
2.	Mamelodi Sundowns	34	19	9	6	44	22	66	
3.	Orlando Pirates	34	16	12	6	42	22	60	
4.	Kaizer Chiefs	34	16	11	7	43	22	59	
5.	Hellenic	34	16	8	10	51	39	56	
6.	Umtata Bucks	34	14	8	12	42	40	50	
7.	Vaal Professionals	34	12	12	10	41	37	48	
8.	Qwa Qwa Stars	34	12	12	10	39	39	48	
9.	Real Rovers	34	11	10	13	46	52	43	
10.	Jomo Cosmos	34	10	12	12	33	37	42	
11.	Wits University	34	11	8	15	37	43	41	
12.	Manning Rangers	34	10	11	13	30	43	41	
13.	Bloemfontein Celtic	34	10	9	15	35	37	39	
14.	Witbank Aces	34	10	6	18	38	52	36	
15.	Moroka Swallows	34	7	13	14	35	47	34	
16.	Amazulu	34	7	13	14	35	52	34	
17.	African Wanderers	34	7	12	15	38	54	33	
18.	Rabali Blackpool	34	5	10	21	34	56	19	***

*** Blackpool deducted 6 points for fielding ineligible players.

2nd Division Regional Winners:

Camps Bay (Western Cape)

Pretoria City (Northern Transvaal)

Crystal Brians (Kwazulu/Natal)

Stocks Birds (Northwest Region)

After promotion play-offs, Pretoria City and Crystal Brains won promotion to NSL First Division for 1996 season.

African Wanderers and Rabali Blackpool got relegated.

Pretoria City were apparently renamed Supersport United.

1996–97

		P	W	D	L	F	A	Pts
1.	Manning Rangers	34	23	5	6	53	28	74
2.	Kaizer Chiefs	34	18	12	4	56	23	66
3.	Orlando Pirates	34	18	10	6	43	27	64
4.	Umtata Bucks	34	16	9	9	45	29	57
5.	Hellenic	34	16	7	11	46	31	56
6.	Mamelodi Sundowns	34	13	11	10	35	30	50
7.	Jomo Cosmos	34	11	16	7	32	27	49
8.	Cape Town Spurs	34	14	6	14	40	45	48
9.	Supersport United	34	10	16	8	40	35	46
10.	Bloemfontein Celtic	34	13	5	16	38	39	44
11.	Moroka Swallows	34	11	10	13	33	35	43
12.	Wits University	34	11	8	15	27	31	41
13.	Qwa Qwa Stars	34	10	8	16	39	49	38
14.	Amazulu	34	9	10	15	34	46	37
14.	Vaal Professionals	34	10	6	18	38	49	36
16.	Real Rovers	34	8	12	14	35	46	36
- -								
17.	Warriors	34	10	5	19	32	50	35
18.	Witbank Aces	34	4	7	23	26	72	19

Promoted: Santos and African Wanderers.

1997–98

		P	W	D	L	F	A	Pts	
1.	Mamelodi Sundowns	34	19	11	4	48	25	68	*
2.	Kaizer Chiefs	34	17	12	5	52	35	63	
3.	Orlando Pirates	34	15	12	7	52	33	57	
4.	Cape Town Spurs	34	15	12	7	51	35	57	
5.	Manning Rangers	34	16	9	9	58	47	57	
6.	Bush Bucks	34	14	12	8	42	38	54	
7.	Jomo Cosmos	34	13	12	9	31	31	51	
8.	Wits University	34	13	9	12	39	34	48	
9.	Qwa Qwa Stars	34	12	10	12	33	34	46	
10.	Hellenic	34	12	8	14	45	42	44	
11.	Moroka Swallows	34	12	6	16	30	42	42	
12.	Bloemfontein Celtic	34	12	5	17	38	46	41	
13.	Vaal Professionals	34	8	14	12	36	44	38	
14.	Supersport United	34	7	15	12	34	37	36	

15.	Amazulu	34	8	9	17	36	46	33
16.	Santos	34	10	3	21	34	61	33

- -

17.	African Wanderers	34	7	10	17	43	56	31
18.	Real Rovers	34	8	7	19	34	50	31
18.	Real Rovers	34	8	7	19	34	50	31

* Champions

Promoted: Dynamos and Seven Stars.

1998–99

		P	W	D	L	F	A	Pts
1.	Mamelodi Sundowns	34	23	6	5	70	26	75
2.	Kaizer Chiefs	34	23	6	5	73	34	75
3.	Orlando Pirates	34	17	9	8	55	28	60
4.	Manning Rangers	34	17	9	8	60	38	60
5.	Seven Stars	34	15	7	12	40	41	52
6.	Qwa Qwa Stars	34	13	11	10	43	39	50
7.	Bloemfontein Celtic	34	13	8	13	33	34	47
8.	Supersport United	34	11	13	10	45	38	46
9.	Bush Bucks	34	13	5	16	48	57	44
10.	Jomo Cosmos	34	11	10	13	37	39	43
11.	Wits University	34	9	13	12	31	39	40
12.	Hellenic	34	8	16	10	32	43	40
13.	Cape Town Spurs	34	9	12	13	52	50	39
14.	Amazulu	34	10	9	15	40	53	39
15.	Moroka Swallows	34	9	10	15	29	44	37
16.	Santos	34	7	14	13	36	54	35

- -

17.	Dynamos	34	7	8	19	20	51	29
18.	Vaal Professionals	34	5	6	23	38	74	21

Promoted: African Wanderers and Thembisa Classic.

NB: Cape Town Spurs and Seven Stars merge to form Ajax Cape Town for 1999–2000. The Spurs franchise will be sold to the highest bidder.

1999–2000

		P	W	D	L	F	A	Pts
1.	Mamelodi Sundowns	34	23	6	5	68	34	75
2.	Orlando Pirates	34	18	10	6	72	36	64
3.	Kaizer Chiefs	34	16	12	6	40	22	60
4.	Ajax Cape Town	34	15	8	11	43	39	53

5.	Manning Rangers	34	14	10	10	54	49	52
6.	Wits University	34	12	15	7	36	29	51
7.	Jomo Cosmos	34	12	14	8	49	32	50
8.	Hellenic	34	13	8	13	62	45	47
9.	Thembisa Classic	34	13	5	16	44	64	44
10.	Supersport United	34	11	10	13	51	48	43
11.	Santos	34	9	16	9	50	52	43
12.	Moroka Swallows	34	11	9	14	39	52	42
13.	Bush Bucks	34	10	11	13	48	48	41
14.	Bloemfontein Celtic	34	10	10	14	46	56	40
15.	Free State Stars	34	9	13	12	29	38	40
16.	African Wanderers	34	11	6	17	38	50	39
17.	Amazulu	34	9	9	16	32	44	36
18.	Mother City	34	2	4	28	22	85	10

2000–01

		P	W	D	L	F	A	Pts
1.	Orlando Pirates	34	16	13	5	60	34	61
2.	Kaizer Chiefs	34	16	12	6	41	25	60
3.	Mamelodi Sundowns	34	17	8	9	58	32	59
4.	Jomo Cosmos	34	15	11	8	47	27	56
5.	Santos	34	15	11	8	40	32	56
6.	Free State Stars	34	15	10	9	40	30	55
7.	Ria Stars	34	13	12	9	43	40	51
8.	Supersport United	34	12	11	11	42	35	47
9.	Lamontville Golden Arrows	34	11	12	11	38	39	45
10.	Umtata Bush Bucks	34	12	8	14	38	45	44
11.	Ajax Cape Town	34	10	10	14	37	46	40
12.	Thembisa Classic	34	9	12	13	26	40	39
13.	Wits University	34	8	14	12	33	43	38
14.	Hellenic	34	7	15	12	32	40	36
15.	Moroka Swallows	34	7	14	13	35	45	35
16.	Manning Rangers	34	9	7	18	49	60	34
17.	Bloemfontein Celtic	34	9	10	15	35	46	34 [−3]
18.	African Wanderers	34	6	8	20	31	66	26

NB: Bloemfontein Celtic deducted three points for fielding ineligible player. Celtic deducted three points for fielding ineligible player.

Promoted: Amazulu (Durban) and Black Leopards (Thohoyandou).

2001–02

		P	W	D	L	F	A	Pts
1.	Santos	34	18	10	6	49	30	64
2.	SuperSport United	34	17	8	9	53	42	59
3.	Orlando Pirates	34	15	12	7	43	31	57
4.	Jomo Cosmos	34	16	9	9	39	29	57
5.	Mamelodi Sundowns	34	15	11	8	47	32	56
6.	Moroka Swallows	34	15	8	11	44	43	53
7.	Wits University	34	13	11	10	39	30	50
8.	Black Leopards	34	13	10	11	58	48	49
9.	Kaizer Chiefs	34	12	13	9	38	33	49
10.	Manning Rangers	34	12	9	13	48	45	45
11.	Free State Stars	34	11	11	12	36	32	44
12.	Ria Stars	34	11	10	13	42	47	43
13.	Lamontville Golden Arrows	34	10	12	12	35	37	42
14.	Ajax Cape Town	34	11	8	15	39	42	41
15.	Umtata Bush Bucks	34	10	5	19	47	70	35
16.	Hellenic	34	8	10	16	35	54	34
-	-	-	-	-	-	-	-	-
17.	Amazulu	34	6	12	16	33	50	30
18.	Thembisa Classic	34	2	13	19	29	59	19

First Division-Western Cape Stream:

		P	W	D	L	F	A	Pts
1.	Santos	30	26	1	3	88-	19	79 *
-	-	-	-	-	-	-	-	-
2.	Seven Stars	30	24	3	3	77-	23	75
3.	Trinitarians	30	17	5	8	52-	38	56
4.	Avendale	30	16	4	10	48-	29	52
5.	Wynberg St Johns	30	14	8	8	42-	30	50
6.	Vasco da Gama	30	12	8	10	59-	45	44
7.	Saxon Rovers	30	11	10	9	39-	39	43
8.	FNB Rangers	30	13	2	15	51-	65	41
9.	Mutual	30	12	4	14	40-	61	40
10.	Edgemead	30	10	6	14	42-	46	36
11.	Battswood	30	10	5	15	39-	41	35
12.	Bellville	30	8	7	15	33-	45	31
13.	Camps Bay	30	6	10	14	29-	53	28
14.	Newtons	30	6	6	18	33-	56	24
15.	Norway Parks	30	4	11	15	21-	52	23
16.	Stephanians	30	3	6	21	23-	74	15

* Promotion Play-off

Final Table:

1.	African Wanderers	6	3	3	0	8-	5	12 *
2.	Santos	6	2	4	0	11-	4	10 *

- -

3.	Thembisa Classic	6	1	2	3	9-	8	5
4.	Black Leopards	6	0	3	3	4-	15	3

* Promoted

2002–03

1.	Orlando Pirates	30	18	7	5	41	16	61
2.	SuperSport United	30	16	7	7	54	37	55
3.	Wits University	30	15	9	6	39	29	54
4.	Moroka Swallows	30	15	8	7	52	36	53
5.	Lamontville Golden Arrows	30	15	6	9	33	27	51
6.	Kaizer Chiefs	30	14	8	8	42	26	50
7.	Dynamos	30	12	4	14	39	37	40
8.	Jomo Cosmos	30	10	10	10	33	34	40
9.	Santos	30	11	6	13	33	28	39
10.	Mamelodi Sundowns	30	11	6	13	30	30	39
11.	Black Leopards	30	11	3	16	40	42	36
12.	Manning Rangers	30	9	8	13	31	39	35
13.	Ajax Cape Town	30	9	6	15	31	44	33
14.	Hellenic	30	10	3	17	33	47	33

- -

15.	Umtata Bush Bucks	30	8	7	15	29	47	31
16.	African Wanderers	30	4	6	20	21	62	18
-.	Free State Stars	bought out						
-.	Ria Stars	bought out						

NB: Free State Stars (Qwa-Qwa) and Ria Stars (Polokwane) were bought out by the League for 8 million rand (roughly USD 800,000) each in order to reduce fixture congestion.